The Neglected Brother

The Neglected Brother
A Study of Henry Kingsley

William H. Scheuerle

Florida State University Press
Tallahassee / 1971

A Florida State University Press Book

PRINTED FOR THE PUBLISHER BY
THE E. O. PAINTER PRINTING COMPANY
DELEON SPRINGS, FLORIDA

To
MILDRED ADAMS ALDRICH
A fellow lover of Victorian novels and a friend

Acknowledgments

DURING THE YEARS that this book has been in preparation, I have incurred many obligations that it is now a pleasure to acknowledge. I am grateful to Cecil Y. Lang, University of Virginia, for introducing me to Henry Kingsley and for his detailed criticism of the first draft of this manuscript; to William E. Morris, Elton E. Smith, and Robert Zetler, my associates at the University of South Florida, for reading the work in progress and offering many thoughtful suggestions; to R. B. Martin, Princeton University, Walter E. Houghton, Wellesley College, and John Byrne, St. Procopius College, for sharing information about Henry Kingsley with me; to Dennis Robison, Reference Librarian, University of South Florida, for obtaining numerous books that I needed; to Jane F. Scheuerle, for faithfully following this study through every stage; and to Mildred Adams Aldrich, to whom this book is dedicated, for countless helps, but mainly for her enthusiasm about Henry Kingsley.

I am especially indebted to Houghton Mifflin Company and the Houghton Library, Harvard University, for permission to study and quote from the Ticknor and Fields cost books; to the Houghton Library, the *Harvard Library Bulletin,* and Robert Lee Wolff for their permission to quote from both the unpublished Kingsley letters and those published by Professor Wolff in the *Bulletin;* to Geoffrey Serle and the Melbourne University Press for their permission to quote from *The Golden Age;* to R. B. Martin and Faber & Faber, Ltd. for their permission to quote from *The Dust of Combat;* and to Laurence Pollinger, Ltd., the Estate of the late Mrs. Frieda Lawrence, and the Viking Press, Inc., for their permission to reprint material from D. H. Lawrence's *Kangaroo* (copyright 1923 by Thomas Seltzer, Inc., renewed 1951 by Frieda Lawrence).

Sections of this book have appeared previously in slightly different forms. I wish to thank *Australian Literary Studies* and the University of Tasmania for permission to reprint "Romantic Attitudes in *Geoffrey Hamlyn*"; *Victorian Poetry* and the University of West Virginia for permission to reprint " 'Magdalen at Michael's Gate': A Neglected Lyric"; *Victorian Newsletter* and New York University for permission to reprint "Henry Kingsley and the Governor Eyre Controversy"; and the University of Nebraska for permission to reprint my introduction to the Bison Book edition of *Ravenshoe*.

The writing of this book was supported in part by grants from the American Philosophical Society and the National Endowment for the Arts and Humanities.

Contents

Introduction

"I WORSHIPPED his books as a boy; today I find them full of faults—often preposterous, usually ill-constructed, at times unnatural beyond belief. . . . And yet each time I read *Ravenshoe*—and I must be close upon 'double figures'—I like it better. Henry did my green unknowing youth engage, and I find it next to impossible to give him up, and quite impossible to choose the venerated Charles as a substitute in my riper age," wrote Sir Arthur Quiller-Couch in 1895 about Henry Kingsley, Charles Kingsley's younger brother and fellow novelist.[1]

Other admirers—Clement Shorter, Justin McCarthy, Walter Frewen Lord, Michael Sadleir, S. M. Ellis, Angela Thirkell, Robert Lee Wolff—all agree that Henry Kingsley can never be considered a major novelist; even his best works are characterized by a carelessness that cannot be overlooked. But he is a gifted and spirited storyteller, whose prose at its best has a quiet force and a felicity that make it worthy to be placed beside that of the finest literary craftsmen. In his earlier novels, he had the ability to create fresh descriptions of manly and noble action and beautiful Australian and English sea and landscape scenes. And, above all, his own enjoyment of life infuses his best romances with a vigor and joviality that still captivate readers.

Kingsley gained literary prominence with his first two novels, *The Recollections of Geoffry Hamlyn* and *Ravenshoe*. When he followed those works with two other successes, *Austin Elliot* and *The Hillyars and the Burtons*, Kingsley's reputation was estab-

---

1. *Adventures in Criticism* (New York, 1925), p. 67.

1

lished, and he seemed destined to be as famous as his brother Charles. But during the succeeding years, when he should have been at the peak of his creativity, he produced a string of distinctly mediocre books—some potentially fine, but crowded with absurdities and redundancies that a more disciplined author would have eliminated. Then he settled into a long period of literary stagnation. From this time came what is probably his most erratic novel, *Oakshott Castle, Being the Memoirs of an Eccentric Nobleman*, which was all but labeled the "worst novel ever written." Although *Reginald Hetherege*, one of his later novels, revealed touches of his earlier artistry, it, for the most part, was labored.

The few critics who have attempted to account for the swift deterioration of Kingsley's literary powers disagree as to the causes. George Saintsbury explains it as merely another example of a man who wrote himself out; Michael Sadleir blames it on a "mental abnormality"; and S. M. Ellis attributes it to "financial difficulties."

Henry Kingsley was just one of the many artists frustrated and defeated by the problems of survival in Victorian England. But since he was popular during his age—practically all of his novels were reviewed in the major journals, such as the *Saturday Review* and the *Athenaeum*, and Mudie Circulating Library purchased large quantities of his earlier novels—and since he commanded the respect of such important contemporaries as Swinburne, Lewis Carroll, Leslie Stephen, Thomas Huxley, Matthew Arnold, and George Meredith, he should not be allowed to sink permanently into a literary limbo. "It is," as the English novelist Angela Thirkell declared in 1950, "high time that attention was recalled to [Henry] Kingsley. . . . He has long been overshadowed in the public mind by his elder brother Charles Kingsley."[2]

Henry Kingsley's lack of fame, however, has continued. Although briefly mentioned in some recent surveys of the nineteenth-century British novel, Henry Kingsley is still virtually ignored by most critics, as can be noted, for example, by his omission from the important study *Victorian Fiction: A Guide to Research* (1964).

To recall attention to Henry Kingsley is the main purpose of this book, and, more specifically, to present a fair evaluation of his work and to examine the complex reasons for his artistic decline.

2. "Henry Kingsley," *Nineteenth-Century Fiction,* V (December, 1950), 175.

Because he still entertains a dedicated coterie, Henry Kingsley deserves such a study. This book is not meant to be a biography per se; it is, instead, a chronological examination of Henry Kingsley in terms of his life, his works, and the relationship between them. This approach is a natural one, for a strong autobiographical strain exhibits itself in all Kingsley's works. From his writings, two Henry Kingsleys clearly emerge: the carefree, irresponsible, simple boyish man who loved life and romantically longed for adventures, and the insecure, suffering man who not only had to compete with a very successful older brother but also had to combat poverty, a rapidly deteriorating artistic imagination, and a fatal cancer. Unfortunately, the harshness of life finally dimmed his childlike eye for beauty, fun, and romance. Henry Kingsley's last works are a forlorn testimony to the decline of a writer who, with all of his weaknesses, had been once able to charm readers with his storytelling.

I

1830-1859

HENRY KINGSLEY was born into a family that was excessively proud of its ancestors. In order to claim the earldom of Huntingdon, one branch of the Kingsley family foolishly "flung its money away" trying to establish Robin Hood as its progenitor.[1] More probably, though, the Kingsleys descended from the twelfth-century Sir Ranulph de Kingsley of Cheshire, who succeeded in gaining the favor of Ranulph, Earl of Chester, and winning for "his heirs and assigns forever" the office of "Baliwick and Keeping of the Forest of Delamere . . . with divers other liberties." To perpetuate this hereditary accolade, the Kingsley descendants prominently displayed a horn, the symbol of the forestry rights, on their heraldic trappings.

Although, for the most part, Sir Ranulph's heirs were content to be influential—but now forgotten—country squires, the line occasionally produced a national figure. Among Kingsley's ancestors was the staunch Puritan Colonel George Fleetwood, one of the commissioners for the trial of Charles I. Because of his signature on Charles' death warrant, Colonel Fleetwood was convicted of high treason at the Restoration, with his life spared but his estate confiscated by the Crown and given to the Duke of York. Almost as if to vindicate his anti-Royalist ancestor, Henry Kingsley liked to praise Oliver Cromwell as "the most tolerant of English rulers" and "the greatest of Englishmen" (*Fireside Studies*, I, 136–37). Less sensational but equally outstanding was William Kingsley (1584–1647), Archdeacon of Canterbury, who married Damaris Abbot of

1. George Henry Kingsley, *Notes on Sport and Travel*, with a Memoir by his daughter Mary H. Kingsley (London, 1900), p. 2.

4

Guildford, niece of Robert Abbot, Bishop of Salisbury, and of George Abbot, Archbishop of Canterbury and founder of the Guildford Hospital.

The most distinguished or, at least, the best known ancestor was Lieutenant-General William Kingsley (1698–1769), whose portrait by Reynolds hung in a prominent place in the Chelsea Rectory, where the young Henry lived during his boyhood. Stories of General Kingsley's heroic actions at Dettingen, Fontenoy, and finally Minden, where his horse was shot from under him, fascinated Henry Kingsley, as well as his older brothers and sister. These stories, no doubt, were Henry's first encounter with military feats and manly glory that were to play such an important part in his novels.

On his mother's side, Henry Kingsley's antecedents were plantation owners in Barbados and Demerara. His mother, Mary Lucas Kingsley, was herself born in the West Indies (1785), daughter of Judge Nathaniel Lucas, of Farley Hall, Barbados, and of Barbadian-born Mary Crookenden. Although no archdeacons or generals adorned the Lucas line, Judge Lucas claimed friendship with important contemporaries: John Hunter, the famous eighteenth-century surgeon and teacher of Edward Jenner; Sir Joseph Banks, president of the Royal Society; and Lord Rodney, the receiver of the Comte de Grasse's surrendered sword on the deck of the *Formidable* off the island of St. Lucia in the West Indies, April 12, 1782. In his essay "The Foundation of an Empire," Henry Kingsley also added Edward Gibbon to the list of his grandfather's acquaintances (*Tales of Old Travel Re-Narrated*, p. 314).

In order to educate his studious daughter in an English school, Judge Lucas moved to England, settling at Rushford Lodge, Norfolk. At this time Mary had a personal glimpse of romance. In later years she was fond of recounting a girlhood experience when she had danced with Byron at a Norwick County Ball and had thought that "he looked like a butcher boy, his face was so red."

Henry's father, Charles Kingsley, Senior, was born in 1781, at Battramsley House, New Forest. Inheritor of a considerable fortune when his father died in 1786, Charles was reared and educated to be a country gentleman—first at Harrow and then at Oxford, where he was matriculated at Brasenose College in December, 1800. He returned, however, to Battramsley House after only two months. There he pursued the pleasurable life of an estate owner—shooting and hunting and indulging in his passion for literature, languages, and natural science. Within a few years he met and married Mary Lucas. Mismanagement of funds on the part of the trustees who had looked after the estate during his minority soon, however, forced Charles and his new wife to sell the dwindling estate and to seriously consider a profession for him. At first he intended to purchase a military commission, but his late age and financial necessity led him, with some reluctance, to Trinity Hall, Cambridge, to study divinity. Finally, nine years later, in 1816, at the age of thirty-five, he took the degree of LL.B. at Sidney Sussex College and accepted his first curacy—his apprenticeship—in the Fens, from which he shortly moved to Holne, in Devonshire, and then in 1819 to Burton-on-Trent, where he remained for two years; early in 1821, there was another move, to North Clifton, near Newark. Multiplying his responsibilities during these early years of his ministry was the growth of his family: Gerald (1816–44),[2] Charles (1819–75), Herbert (1820?–34), Louisa Mary (b.d. 1823).

Finally, in January, 1824, after occupying insignificant charges for nearly eight years following his late ordination, the Reverend Charles Kingsley moved his ever increasing family to Barnack, near Stamford, in the Northamptonshire Fens, one of the best livings in the diocese. This appointment had been offered him by a former Cambridge acquaintance, Dr. Herbert Marsh, recently consecrated Bishop of Peterborough, with the stipulation that the Reverend Kingsley should hold the living until the Bishop's son, Herbert —then seventeen—could be ordained. In Barnack Rectory the rest of the Kingsley children were born: George Henry (1826–92), Charlotte (1828–82), and Henry (on January 2, 1830).

Certainly Barnack Rectory, a rambling fourteenth-century house, was a seemingly auspicious setting for the birth of a novelist. The romantic Mary Lucas Kingsley, who superstitiously believed in the effects of prenatal influences—especially the beauty of nature—on a child, must have been delighted during her last pregnancies. Surrounded by the uncanny cries of the water fowl and the wild beauty of the marshes, with their mysterious mists and fires, the rectory had the additional and indispensable, if inevitable, glamour of an amiable apparition called "Button Cap," who, wearing flopping slippers, a flowered dressing-gown, and the buttoned cap aforesaid,

2. For R. B. Martin's argument that Charles was the oldest child, see *The Dust of Combat, A Life of Charles Kingsley* (London, 1959), p. 21n1.

haunted the ancient house, turning over the pages of the books in the library or, at times, with a poltergeist fury, rolling the barrels in the cellar and then returning contritely to the Great North Room.

But ill luck seemingly hung over Henry from his birth. When he was still an infant, probably less than a year old, his brother George and sister Charlotte, provoked no doubt by sibling jealousy, wheeled Henry into a garden pond and abandoned him, in the hope of drowning the new favorite. As Mary Kingsley later recounts the tale, "No harm, however, was done, owing to the gardener, under Providence, having a need of that barrow. Chastisement was administered where deserved."[3] Physically, Henry suffered no lasting effects from his near drowning, and though his future novels stress comparable sibling rivalries, the evidence is too tenuous to allow us to assume that his childhood drama had any permanent psychological effects. It seems more likely that this recurrent theme in his novels owes its origin to its frequent general appearance in Victorian fiction. Symbolically, however, this incident forbodes many future personal disasters for Kingsley.

When Henry was not yet two years old, Herbert Marsh was ordained, and the Reverend Charles Kingsley fulfilled his part of the bargain and moved his family from Barnack to lodgings at Ilfracambe. Relying upon a former acquaintanceship with Sir James Hamlyn-Williams of Clovelly Court, Devonshire, Mr. Kingsley shortly obtained a curacy at Clovelly and upon the Rector's death the following year was presented the living.

Although the income was small, both Mr. and Mrs. Kingsley enjoyed the sunshine and warmth of Devonshire after the cold mistiness of the Fens and were pleased with Clovelly, a picturesque fishing village of white-washed cottages with bright green doors and trim nestled in one of the ravines that occasionally cleave the steep wall coast of Barnstaple Bay. Its pier, where the fishermen unloaded their mackerel and herring boats, dates from Richard II's time. The rectory itself and a few other houses were situated on a high plateau, four hundred feet above the breaking sea, but most of the cottages lined the stair-like street that descended from the plateau to the harbor. It was so narrow and steep that donkeys were the only means of transportation.

The older Kingsley boys, with Henry toddling along, were

3. *George Henry Kingsley*, p. 5.

caught up in the adventures offered by this setting. On the beach and among the crags, they collected sea shells, wild flowers, and birds' eggs, which they learned to classify under their father's directions. From the rectory they could see Lundy Island, with its lone lighthouse and fantastic rocky coast. The fishermen, who used the island as a port, told the boys stories about pirate treasure buried there long ago and about Sir Lewis Stukeley, who in 1618 had betrayed his cousin Sir Walter Raleigh and had died ostracized in the old Moresco Castle, whose ruins still remained on the island. Smugglers, it was whispered, still sought a haven in the isolated coves.

Henry, of course, was too young at that time to understand all of the stories, but his remembrance of the fishermen and the numerous shipwrecks that occurred off the rocky coast influenced many of his later novels. Vivid shipwreck scenes figure prominently in *Ravenshoe* and *Oakshott Castle*, for example. Sea life and tragedies were impressed upon his mind, no doubt, because he and his brothers usually accompanied their father down the long street from the rectory when the Vicar held parting services at the harbor for the fishing fleet. His voice muffled by the men's huskier ones and by the weeping of the women, Henry, nevertheless, joined with the others to sing the customary Psalm 121, affirming that "The Lord shall preserve thy going out and thy coming in from this time forth and even for evermore." When tragedy struck, the entire Kingsley family gathered for the solemn burial services.

Feeling settled at last in this locale, the Kingsleys sent Charles and Herbert, twelve and eleven respectively, away to school, first to preparatory school in Clifton, Bristol, headed by the Reverend John Knight, and then, a year later in 1832, to Helston Grammar School in Cornwall, where the Reverend Derwent Coleridge, second son of Samuel Taylor Coleridge, was Headmaster. During their second year at Helston, both brothers became seriously ill. Charles recovered from his attacks of brain fever and English cholera, but the convalescing Herbert took a turn for the worst and died from a case of rheumatic fever, which had severely damaged his heart.

Four-year-old Henry was naturally frightened and bewildered by his brother's sudden death and the grief that befell the household that spring. When he saw that Charles, who had been greatly shocked by the death, now preferred solitary walks instead of his usual romps with his youngest brother and when he heard his parents' concern over Charles' health and melancholy, his fears and confusion were exacerbated. Henry imagined that Charles also was going to die. But when no further tragedy occurred, Henry forgot his worries and was soon again exploring the crags and pestering the fishermen to take him out to sea in their boats.

In 1836, Lord Cadogan presented to Mr. Kingsley an excellent living at St. Luke's Church, Sidney Street, Chelsea, and, although Mr. and Mrs. Kingsley regretted leaving Clovelly, they realized that the increased income from the new position meant more opportunities for their growing sons.

Chelsea in the 1830s and 1840s was outgrowing its rural confines and becoming a suburb of London. The completion in 1831 of Belgrave, Eaton, and Lowndes Squares, with their connecting streets, had definitely joined the cobbled-stone streets of Chelsea with the busier ones of the Metropolis. And with the rise in population from approximately 20,000 at the beginning of the nineteenth century to 40,243 by 1841, Chelsea could no longer be called a large village. The days that Thomas Carlyle described when he was newly arrived at Chelsea in 1834 were passing: "We lie safe down in a little bend of the river, away from all the great roads; have air and quiet hardly inferior to Craigenputtock, an outlook from the back-windows into mere leafy regions with here and there a red high-peaked old roof looking through; and see nothing of London except by day the summits of St. Paul's Cathedral and Westminster Abbey, and by night the gleam of the great Babylon affronting the peaceful skies."[4] St. Luke's itself was a sign of the expansion. Just twelve years before Mr. Kingsley became its second Rector, this neo-Gothic church had been built to replace the Chelsea Old Church, which had grown too small for the increasing congregation.

A little distance from St. Luke's, next to the river, was the Chelsea Rectory, a many-roomed Georgian house with ivy covering its brownish-grey bricks. It was outstanding only for its huge, high-walled garden. There the younger Kingsley children climbed the many old poplars, dreamed under the mulberry that—as legend goes—shaded Queen Elizabeth when she had once paused in Chelsea, ran on the many graveled paths, and played among the pollard limes and giant acacias.

4. *Letters of Thomas Carlyle*, ed. Charles Eliot Norton (London, 1889), II, 412–13.

Near the rectory on the river side at the corner of Church Street stood the decaying Old Church. Originally erected in the fourteenth century, it was even then in 1836 mostly rebuilt in a nondescript style. Although not remarkable for its architecture, the church is noted for its historical associations. Still present are the black marble monument that Sir Thomas More erected to himself in 1532 and the sadly neglected tomb of Jane Dudley (d. 1555), Duchess of Northumberland, mother-in-law of Lady Jane Grey, and the mother of Queen Elizabeth's Leicester. From the pulpit Dr. John Donne had preached the funeral sermon of George Herbert's mother, and in the churchyard lay now dimly remembered one-time celebrities: Jean Cavalier, leader of the Huguenot Camisards; Thomas Shadwell, the Poet Laureate whom Dryden derided in *MacFlecknoe* and *Absalom and Achitophel*; Henry Woodfall, the publisher of "Junius"; Sir Hans Sloane, whose museum and library formed the nucleus of the British Museum.

This ancient structure with its imposing history, its low, dark passages and highly decorated tombs so impressed—and probably frightened—the boy Henry that years later he recreated it imaginatively in his fourth novel, *The Hillyars and the Burtons.* Joe and Jim Burton roam among the large and costly monuments of the old Chelsea families: the life-size effigies of Lord Dacre in armor and Lady Dacre in a long cloak, with their dogs at their feet; the simple figure of Thomas Lawrence—John Hillyar, in the novel—who, with his family, prefers "to kneel, with folded hands, until the last trump sound from the East, or until Chelsea Church crumble into dust." Through Joe, Kingsley crystalized his own memories of the church: "Four hundred years of memory . . . are crowded into that dark old church, and the great flood of change beats round the walls, and shakes the door in vain, but never enters. The dead stand thick together there, as if to make a brave resistance to the moving world outside, which jars upon their slumber. It is a church of the dead. I cannot fancy any one being married in that church—its air would chill the boldest bride that ever walked to the altar. No; it is a place for old people to creep into, and pray, until their prayer is answered and they sleep with the rest" (Vol. I, ch. 13).[5]

Also, as his novels reveal, Kingsley must have explored the old

5. The chapter or page number within parentheses following quotations from Henry Kingsley's works in the text are to the first edition listed in the Bibliography.

mansions that still stood in the Chelsea of his day, especially Essex House, formerly the palace of the Earls of Essex, a deteriorating estate with an overgrown but magnificent garden. Although razed in 1842, when Kingsley was twelve, it used to stand near the rectory in Church Place, and from its dormer window at the north end, Kingsley said that he could look right down on the top of the trees in the rectory garden and see beyond "the new tavern, the Cadogan Arms, and away to the north-east St. Luke's Church." Like the old church, Essex House is important in *The Hillyars and the Burtons,* when it becomes the Burtons' home:

> There was no house to move into, except into a very large house which stood by itself, as it were fronting the buildings opposite our forge; which contained twenty-five rooms, some of them very large, and which was called by us, indifferently, Church Place or Queen Elizabeth's Palace.
>
> It had been in reality the palace of the young Earl of Essex; a very large three-storied house of old red brick, with stone-mullioned windows and doorways. Many of the windows were blind, bricked up at different times as the house descended in the social scale. The roof was singularly high, hanging somewhat far over a rich cornice, and in that roof there was a single dormer window at the north end.
>
> The house had now been empty for some time, and it had always had a great attraction for us children. In the first place, it was empty; in the second place, it had been inhabited by real princesses; and in the third, there was a ghost, who used to show a light in the aforementioned dormer window the first Friday in every month (Vol. I, ch. 2).

The ghost is a "little old lady, in grey shot-silk and black mittens." No doubt when Henry was writing this novel he had enlivened his recollections of his boyhood life among the old Chelsea mansions with remembered tales about the Barnack ghost "Button Cap," told to him by Charles and Gerald.

In April, 1844, Henry started to attend King's College School in the Strand, a four-mile walk from Chelsea. Presumably, he had been enrolled in a local school previously or had been tutored by his father or possibly even Charles, whom he visited when Charles became curate at Eversley on July 3, 1842.

The rectory had become a lonely place for a young boy. With a large semi-urbanized parish to supervise, his parents were busy establishing clubs and schools, visiting the poor, organizing committees, and dispensing considerable sums of money in charity. Little time was left to indulge their youngest son. District visitors and parish councillors instead of lively brothers now filled the house: Charles was at Cambridge and then Eversley and had been married on January 10, 1844; George was studying medicine at St. George's Hospital; and his oldest brother, Gerald, was a lieutenant in the Royal Navy.

Since his parents prohibited their children from going to plays or learning to dance, Henry, always a voracious reader, spent many hours in his father's well-stocked library dreaming over rousing accounts of the West Indian islands, the Spanish Main, and other faraway places and poring over illustrated treatises on natural history. His desire for travel and adventure that led him eventually to Australia grew stronger in this period of loneliness. From fiction he enthusiastically chose such friends as Robinson Crusoe, Uncle Toby, and Mr. Pickwick and fell in love, in turn, with Mrs. Burney's Evelina and Scott's Flora MacIvor and Julia Mannering. The many references in his future novels to literary characters show that Kingsley knew them firsthand.

While Henry was dreaming his schoolboy fantasies and storing up material for his later romances, Lieutenant Gerald Kingsley was heroically living the adventures. He had served on H.M.S. *Pique* in the bombardment of St. John d'Arce on the Syrian Coast in 1840 and was second in command on H.M.S. *Royalist* when it left England in 1843 for the tropics. This second gunboat, however, was a doomed ship. In May, 1844, fever struck down the Commander and then Gerald on September 17 in the Gulf of Carpentaria. By the time Second Master Parkinson had taken command of the leaking ship and had sailed it into Singapore in November, 1844, all of the officers and half of the crew had perished from the fever. But it was not until February 24, 1845, that Mr. Kingsley was informed of his son's death, and then in a shocking manner. Reading in the Chelsea Public Library, he overheard a man near him say: "Dreadful bad business this about the *Royalist*—every single officer on board her dead—those who did not die of fever were eaten by cannibals."[6] The stunned Mr. Kingsley fainted.

Henry stayed at King's College until 1848, passing from the Junior Department to the General Literature and Science Depart-

6. George Henry Kingsley, p. 4.

ment. But the most important event for him that year was his meeting with William Makepeace Thackeray. When Becky Sharp had appeared in 1847, Kingsley gave up his other fictitious heroines and "loved as we had never loved before." His delight must have been inexpressible when John William Parker, the publisher of novels and *Fraser's Magazine,* invited Henry to meet Thackeray at dinner. Parker, whose son, John, had been Charles Kingsley's fellow student at King's College, had always taken an interest in his son's friends, especially those with literary talents. Already contracted with Charles to publish in *Fraser's* his article "Why Should We Fear the Romish Priests" and *Yeast,* a novel dealing with the social and religious problems of the day, Parker had also noted ability in Henry's schoolboy writings. Too shy to speak to Thackeray at the time of their meeting, Henry later vividly remembered his feelings: "There before him was the great man, the great man himself, at last; there was the head of hair so familiar afterwards, though not so grey sixteen years ago; there were the spectacles and the wonderful uplooking face. . . . This lad engaged himself entirely in watching Thackeray, and as he did so, he came to this conclusion—that the man who had written the most remarkable tale (*Vanity Fair*) he had ever read, had the most remarkable face he had ever seen."[7]

Although little is known of Kingsley's actual school life, hints of possible schoolboy difficulties are given by J. M. Ludlow, who, with Charles Kingsley and J. F. D. Maurice, edited *Politics for the People,* a journal advocating Christian Socialism: "His family were at one time in great trouble about him, he having got into bad courses while at King's College. It was then I first knew him, and I liked the lad notwithstanding his misdoings. There was a good deal of resemblance in character between Charles and Henry, but Henry was much weaker, and with lower aims, though a really good fellow at bottom."[8] It may be that the excessive smoking and drinking that we hear so much about in later years began during those school days. At any rate, it seems as if Henry must have frittered away some academic opportunities, for he did not matriculate at Worcester College, Oxford, until March, 1850—after, that is, a two-year stint at Colebrook, studying under Charles' former Cambridge tutor, the Reverend Thomas Drosier.

7. "Thackeray," *Macmillan Magazine,* IX (February, 1864), 362.
8. Quoted from Martin, *The Dust of Combat,* pp. 97–98.

But the two years of tutoring were virtually wasted, for at Worcester he engaged in a life of strenuous athletics and exuberant social pleasures. Sir Edwin Arnold, his friend at both King's College School and Oxford, relates that the roisterous Henry was "always generous, manly, and of an inner temper nobler than his external manners. I wagered him £10 one day that he could not 'run a mile, row a mile, and trot a mile' within fifteen minutes; yet he accomplished this remarkable feat."[9] Later, he won the Diamond Sculls at Henley. Another Oxford friend, John Cordy Jeaffreson, remembers that Henry gloried so in his athletic ability that "he desired the 'cheesey death' in his merry boyhood to close a brief and brilliant career. He would fain fall back in his outrigger and expire suddenly at the close of a triumphant match with the champion sculler of the whole universe. To perish of violent delight as his boat shot past the goal, three clear lengths ahead of the universal champion's outrigger, as the acclamations for the conqueror rent the air and rose to the blue sky, would be a blissful exit."[10]

Other contemporaries testify not only to Kingsley's addiction to athletics but his inclination to overindulgences: wine-drinking breakfasts and suppers and rags and riots. On one occasion he challenged W. G. Wilkinson, a fellow student and later a clergyman at Aldeburgh, to a contest to determine which one could smoke more continuous pipes of Cavendish and the stronger Latakia. Lasting many hours, the smoking contest finally ended in a tie. Whether Kingsley suffered any serious aftereffects at that time is not known, but Wilkinson became so ill that he gave up smoking permanently. It is unfortunate that Kingsley did not follow suit, for there is little doubt that his continual excessive smoking led eventually to his early death from cancer of the trachea and tongue.

One of the most eccentric of his college activities was his cofounding with Sir Edwin of the short-lived Fez Club, a secret society of fifty men dedicated to misogamy, misogyny, and "celibate freedom." Possibly, Henry had originally conceived the idea from reading Sir Walter Scott's *The Antiquary*, for an ideal Patron Saint of the club would be Jonathan Oldbuck of Monkbarns, the antiquary, who lamented that "All ancient legislators, from Lycur-

9. Clement K. Shorter, Introduction to *The Recollections of Geoffry Hamlyn* (New York, 1894), p. xiv. Whether or not this impossible feat was a single sport I do not know.

10. S. M. Ellis, *Henry Kingsley 1830–1876* (London, 1931), p. 33.

gus to Mahommed agree in putting them [women] in their proper
and subordinate rank, and it is only the crazy heads of our old
chivalrous ancestors that erected their Dulcineas into despotic
princesses." At luxurious breakfasts held at Dickenson's Coffee
House in the Turl, the befezzed and costumed woman-haters—
smoking oriental tobacco from oriental pipes—would relate stories
"which would serve to confirm members in their conviction that
women must be held in subjection as weak-minded and incorrigi-
bly frivolous creatures."

During his long vacation in 1851, Henry accompanied his parents
and Charles on a two-month trip to Germany. For both Charles
and Henry this was their first trip to the Continent, and to cele-
brate their holiday they decked themselves in new brown felt hats,
broad-brimmed with very high and pointed crowns. The very
splendor of these wide-awake hats is one reason for an unusually
fine firsthand account of the Kingsleys' crossing of the channel.

When the packet-boat left St. Katherine's Wharf that drizzly
July morning, on board were Thackeray and his two daughters,
Anne and Harriet (Minny), beginning their grand tour of Europe.
As Anne Thackeray, then thirteen, later states, she always distinctly
remembered that trip because she associated the crossing with hats.
The purchase of new hats had apparently occupied the Thackerays
as well as the Kingsleys. Mr. Thackeray had bought himself a new
grey wide-awake, which now, according to his daughter, looked
"commonplace" beside those of the Kingsley boys. And she and her
sister had gently packed into their cramped luggage two new,
brilliantly ribboned bonnets which "would bring us triumphantly
out of every crisis."

The channel crossing was stormy, Anne Thackeray tells us: "The
waves were curling unpleasantly round about the boat. I sat by
Mrs. Kingsley, miserable, uncomfortable, and watching in a dazed
and hypnotized sort of way the rim of Charles Kingsley's wide-
awake as it rose and fell against the horrible horizon."[11] Towards
evening the weather became more fierce, and as the steamer pitched
and tossed many women became sick on the cabin floor. Finally,
the two families arrived at Antwerp. After traveling together by
steamer to Cologne, they separated, and the Kingsleys settled at
Ems for two weeks.

11. Anne Thackeray Ritchie, *Chapters from Some Unwritten Memoirs* (New
York, 1895), p. 106.

After visiting the mineral baths at Ems, climbing the nearby mountains, and making short excursions in the vicinity of Coblenz, Charles and Henry left their parents and set out for a two-week walking trip through the Eifel and the country around the Moselle. This hike must have especially pleased and invigorated the athletic Henry, who, doubtless, wanted to prove to the older and taller Charles that his baby brother had become a man.

Trudging about fifteen miles per day with knapsacks that increased in weight daily from a steady accumulation of fossils and minerals, the two now-bearded brothers traveled through, as Charles said, "such wonders, I don't know where to begin . . . the whole country [is] the strangest jumble, alternations of Cambridgeshire ugliness (only lifted up 1,200 feet high) with all the beauties of Devonshire." One night, after losing their way, they found themselves "at the top of a cliff 500 feet high, with a roaring river at the bottom, and *no* path. So down the cliff face we had to come in the dark, or sleep in the forest to be eaten by wild boars and wolves, of which latter, one was seen on our route yesterday 'as high as a table.' And down we came, knapsacks, fishing-rods, and all; which process must not be repeated often if we intend to revisit our native shores."[12]

Nearing the end of their jaunt, the Kingsley brothers had reason to regret buying the wide-awake hats which had so fascinated Anne Thackeray. As they were about to enter Treves, they were arrested by a constable sent by the Mayor of Bittsburg and were thrown into prison, where "we had the pleasure of spending a night . . . among fleas and felons, on the bare floor." The Germans—"barbarians," as Charles called them—had mistaken the brothers' fishing-rods for "*todt-instrumenten*," some strange type of deadly weapon, and their wide-awakes "for Italian hats, and got into their addle pates that we were emissaries of Mazzini and Co. distributing political tracts." The next morning they were freed "with much laughter and many curses from the police" at Treves: "Luckily the police-inspector here was a gentleman, and his wife and daughter ladies . . . they did all they dared for us." This affair had, of course, attracted much attention among the local inhabitants, who, as a way of apology, feted and lionized the two Englishmen.[13] That same evening Mr.

12. *Charles Kingsley: His Letters and Memories of His Life,* Edited by his Wife (London, 1877), I, 234–35.
13. *Ibid.,* I, 237.

and Mrs. Kingsley arrived, and the reunited family set off on the last part of the trip—a slow journey to Bonn, Brussels, Waterloo, Ghent, and Bruges, before sailing for London from Ostend.

If Charles, at any time during their walking tour, had advised Henry about his conduct at college, Henry soon forgot the advice when he arrived back at Worcester. His entire college career is distinguished only by his athletic and social excesses. And like many other undisciplined boys, Kingsley borrowed heavily to pay for his pleasures. At one point, he was so pestered by anxious trades-men that his friend Cordy Jeaffreson backed a bill for £80.

Probably the best testimonies of the wasted college days occur in Kingsley's own novels, in which Worcester, renamed St. Paul's, figures prominently. The academic settings serve merely as arenas for boyish horseplay. The experiences he narrates usually concern "intoxicated and frantic young men" setting midnight bonfires in the Quad or enthusiastic scullers "rowing like madmen." Scenes of this kind—and they are numerous—ring with authenticity; indeed, in *Ravenshoe*, Charles Ravenshoe's outburst to John Marston, his college friend, at the idea of spending the best years of his life to get a "first" may easily have reflected the author's own thoughts:

> You're going to spend the best years of your life, and ruin your health, to get a first. *A first! A first!* Why that miserable little beast, Lock, got a first. A fellow who is, take him all in all, the most despicable little wretch I know! If you are very diligent you may raise yourself to *his* level! And, when you have got your precious first, you will find yourself utterly unfit for any trade or profession whatever (except the Church, which you don't mean to enter). What do you know about modern languages or modern history? If you go in the law, you have got to begin all over again. They won't take you in the army; they are not such *muffs*. And this is what you get for your fifteen hundred pounds! . . . I shouldn't care if I *was* a waterman. I'm sick of all this pretension and humbug; I'd sooner be anything than what I am, with my debts, and my rustication, and keeping up appearances. I wish I was a billiard marker; I wish I was a jockey; I wish I was Alick Reed's Novice; I wish I was one of Barclay and Perkins's draymen. Hang it! I wish I was a cabman! (Vol. I, ch. 8).

Kingsley, though not rusticated, suddenly left Worcester after three years without taking a degree. What actually caused the de-

parture remains unknown. Perhaps it was his penchant for riotous
living that either prompted or compelled him to leave, but since
the college minutes for 1853 register no mark against Kingsley's
name one suspects that Roland Evans' impulsive act in *Stretton*
mirrors Kingsley's own feelings at that time. Roland shouts his
dissatisfaction with college life: "I am sick of my life, and for no
reason—at least, for no reason which these wretched Philistines
can give me. I have always had everything which could make life
beautiful since I was a child, and I am sick of it. What is before
me? The schools? Bah! A double-first and then the compliments
due to the honour of my college. And then to drop back on my
position as a country gentleman? I tell you that I am utterly sick
of, and that I utterly loathe, my whole future career. From this
moment I give it up. For me to drop back on to Oxford honours
and turnips—I'll have none of it. Viva la Revolution! I am for
India" (Vol. II, ch. 3). Kingsley's further explanation of Roland's
actions sounds self-defensive: "In looking for a precedent for his
remarkable conduct, just look at your own when you were twenty-
one. Did you not do things then that you would not do now? Did
you not do generous and carelessly foolish things which you would
not do now? . . . In the Australian madness of 1852, how many
men do I know who, sick of things here, gave up safe positions in
England out of the pure old English spirit of adventure?" (Vol. II,
ch. 5).

Opportunely in March, 1853, an unexpected legacy of £500 from
his great aunt enabled him to pay off his many college debts and
to secure passage for Australia, then in the height of gold-rush fever.
Armed with letters of introduction and accompanied by two friends,
Venables and Irvine, the naïve twenty-three-year-old youth set out
on a Micawber-like voyage, confident that something worthwhile
would turn up.

But impractical Kingsley became no esteemed colonial magistrate. Instead of the wealth, fame, glory that he so ardently sought,
he encountered cruelty, harshness, and privation. Unprepared as
he was for any coarseness and crudity, his bewilderment was
doubtless excessive. Certainly, he trembled underneath his facade
of boldness when, suddenly, he was free of all supervision—parietal
or parental. Probably a passage in *The Recollections of Geoffry
Hamlyn* accurately transcribes Kingsley's own feelings when he left
England and arrived in Melbourne: "Only those who have done

so know how much effort it takes to say, 'I will go away to a land where none know me or care for me, and leave for ever all that I know and love.' And few know the feeling which comes upon all men after it is done,—the feeling of isolation, almost of terror, at having gone so far out of the bounds of ordinary life; the feeling of self-distrust and cowardice at being alone and friendless in the world, like a child in the dark" (Vol. I, ch. 17).

According to the *Melbourne Argus*, Victoria was a land of madness in 1853, when Kingsley arrived. It had just recently, in November, 1850, achieved its independence from New South Wales, and the discovery of gold almost a year later, in August, 1851, had swelled its population from 77,000 (1851), mainly in pastoral occupations, to nearly 200,000 (1853), with about 80,000 roaming around the goldfield. These people had flocked from all walks of life and from all countries. The great majority of the young and single men —like Kingsley—were there to find adventures and riches and to return home as quickly as possible. But many others, such as miners from Cornwall and Derbyshire, clerks and shopkeeper assistants from London, bankers from Bristol, small farmers from the provinces, and families from country towns had decided to migrate permanently.[14] Australia, as Kingsley later wrote, was not only a "cesspool for a vast quantity of nameless rubbish, convicted and unconvicted; but it gave an opening also for really honest, upright fellows" (*The Hillyars and the Burtons*, Vol. II, ch. 18). It was a melting pot for "all the unfortunates of the earth": "The English factory labourer and the farmer-ridden peasant; the Irish pauper; the starved Scotch Highlander. I hear a grand swelling chorus rising above the murmur of the evening breeze; that is sung by German peasants revelling in such plenty as they never knew before, yet still regretting fatherland, and then I hear a burst of Italian melody replying. Hungarians are not wanting, for all the oppressed of the earth have taken refuge here" (*Geoffry Hamlyn*, Vol. III, ch. 13).

With this influx of people the once pastoral hamlet of Melbourne, of course, changed. A correspondent for the *Sydney Morning Herald* wrote of it on November 4, 1852: "I must say that a worse regulated, worse governed, worse drained, worse lighted, worse watered town of note is not on the face of the globe; and that a population more thoroughly disposed, in every grade to

14. Geoffrey Serle, *The Golden Age* (Melbourne, 1963), pp. 47–48.

cheating and robbery, open and covert, does not exist; that in no other place does immorality stalk abroad so unblushingly and so unchecked; that in no other place does mammon rule so triumphant; that in no other place is the public money so wantonly squandered without giving the slightest protection to life or property; that in no other place are the administrative functions of Government so inefficiently managed; that, in a word, nowhere in the southern hemisphere does chaos reign so triumphant as in Melbourne."[15]

Probably exaggerated, this report, nevertheless, rings true. Kingsley tells us in *The Hillyars and the Burtons* that the discovery of Australia opened "a career for young gentlemen possessed of every virtue, save those of continence, sobriety, and industry, who didn't choose to walk, and couldn't afford to ride; and, viewed from this point, its discovery ranks next in importance after the invention of soda-water—a sort of way of escaping cheaply from the consequences of debauchery for a time" (Vol. II, ch. 18) . Other accounts record barefooted prostitutes "decked out in the richest and brightest of silks and satins," once respectable matrons in gaudy jewelry and ribboned bonnets, and even gold-shod-and-harnessed horses parading the streets. And everywhere were seen drunken diggers arrayed in their blue-or-red jerseys and their thick moleskin trousers. It was, one Anglican clergyman said,"the French Revolution without the guillotine."[16]

In the meantime, life on the goldfields was primitive. The diggers' cotton tents were insufficient to protect them from the ubiquitous fleas, flies, and mosquitoes and the unaccustomed heat and rain. The diggings, needless to say, were unhealthy places. Dysentery, malnutrition, typhoid, numerous respiratory diseases, resulting from sleeping on wet ground, as well as the hard physical labor either seriously injured or killed thousands of diggers. And just as many soon wearied of the hardships and returned to the swollen cities. An anonymous author amusingly writes of the diggers' disillusionment:

> "Well it don't suit me," said Tom, "I'm sure;
> That crowbar makes my hands too sore

15. *Ibid.*, p. 67.
16. J. H. Kerr, *Glimpses of Life in Victoria* (Edinburgh, 1872), p. 127; J. D. Mereweather, *Diary of a Working Clergyman in Australia and Tasmania, 1850–1853* (London, 1859), p. 214, as quoted in Serle, pp. 29–30.

And miserably soaked, all day I've stood,
Rocking the cradle, knee-deep in mud.
Now mucking at cooking, and slushing all day;
Now delving through dirty rocks and clay.
Gold digger! bah! It's all my eye
And that you'll say, lads, by-and-by.
You're welcome to your golden joys,
Your duffs and Johnny cakes, and doughboys,
Your vile lobscouse and milkless teas,
Your endless bacon fry and cheese,
Your dreary nights and weary days,
Your barb'rous, semi-savage ways;
Farewell to all your toil and strife,
And welcome quiet, cleanly life."[17]

But the majority stayed on the fields, driven on by a single-mindedness of greed or dreams.

For five years, Kingsley lived and struggled in this land, drifting from one job to another, sometimes walking more than two hundred miles "between Monday morning and evening church on the next Sunday evening" (*Tales of Old Travel Re-Narrated*, p. 119). He labored first on the newly discovered gold fields, then served with the Sydney Mounted Police, was briefly employed as an agricultural worker and stock driver, and finally returned to the gold fields. Since Kingsley was ashamed of his failures and completely cut himself off from his family during this time, the only actual accounts we have of him during these years are occasional personal allusions in his works and a few secondhand accounts recorded years later. In 1867 Henry's brother George, then traveling in Auckland, met a Mrs. Brackenbury, who had encountered Henry "fishing off the Gold Fields." "She was," George writes, "paralysed at the scientific manner in which he, a most ruffianly looking scoundrel of a miner, described the fish which he had caught; and took him in and was good to him, the old dear, when he was ill."[18] And in 1931, the ninety-four-year-old Henry J. Campbell, an old friend of the Kingsleys, recalled that upon his arrival in Melbourne in the early part of 1857 he presented a letter of introduction Charles Kingsley had given him to Martin Howy Irving, Professor of Classics and English at the newly created University of Melbourne. A former

17. *Ibid.*, p. 74.
18. George Henry Kingsley, pp. 49–50.

friend of both Charles and Henry in Chelsea, and Henry's school-
mate at King's College School, Irving informed Campbell that
Henry was at the Caledonian Gold Fields thirty miles from Melbourne. Campbell, as he remembers, "walked out to the camp, and
joined his party, and he took me as his mate; I slept in his tent,
helped with the rough cooking, and we 'toiled and moiled' and met
with nothing but disappointment, for it was a very poor diggings.
. . . There was one thing that varied the monotony of digging for
gold in hope and finding always Hope Deferred, and that was our
Sunday's work, which was called Prospecting—poking about the
gullies in the Dandenong Ranges. This always tempted Harry
Kingsley, for he was always keeping his eyes open for 'Colour' in
describing Bushrangers' haunts for the book he was even then
writing. . . . If I remember rightly, Henry Kingsley went to Daisy
Hill, and I went with another of the party to Bendigo, and I never
heard of H.K. till I returned home in 1862."[19]

In his quasi-autobiographical short story "My Landladies," published in 1872, Kingsley humorously describes one of his less congenial tent-mates, Harris, an old bricklayer from London who used
to return to the tent extremely drunk every Saturday night and
have to be put to bed. One Saturday night, as Kingsley tells us,
he kicked Harris out of the tent into the rain to cool off. Instead
of reforming, "like a decent man," Harris spent the weekend nights
elsewhere and returned in a "crapulous state" about noon every
Monday. Kingsley endured Harris' drunkenness because the old
man "had a nose for gold like a hound," but finally the breakup
occurred:

> This dreadful old man of the sea who had fastened himself
> on my back had an equally dreadful dog. I cannot describe
> all this dog's specialities, further than that he used diligently
> to howl all night. Also, when he came home drunk with his
> master, my dog Rover used to get him down and make night
> hideous. The number of times the silent Australian forest has
> seen me out in my shirt, bare-legged, separating those two dogs,
> with barefooted kicks, for which Rover cared not one penny,
> and which the other dog resented by biting my tendon Achil-
> les—the number of times, I say, when I have exhibited my
> legs to the blacks who slept outside our tent I am unable to
> remember.

19. Ellis, pp. 46–48.

... The end came in this way.

There were a great many Scotch on the Red Hill; and being a very thrifty people, they helped to build a church before the Anglicans, who came soon after. The church was of course Presbyterian, and I went the first Sunday; and Rover, my dog, followed: a fact I did not notice till I came to the church-door. I saw many others with their dogs, for some of the Scotch shepherds had heard of the church being opened. One grey-headed old Scotchman who spoke to me told me that he had started at two o'clock in the morning and had walked eighteen miles to worship in the church of his fathers once more before he died. . . . I went in with him and our dogs came also. I do not profess to be an extremely religious person, but the sensation of worshipping among one's fellow-men after an interval of three years would make any man sensitive and sentimental.

I am afraid that old memories of my father's church were crowding on me so strongly that my cheeks were wet when the first hymn was sung. The whole thing was destroyed by that tipsy old vagabond Harris. I could have killed him.

He not only came to church extremely drunk, but he brought his dog. Rover, who was as good as gold with the dear old Scotch shepherd's dog, saw old Harris's dog and fell on him tooth and nail. The whole service was stopped, and I had to get Rover away, with angry glances from the congregation. . . . I could live with old Harris no longer.[20]

The last year or so Kingsley spent as a "sundowner" (a tramp who arrives at out-stations at sunset, seeking food and lodgings). Thus, his great adventure was ending. He had met with increasing disappointment and futile monotony on the gold fields and repulsive brutality in the Mounted Police. Ellis relates that Kingsley, "with his sensitive nature, did not like witnessing the executions in cold blood of the captured bushrangers . . . and left the Mounted Police for this reason."[21] And now he was realizing humiliating treatment as a virtual beggar in the lonely and, at times, hostile country. But as *The Recollections of Geoffry Hamlyn, The Hillyars and the Burtons,* and the Australian sections of *Reginald Hetherege* amply demonstrate, the experiences were eventually rewarding.

20. *Temple Bar,* XXXVI (1872), 372–73.
21. Ellis, p. 45.

Kingsley began *Geoffry Hamlyn* in Australia during his last few months there, after finally finding some comfort at the end of almost five years of restlessness. Miss Rose Browne, daughter of Thomas Alexander Browne—the "Rolf Boldrewood" who became famous for his romantic and didactic novels of the Australian cattle stations and diggings—writes that "one evening two sun-downers came to her father's station, Squattle-Sea Mere, near Port Fairy, Victoria in the Fifties. Next morning one of the men revealed himself as Kingsley, and after a long and interesting talk with him 'Rolf Boldrewood' advised him to write a book. On leaving, he gave him an introduction to Mr. [William] Mitchell, of Langa-willi Station ["Home of the Parrots"], in the Western District."[22] Browne adds to the reminiscence in his *Old Melbourne Memories*: "It was at Langa-willi that *Geoffry Hamlyn*, that immortal work, the best Australian novel and for long the only one, was written. . . . I like to think of them both [Kingsley and Mitchell] spending the evening sociably in their own way, both rather silent men—Kingsley writing away till he had covered the regulation number of sheets or finished the chapter, perhaps when the bushrangers come to Garoopna . . . the old housekeeper coming in with the glasses at ten o'clock! then a tumbler of toddy, a smoke on the verandah, or over the fire if in winter, and so to bed."[23]

Just as abruptly as he had left England, Henry Kingsley returned to it. And as a search for adventure probably initiated the first flight, a longing for England and home motivated the second. Two years after his return Kingsley wrote, "If our reader has never been to Australia, he will hardly understand what are the sensations of a man, long banished, when he first realizes to himself the fact, 'I am going home.' Home! No one ever says, 'I am going to Europe, sir,' or 'I am going to England, sir!' "[24]

In September, 1858, shabbily dressed—almost threadbare—and a failure in every sense, he arrived at Chelsea. Kingsley, so the story goes, was afraid that his parents might have died during the five years of silence and paced up and down outside of the rectory for over an hour, dreading the news he might hear. Finally, taking heart of grace, he knocked, and was relieved to learn that his parents were living at Eversley, Hampshire, where his brother

22. *Ibid.*, p. 49*n*1.
23. London, 1896, pp. 172–73.
24. "Travelling in Victoria," *Macmillan Magazine*, III (December, 1860), 141.

Charles, now a great celebrity, was still curate.[25] The postponed homecoming was a joyous one. Free of hardships and happy in the midst of his family and familiar scenery, Kingsley settled down and finished *Geoffry Hamlyn*, which Charles recommended to Alexander Macmillan, his own publisher.

Enthusiastic about the manuscript, Macmillan wrote to his friend James Mac Lehose on October 27, 1858: "A younger brother of Kingsley's—Henry by name—who has spent many years in Australia, principally in the back-woods, is writing a story of Australian life—chiefly back-woods, partly in England. I have seen about 100 pages of it, and so has Mrs. Macmillan. We are both delighted with it, and augur good things from it. He has his brother's power of describing, but he does not write in the same style at all; it is wonderfully quiet and yet powerful—a kind of lazy strength which is very charming; some of the characters too are drawn with a masterly hand. Convicts, emigrant gentlemen from decayed families, farmers emigrant from various reasons—these are characters he draws. Each one stands firm and clear on his feet, like a man in actual life. I will tell you more about it when I know more. Henry I saw at Eversley in the Autumn, and liked exceedingly."[26]

It is probably owing to Kingsley's contentment at this time that *Geoffry Hamlyn* is not entirely representative of his work. It was begun in a peaceful Australian setting after his romantic, foolish, and disillusioning adventure, and it was completed in a comparable serenity at Eversley, in a cottage adjoining that of his parents. Although he lived at Eversley during most of the writing of his next three novels, he was never again able to write such a totally jovial and delightful book. His later novels are either clouded by a melancholy that slowly deepens as he grows older and more despondent or else puffed up by a forced heartiness that only calls attention to their hollowness. *Geoffry Hamlyn*, however, was revised and finished in the bloom of his homecoming. He was a true prodigal son. There is no doubt that a rivalry—felt at least on Henry's part—existed between the two Kingsley brothers, and Henry's fear of fraternal competition became more acute as Charles

25. By 1858, Charles Kingsley had published *Alton Locke* (1850), a fictitious autobiography of a Chartist Leader, and his historical novels *Hypatia* (1853) and *Westward Ho!* (1855).

26. *Letters of Alexander Macmillan*, ed. with Introduction by his son George A. Macmillan (Printed for Private Circulation, 1908), pp. 5–6.

won yet more honors. But in 1858, for a short time, Henry was not just Charles Kingsley's younger brother but an important figure himself—an adventurer—and even successfully competing with him in Charles' own trade. Indeed, after *Geoffry Hamlyn* appeared, Anne Thackeray recalls visiting the Kingsleys with her father: "I remember hearing Mrs. Kingsley—saying to my father, 'You know my son Charles, I should like you to know my son Henry too,' and took up some new books which were lying on the table and put them into my father's hand. 'He also can write books,' she said, smiling with motherly pride."[27]

27. Letter to C. K. Shorter, "Introduction," pp. xix–xx. Henry, of course, had met Thackeray twice before: in 1848, with John Parker, and in 1851, on his continental trip.

II

The Recollections of Geoffry Hamlyn

Geoffry Hamlyn was published in that *annus mirabilis* 1859, but Kingsley's novel bears little similarity to the two epoch-making "first novels" of that year: *Adam Bede* and *The Ordeal of Richard Feverel* are both psychological analyses, founded on the principle that art has a social and moral mission. No scientific or even quasi-scientific study of characters exists in the romantic *Geoffry Hamlyn*, and, if any moral purpose manifests itself in Kingsley's work, it is one that swings closer to the then current Thomas Hughes spirit of fiction than to that of George Eliot and Meredith. Unlike the Tom Brown novels, however, especially *Tom Brown's School Days* (1857), *Geoffry Hamlyn* does not plead for needed improvements in established customs. Never does Kingsley produce a rigidly narrow didactic novel to propagate a particular creed as does his brother Charles in most of his major works. He stresses and lovingly portrays the simple standards of loyalty, generosity, bravery, and friendship that align him with his brother's and Hughes' "Muscular Christianity." *Geoffry Hamlyn* emphasizes and re-emphasizes a life that consists of honor, manly strength and gentility, womanly beauty and virtue, and wholesome comradeship. In other words, this is the life that begets the ideal English gentleman and the model English matron.

Favorable reviews attest the nineteenth-century popularity of the novel. The *Athenaeum*, after listing some of its obvious defects, guaranteed that "Mr. Henry Kingsley, however, has written a book which the public will be more inclined to read than to criticise, and we commend them to each other."[1] The *North British Review* more

1. XXXII (May 7, 1859), 610.

enthusiastically acclaimed: "*Geoffry Hamlyn* is a fresh, vivid, and picturesque book. The narrative is lively throughout,—it never flags nor tires."[2] Most important of all, Mudie's chain of circulating libraries ordered five hundred copies—the Victorian equivalent of adoption by a major book club. ("I would rather have Mudie and the British Matron on my side," said Meredith, "than the whole British press.") Its publisher, Alexander Macmillan, was so pleased with the novel that he sent a copy of it to Tennyson, hoping that the Poet Laureate would find it a "relief from metaphysico-theological controversy."[3] In the United States, Ticknor and Fields, Kingsley's American publisher for his first six novels, published 3,706 copies of the novel between May 28, 1859 and June 21, 1869.[4]

The English and American receptions, however, were moderate compared to the Australian. For many of the colonists *Geoffry Hamlyn* was the Great Australian Novel; it and Kingsley's later work *The Hillyars and the Burtons* together were termed by Alfred Deakin (1857–1919), the Australian statesman, the "Charter of Australia."[5] Marcus Clarke, mainly known now for his novel *For the Term of His Natural Life* (1874), dealing with the convict settlements in Australia, wrote in 1869 that the setting for his earlier novel *Long Odds* was England because *Geoffry Hamlyn* was already the "best Australian novel that has been, and probably will be."[6] In the late nineteenth century, writing an appreciative account of Kingsley from an Australian point of view, Desmond Byrne remarked that Kingsley "was the first to describe in fiction the rural life of the country, to recognize the beginning of an aristocracy of landholders, and to commemorate the pervading spirit of cheerful confidence to which so much of the rapid development of Australia was due."[7] And even today in Australia *Geoffry Hamlyn* is regarded as the first Australian novel "of note, written by a novelist of note": "*Geoffry Hamlyn* marks the beginning of a period when writers saw in the Australian scene a wider

2. XXXI (1859), Article V, 393. See also L.T. Hergenhan, "*Geoffry Hamlyn* Through Contemporary Eyes," *Australian Literary Studies*, II (December, 1966), 289–95.

3. *Letters of Alexander Macmillan*, p. 23.

4. Ticknor and Fields Cost Books, Houghton Library, Harvard University.

5. Letter by Sir George Otto Trevelyan, *Times Literary Supplement*, June 21, 1923, 422.

6. Quoted in Robert Lee Wolff, "Henry Kingsley," *Harvard Library Bulletin*, XIII (Spring, 1959), 198.

7. *Australian Writers* (London, 1896), p. 107.

wealth of source material embracing the whole ambit of human experience and not simply a highly coloured background against which picaresque tales could be easily set."[8]

Pride naturally entered into the early Australian appreciation of the work, but the novel's reception in the colony cannot be accredited wholly to mere prejudice shading into provincial chauvinism. *Geoffry Hamlyn* is an exhilarating and original romance. Unlike Charles Reade—doubtless the greatest researcher in English fiction—who, in order to authenticate the Australian setting for sections of *It Is Never Too Late To Mend* (1856), had assiduously interviewed returning travelers, Kingsley had wandered, labored, and struggled in the primitive land. He had seen and felt the fetal stirrings of the new nation, and with his intense powers of observation he had recorded them. Melbourne, heaving lustily "through the unbroken solitude of a primeval forest"; the rugged woodlands, untamed mountains, and treacherous rivers of the new continent; and the then unheard of adventures such as kangaroo hunts, wild bull roundups, and bushranger raids are superbly described. Like their fellow Englishmen, the colonists could thrill to the excitement generated by Kingsley's, at times, breathless style. Such a scene as Sam Buckley's wild ride on Widderin is still an example of great descriptive narrative. Although lengthy, the excerpt deserves to be quoted in its entirety; cutting would ruin the scene's total effect.

Aware of an imminent bushranger attack on the Brentwood house, where Alice, his fiancée, is alone, Sam Buckley rides desperately to the rescue:

> The Doctor . . . was making good work of it across the plains, when he heard the rush of horse's feet behind him, and turning, he saw Widderin bestridden by Sam, springing over the turf, gaining on him stride after stride. In a few minutes they were alongside of one another. . . .
>
> Sam only waved his hand in good-bye, and sped on across the plain like a solitary ship at sea. He steered for a single tree, now becoming dimly visible, at the foot of the Organ hill.
>
> The good horse, with elastic and easy motion, fled on his course like a bird; lifting his feet clearly and rapidly through the grass. The brisk south wind filled his wide nostrils as he turned his graceful neck from side to side, till, finding that

8. Clive Hamer, "The Surrender to Truth in the Early Australian Novel," *Australian Literary Studies*, II (December, 1965), 103.

work was meant, and not play, he began to hold his head straight before him, and rush steadily forward.

And Sam, poor Sam! all his hopes for life are now brought down to this: to depend on the wind and pluck of an unconscious horse. One stumble now, and it were better to lie down on the plain and die. He was in the hands of God, and he felt it. He said one short prayer, but that towards the end was interrupted by the wild current of his thoughts.

Was there any hope? They, the devils, would have been drinking at the Mayfords', and perhaps would go slow; or would they ride fast and wild? After thinking a short time, he feared the latter. They had tasted blood, and knew that the country would be roused on them shortly. On, on, good horse!

The lonely shepherd on the plains, sleepily watching his feeding sheep, looked up as Sam went speeding by, and thought how fine a thing it would be to be dressed like that, and have nothing to do but to ride blood horses to death. Mind your sheep, good shepherd; perhaps it were better for you to do that and nothing more all your life, than to carry in your breast for one short hour such a volcano of rage, indignation and terror, as he does who hurries unheeding through your scattered flock.

Here are a brace of good pistols, and they, with care, shall give account, if need be, of two men. After that, nothing. It were better, so much better, not to live if one were only ten minutes too late. The Doctor would be up soon; not much matter if he were, though, only another life gone.

The Organ hill, a cloud of misty blue when he started, now hung in aerial fluted cliffs above his head. As he raced across the long glacis which lay below the hill, he could see a solitary eagle wheeling round the topmost pinnacles, against the clear blue sky; then the hill was behind him, and before him another stretch of plain, bounded by timber, which marked the course of the river.

Brave Widderin had his ears back now, and was throwing his breath regularly through his nostrils in deep sighs. Good horse, only a little longer; bear thyself bravely this day, and then pleasant pastures for thee till thou shalt go the way of all horses. Many a time has she patted, with kind words, thy rainbow neck, my horse; help us to save her now.

Alas! good willing brute, he cannot understand; only he knows that he will run till he drop. Good Widderin! think of the time when thy sire rushed triumphant through the shouting thousands at Epsom, and all England heard that Arcturus had won the Derby. Think of the time when thy grandam, carrying Sheik Abdullah, bore down in a whirlwind of sand on the toiling affrighted caravan. Ah! thou knowest not of these things, but yet thy speed flags not. We are not far off now, good horse, we shall know all soon.

Now he was in the forest again, and now, as he rode quickly down the steep sandy road among the bracken, he heard the hoarse rush of the river in his ears, and knew the end was well-nigh come.

No drink now, good Widderin! a bucket of champagne in an hour's time, if thou wilt only stay not now to bend thy neck down to the clear gleaming water; flounder through the ford, and just twenty yards up the bank by the cherry-tree, we shall catch sight of the house, and know our fate.

Now the house was in sight, and now he cried aloud some wild inarticulate sound of thankfulness and joy. All was as peaceful as ever, and Alice, unconscious, stood white-robed in the verandah, feeding her birds.

As he rode up he shouted out to her and beckoned. She came running through the house, and met him breathless at the doorway.

"The bushrangers! Alice, my love," he said, "We must fly this instant, they are close to us now" (Vol. III, ch. 8).

The swiftness of the prose, the control of the tempo, the rhythm of the language epitomize the early Kingsley when he possessed not only an instinct for beautiful prose but the ability to create it, a mastery over form that lifts *Geoffry Hamlyn* out of the range of usual adventure stories.

The novel opens with a prologue. Three of the main characters, Major Buckley, Captain Brentwood, and the narrator, Geoffry Hamlyn, are sitting in the verandah at Baroona, the Buckleys' Australian estate, discussing past circumstances in their lives. The year is 1857. Suddenly, Hamlyn surprises the group (increased by the entrance of Mrs. Buckley) with an account of their history, which he has secretly written. By one of Kingsley's typically informal intrusions, the curious reader is led by Hamlyn into Kingsley's fictional world of romantic characters living in a strangely new setting:

The reader will probably ask:
"Now who on earth is Major Buckley? and who is Captain

Brentwood? and last, not least, who the Dickens are you?" If you will have the patience, my dear Sir, you will find it all out in a very short time—Read on.

The first third of the novel takes place in England, mostly in Dartmoor, Devonshire. Although Henry had moved from this county when he was six, Devonshire so impressed both him and Charles that between them they used it as a setting for five novels. His memories of it refreshed by later visits, Henry, in *Geoffry Hamlyn*, vividly reproduces the locale:

> Those who only know the river Taw as he goes sweeping, clear and full, past orchards and farmhouses, by woods and parks, and through long green meadows, after he has left Dartmoor, have little idea of the magnificent scene which rewards the perseverance of any one who has the curiosity to follow him up to his granite cradle between the two loftiest eminences in the west of England.
>
> On the left, Great Cawsand heaves up, down beyond down, a vast sheet of purple heath and golden whin, while on the right the lofty serrated ridge of Yestor starts boldly up, black against the western sky, throwing a long shadow over the wild waste of barren stone at his feet. . . .
>
> It is an evil, depressing place. Far as the eye can reach up the glen and to the right, it is one horrid waste of grey granite; here and there a streak of yellow grass or a patch of black bog; not a tree nor a shrub within the sky-line. On a hot summer's day it is wearisome enough for the lonely angler to listen to the river crawling lazily through the rocks that choke his bed, mingled with the clocking of some water-moved boulder, and the chick-chick of the stone chat, or the scream of the golden plover over head. But on a wild winter's evening, when day is fast giving place to night, and the mist shrouds the hill, and the wild wind is rushing hoarse through tor and crag, it becomes awful and terrible in the extreme (Vol. I, ch. 5).

Kingsley does more than merely describe the countryside. Characteristically, Great Cawsand, intensely objectifying evilness in the impending action, becomes a symbolic counterpart of the characters and situation: William Lee, a transported convict, has arranged a secret rendezvous in order to blackmail George Hawker, the novel's villain. The device is only too familiar, in Victorian fiction as in Elizabethan drama, but Kingsley handles it discreetly and successfully.

Although the other example of Kingsley's effective use of nature occurs in the Australian section of the novel, it can most efficiently be discussed here. A lengthy description of an approaching storm becomes a vehicle to reflect and to heighten the emotional state of Mary Thornton Hawker, who is about to hear that the notorious bushranger Captain Touan is, in reality, her supposedly dead husband, George:

> She sat still listening . . . eating nothing. Lee's words outside had, she knew not why, struck a chill into her heart, and . . . she shivered, although the night was hot. Through the open window she could hear all those thousand commingled indistinguishable sounds that make the nightlife of the bush, with painful distinctness. She arose and went to the window.
>
> The night was dark and profoundly still. The stars were overhead, though faintly seen through a haze; and beyond the narrow enclosures in front of the house, the great forest arose like a black wall. Tom and Charles went on talking inside, and yet, though their voices were loud, she was hardly conscious of hearing them, but found herself watching the high dark wood and listening to the sound of the frogs in the creek, and the rustle of a million crawling things, heard only in the deep stillness of night.
>
> Deep in the forest somewhere, a bough cracked, and fell crashing, then all was silent again. Soon arose a wind, a partial wandering wind, which came slowly up, and, rousing the quivering leaves to life for a moment, passed away; then again a silence, deeper than ever, so that she could hear the cattle and horses feeding in the lower paddock, a quarter of a mile off; then a low wail in the wood, then two or three wild weird yells, as of a devil in torment, and a pretty white curlew skirled over the housetop to settle on the sheep-wash dam.
>
> The stillness was awful; it boded a storm, for behind the forest glazed up a sheet of lightning, showing the shape of each fantastic elevated bough (Vol. II, ch. 14).

In examining Kingsley's descriptive artistry and his careful scene planning in *Geoffry Hamlyn*, J. C. Horner has compared this passage with a similar one which occurs two hours later. Tom Troubridge, Mary's cousin-partner, is awaiting Captain Touan's arrival at their estate, Toonarbin: "The night was wonderfully still and dark. As he paused before entering the house, he could hear the bark falling from the trees a quarter of a mile off, and the opossums scratching and snapping little twigs as they passed from bough to bough. Somewhere, apparently at an immense distance, a morepork was chanting his monotonous cry. The frogs in the creek were silent even, so hot was the night" (Vol. II, ch. 14).

The contrasts in the scenes effectively differentiate the emotional states of the two characters. Mary knows not what to fear; she merely apprehends an approaching danger. Her anxiety and fright increase gradually (as does the suspense) as Kingsley slowly creates the signs of the ominous physical storm: Mary loses consciousness of the household behind her as she becomes more engrossed in the outside world, which will literally bring her further desolation. Tom, however, has no such presentiment. Not fearing Touan, he merely identifies the nocturnal sounds, as he listens intently for the bushranger's footsteps. The passage is short because Tom, unlike Mary, does not stare into the night but pauses only briefly before entering the house; he has already prepared himself for the expected battle. Kingsley is now ready to bring Touan on stage: the storm has finally neared the house and the nightsounds have become apparently quieted so that Tom may hear Touan's "stealthy step on the gravel."[9]

The English section of the novel not only introduces most of the principal characters but also sets forth the unwieldy plot-machinery that will transport them to Australia, for eventually all major characters, except one, will find their way to the new land. Although at times this machinery lumbers along incredibly, the main defect in this section lies in the typically Victorian melodrama. Most of the action hinges on the disastrous love affair and elopement of Mary Thornton, the Vicar's willful and flirtatious daughter, with George Hawker, the illegitimate son of the gypsy Madge Hawker, a Scott-like character faintly suggestive of a Madge Wildfire/Meg Merrilies combination, and a miserly old reprobate. George's crimes are Victorian stereotypes: He fathers illegitimate children, forges his father's name, gambles, and mistreats Mary, after running through her small fortune. Finally apprehended for coining, he is transported to Australia, and Mary, penniless, wanders

9. J. C. Horner, "*Geoffry Hamlyn* and its Australian Setting," *Australian Literary Studies*, I (1963), 11–12.

homeward with her child, there to be greeted ecstatically by her aunt and her dying father. Since, she is, after all, married, Mary's circumstances differ essentially from those of poor unwed Hetty Sorrell (*Adam Bede*), but how unfavorably Kingsley's treatment of anguish and desolation compares with George Eliot's or even, for that matter, with Scott's portrayal of Effie Deans in *Heart of Midlothian* (1818)! In this episode, for example, he falls back on shabby triteness and an unconvincing coincidence for sensation. First, Mary is accosted by the usual "handsomely dressed" procuress:

> Mary stepped forward and struck her, so full and true that the woman reeled backwards, and stood whimpering and astonished.
> "Out! you false jade," said Mary, "you are one of those devils . . . who come whispering, and peering, and crowding behind those who are penniless and deserted; but I have faced you, and struck you, and I tell you to go back to your master, and say that I am not for him."

Then immediately she sees "There, under the lamp, on the step . . . a woman, her own image, nursing a baby so like her own that she looked down at her bosom to see if it was safe" (Vol. I, ch. 16). Mary had encountered the lunatic Ellen Lee, George's discarded mistress. In *Daniel Deronda* (1876) George Eliot shows how such a confrontation of wife (or wife-to-be) and mistress with child can be well done, when Gwendolen Harleth encounters Mallinger Grandcourt's all-but-discarded mistress, Mrs. Lydia Glasher.

While the Mary Thornton/George Hawker embroilment dominates the foreground, the staid, noble Buckleys occupy the middle distance. Inextricably connected with the Thorntons, the Buckleys furnish support for the inept, ineffectual Vicar Thornton and advice to the unheeding Mary. It is Major Buckley who journeys unsuccessfully to London to save Mary, and Mrs. Buckley who comforts her when she finally comes home. Major James Buckley, a hero of Waterloo and heir of Clere, the impoverished family estate, represents Kingsley's honorable, soldier-hero type of gentleman, a characterization which degenerates into unintentional caricature in later novels. Agnes Buckley, also a static figure, embraces all of the characteristics of a good, obedient wife and loving mother—the ideal English lady portrayed so often (and sometimes so lifelessly) by many English novelists and apotheosized in Mrs. Sarah Stickney Ellis' *Women of England* series.[10] Occasionally, Kingsley catches Mrs. Buckley perceptively in a short, pregnant description, for example in the Australian section of the novel when the newly arrived immigrants are crossing the Australian ranges: "Mrs. Buckley, with her gown tucked up, was preparing breakfast, as if she had been used to the thing all her life. She had an imperial sort of way of manoeuvring a frying pan, which did one good to see. It is my belief, that if that woman had been called upon to groom a horse, she'd have done it in a ladylike way" (Vol. II, ch. 1).

The reader harbors no doubts that the Buckleys will succeed gloriously in Australia. As if to emphasize the point, Kingsley sends them forth with the prophetic blessing of Madge Hawker, in a scene that, although theatrical, and certainly unadulterated Scott, is nonetheless effective. In all her gypsy tempestuousness and dignity, Madge stands majestically in front of the Buckleys' door, raises her hand, and chants: " 'The blessing of God . . . shall be upon the house of the Buckleys, and more especially upon you and your husband, and the boy that is sleeping inside. He shall be a brave and a good man, and his wife shall be the fairest and best in the country side. Your kine shall cover the plains until no man can number them, and your sheep shall be like the sands of the sea. When misfortune and death and murder fall upon your neighbours, you shall stand between the dead and the living, and the troubles that pass over your heads shall be like the shadow of the light clouds that fly across the moor on a sunny day. And when in your ripe and honoured old age you shall sit with your husband, in a garden of your own planting, in the lands far away, and see your grandchildren playing around you, you shall think of the words of the wild lost gipsy woman, who gave you her best blessing before

10. Twelve years earlier in *The Princess*, Tennyson had immortalized this type of English womanhood:

> Not learned save in gracious household ways,
> Not perfect nay, but full of tender wants,
> No angel, but a dearer being, all dipt
> In angel instincts, breathing Paradise,
> Interpreter between the gods and men,
> Who look'd all native to her place, and yet
> On tiptoe seem'd to touch upon a sphere
> Too gross to tread, and all male minds perforce
> Sway'd to her from their orbits as they moved,
> And girdled her with music.
>   (Part VII, ll. 299–308)

she went away' " (Vol. I, ch. 14). Madge's words accurately presage the action found in the second part of the novel.

When the setting moves to Australia, Kingsley introduces a new world to his readers:

> A new heaven and a new earth! Tier beyond tier, height above height, the great wooded ranges go rolling away westward, till on the lofty skyline they are crowned with a gleam of everlasting snow. To the eastward they sink down, breaking into isolated forest, fringed peaks, and rock-crowned eminences, till with rapidly straightening lines they disappear gradually into broad grey plains, beyond which the Southern Ocean is visible by the white reflection cast upon the sky.
>
> All creation is new and strange. The trees surpassing in size the largest English oaks, are of a species we have never seen before. The graceful shrubs, the bright-coloured flowers, ay, the very grass itself, are of species unknown in Europe; while flaming lories and brilliant parroquets fly whistling, not unmusically, through the gloomy forest, and over head in the higher fields of air, still lit up by the last rays of the sun, countless cockatoos wheel and scream in noisy joy, as we may see the gulls do about an English headland (Vol. II, ch. 1).

Not until D. H. Lawrence published *Kangaroo* (1923) and *The Boy in the Bush* (1924) does a reader encounter this same acute sensitivity by a British novelist to this "strange, strange world . . . with its sun and its marsupials." Echoing Kingsley's fascination, Lawrence also celebrated its lushness and its array of queer charms. But Lawrence's description takes on a different dimension from Kingsley's. Whereas *Geoffry Hamlyn* is a romance of young love and, thus, draws its images from the newness of the land, *Kangaroo*, the more major of Lawrence's two Australian works, is a brooding psychological novel in which its hero, Richard Lovat Somers, labors to maintain his individuality against his wife, his newly found Australian friends, and, most importantly, against the charismatic political leader Benjamin Cooley, the Kangaroo of the title. In order to depict Somers' individualism and isolation, Lawrence found a perfect image in the desolation of the menacing and seemingly ageless Australian bush that both attracted and terrified him. It is this setting that Lawrence turned to continually to emphasize Somers' aloneness:

> That curious sombreness of Australia, the sense of oldness,

with the forms all worn down low and blunt, squat. The
squat-seeming earth. And then they ran at last into real
country rather rocky, dark old rocks, and sombre bush with its
different pale-stemmed dull-leaved gum trees standing graceful,
and various healthy-looking undergrowth, and great spikey
things like zuccas. . . . It was virgin bush, and as if unvisited,
lost, sombre, with plenty of space, yet spreading grey for miles
and miles, in a hollow towards the west. Far in the west, the
sky having suddenly cleared, they saw the magical range of the
Blue Mountains. And all this hoary space of bush between.
The strange, as it were, *invisible* beauty of Australia, which
is undeniably there, but which seems to lurk just beyond the
range of our white vision. You feel you can't *see*—as if your
eyes hadn't the vision in them to correspond with the outside
landscape. For the landscape is so unimpressive, like a face
with little or no features, a dark face. It is so aboriginal, out
of our ken, and it hangs back so aloof. Somers always felt he
looked at it through a cleft in the atmosphere; as one looks
at one of the ugly-faced, distorted aborigines with his wonderful dark eyes that have such incomprehensible ancient shine
in them, across gulfs of unbridged centuries. And yet, when
you don't have the feeling of ugliness or monotony, in landscape or in nigger, you get a sense of subtle, remote, *formless*
beauty more poignant than anything ever experienced before
(Ch. 5).

Opposite in their presentations of this new land, both Lawrence and
Kingsley, nevertheless, in their own ways, recorded two of the most
vivid pictures of the Australian continent.

No wonder Kingsley's description stirred the imagination of the
British readers, accustomed, as they were, to the familiar rural
scenes depicted in their glorious nineteenth-century watercolors:
Constable's fields of grain and his haywains, or Cox's rocky landscapes and old castles, or the early Girtin's hills and streams.
Tennyson caught this traditional landscape perfectly in a stanza
in "The Palace of Art":

> And one, an English home—gray twilight pour'd
>   On dewy pastures, dewy trees.
> Softer than sleep—all things in order stored,
>   A haunt of ancient Peace (11. 85–88).

The very point is that Kingsley, rejecting the thatched cottage
so hallowed by tradition that Forster, in *Howards End* (1910),

could make it stand for a whole way of life, the heart-stirring old rectories, and misty fields, takes the willing reader into a world of strange animals, earthquakes, bushfires, cannibalism, and hot Christmas days, when the thermometer reads 109 degrees in the shade. Vivid descriptions of this new world display Kingsley's talents at their best. Typical is the scene of the first meeting between Sam Buckley and Alice Brentwood:

What a delicious verandah is this to dream in! Through the tangled passion-flowers, jessamines and magnolias, what a soft gleam of bright hazy distance, over the plains and far away! The deep river-glen cleaves the tableland, which, here and there, swells into breezy downs. Beyond, miles away to the North, is a great forest-barrier, above which there is a blaze of late snow, sending strange light aloft into the burning haze. All this is seen through an arch in the dark mass of verdure which clothes the trellis-work, only broken through in this one place, as though to make a frame for the picture. [Sam] leans back, and gives himself up to watching trifles.

See here. A magpie comes furtively out of the house with a key in his mouth, and, seeing Sam, stops to consider if he is likely to betray him. On the whole, he thinks not, so he hides the key in a crevice, and whistles a tune.

Now enters a cockatoo, waddling along comfortably and talking to himself. He tried to enter into conversation with the magpie, who, however, cuts him dead, and walks off to look at the prospect.

Flop! flop! A great foolish-looking kangaroo comes through the house and peers round him. The cockatoo addresses a few remarks to him, which he takes no notice of, but goes blundering out into the garden, right over the contemplative magpie, who gives him two or three indignant pecks on his clumsy feet, and sends him flying down the gravel walk.

Two bright-eyed little kangaroo rats come out of their box peering and blinking. The cockatoo finds an audience in them, for they sit listening to him, now and then catching a flea, or rubbing the backs of their heads with their forepaws. But a buck 'possum, who stealthily descends by a pillar from unknown realms of mischief on the top of the house, evidently discredits cocky's stories, and departs down the garden to see if he can find something to eat.

The scene continues with a playful tousle between a kitten and a puppy, with a magpie serving as a gadfly until

Sam lay sleepily amused by this little drama; then he looked at the bright green arch which separated the dark verandah from the bright hot garden. The arch was darkened, and looking he saw something which made his heart move strangely, something that he has not forgotten yet, and never will.

Under the arch between the sunlight and the shade, bare-headed, dressed in white, stood a girl, so amazingly beautiful, that Sam wondered for a few moments whether he was asleep or awake (Vol. II, ch. 10).

The beginning of a conventional love scene, but Kingsley has filled it with the newness and playfulness and loveliness of young love.

Kingsley seldom presents these scenes merely for the sake of adding local color; most of them either develop a characterization or picturesquely lead into forthcoming action. According to J. C. Horner, *Geoffry Hamlyn*, in fact, was the first novel which utilized the Australian setting as a "fitting background for a romantic tale without any jarring effect and without glaring distortion."[11] Whereas the scene above serves to introduce the two lovers, a graphic picture in the stockyard, describing men attempting to capture wild bulls, climaxes Sam and Alice's romance. Seeing him injured, she realizes that she loves him. Comparably, a sentimental but moving tale of a little boy lost in the bush initiates a discussion between Sam and Cecil Mayford, his rival, about their love for Alice.[12]

Although Kingsley concentrates on reporting the Australian life, his picture of the golden age of squatterdom invests it with a glory that was assuredly not characteristic. Not only does he select the pre-auriferous period of Australian history, when the country had not yet been invaded by a wanton rowdyism, but he eliminates most of the ugliness of the squatting life. As one of his nineteenth-century critics mockingly but truthfully said, Kingsley "made the life too much like a prolonged picnic."[13] The misery, despair, toil, loneliness are all ignored. The Buckleys and their friends have erected in the Australian wilderness a self-contained Arcadian kingdom, consisting of three close-knit, individual households, all en-

11. P. 5.

12. In 1871, Kingsley published this incident separately as a Christmas book entitled *The Lost Child.*

13. Anonymous critic quoted in Byrne, p. 107. The most adverse criticism of *Geoffry Hamlyn* is Joseph Furphy's novel *Such is Life,* written under the pseudonym of "Tom Collins" and first published in 1903.

joying incredible financial success and luxurious living. Actually, young Victoria's England has been transplanted to the new land. The setting differs but the English country life remains. And in order to make the English group a unity in Australia, Kingsley, heedlessly and with great improbability, transports two characters of the inner circle who had remained in England when Major Buckley's expedition emigrated.

One is Frank Maberly, Kingsley's first and most obvious example of a true muscular Christian, who not only runs four miles in a little over twenty minutes but later vaults over a five-barred fence. Completely unnecessary to the Australian scenes, Dean Maberly offers Kingsley an excuse to picture life in the outlying huts, where the freed convict-workers are housed. And when Maberly rides into the bush to talk with these men, Kingsley, unintentionally, gives the reader an opportunity to pinpoint one of the major differences between the Kingsley brothers. Whereas Charles would have given not only the text but the sermon proper, Henry dismisses both in one short sentence and focuses all attention on a description of the individual convicts, stressing well their false solicitude and deep hatred of the clergyman.

The mysterious Dr. Mulhaus figures more prominently in the novel, for he is the center of one of its minor and extraneous mysteries, the kind which Kingsley delights in adding to most of his stories. Not until quite late in the tale, after many hints and clues, does the reader learn that the Doctor is, in reality, the famous Baron von Landstein, a noble, exiled Prussian. Although not irritating to the reader, this concealment serves little purpose except to add unneeded suspense to the already packed novel. But Dr. Mulhaus' pleasing characterization fulfills two major functions: the incongruity of his scholarly bearing and conversation in primitive Australia adds humor; his erudition enables Kingsley to expound copious scientific facts about the country that undoubtedly excited the English reader.

The reason for Kingsley's whitewashed presentation of the squatters is obvious. He was an Englishman inoculated from birth with English taste and morals, and his ancestry had included men similar to Major Buckley and Captain Brentwood. His reading of Dickens and Thackeray only augmented his earlier reverence for the English tradition. Even Kingsley's romantic expedition to Australia initially followed the pattern set up by innumerable English adventurers.[14] It seems improbable that, when he wrote *Geoffry Hamlyn*, Kingsley ever considered portraying his English gentry in any manner except that which had always been reproduced in British novels: ordered and restrained. The Buckleys are such; they could easily have presented themselves in a Jane Austen or Trollope drawing room. In fact, Major Buckley's words concerning dining are closely similar in tone to Archbishop Grantly's dictates about the appropriateness of a large dining room:

> "I think, Doctor," said the Major, "that the habit of dining in the middle of the day is a gross abuse of the gifts of Providence, and I'll prove it to you. What does a man dine for?—answer me that."
>
> "To satisfy his hunger, I should say," answered the Doctor.
>
> "Pooh! pooh! stuff and nonsense, my good friend," said the Major; "you are speaking at random. I suppose you will say, then, that a black fellow is capable of dining?"
>
> "Highly capable, as far as I can judge from what I have seen," replied the Doctor. "A full-grown fighting black would be ashamed if he couldn't eat a leg of mutton at a sitting."
>
> "And you call that *dining*?" said the Major. "I call it gorging. Why, those fellows are more uncomfortable after food than before. I have seen them sitting close before the fire and rubbing their stomachs with mutton fat to reduce the swelling. Ha! ha! ha!—dining, eh? Oh, Lord!"
>
> "Then if you don't dine to satisfy your hunger, what the deuce do you eat dinners for at all?" asked the Doctor.
>
> "Why," said the Major, spreading his legs out before him with a benign smile, and leaning back in his chair, "I eat my dinner, not so much for the sake of the dinner itself, as for the after-dinnerish feeling which follows: a feeling that you have nothing to do, and that if you had you'd be shot if you'd do it. That, to return to where I started from, is why I don't dine in the middle of the day" (Vol. II, ch. 5).

And now Trollope's *Barchester Towers* (1857):

> The archdeacon had again ascended, and was now in the dining-room. "Arabin," said he, speaking in his usual loud clear voice, and with that tone of dictation which was so common to him; "you must positively alter this dining-room, that is, remodel it altogether; look here, it is sixteen feet by

14. See excerpts from *Stretton* quoted above on p. 18.

fifteen; did anybody ever hear of a dining-room of such proportions!" . . .

"It would do very well for a round table," suggested the ex-
warden.

Now there was something peculiarly unorthodox in the
archdeacon's estimation in the idea of a round table. He had
always been accustomed to a goodly board of decent length,
comfortably elongating itself according to the number of
guests, nearly black with perpetual rubbing, and as bright
as a mirror. Now round dinner tables are generally of oak, or
else of such new construction as not to have acquired the
peculiar hue which was so pleasing to him. He connected them
with what he called the nasty new-fangled method of leaving
a cloth on the table, as though to warn people that they
were not to sit long. In his eyes there was something demo-
cratic and parvenue in a round table. . . .

"A round dinner-table," said he, with some heat, "is the
most abominable article of furniture that ever was invented.
I hope that Arabin has more taste than to allow such a thing
in his house" (ch. 21).

And neither Major Buckley nor Archbishop Grantly is far removed
from George Meredith's Dr. Middleton, in *The Egoist* (1879), who
"misdoubted the future as well as the past of the man who did not,
in becoming gravity, exult to dine. That man he deemed unfit for
this world and the next" (ch. 20).

After his disillusionment with his various ill-successes in Australia, the roughness of the frontier, and his personal disappoint-
ments, Kingsley actually encountered comparable well-regulated
elegance being maintained by at least a few Australian colonists.
Rolf Boldrewood describes Langa-willi as "the most perfect place
and homestead in the west" and Mitchell as a "recent importation
. . . cultured and artistic . . . the nearest approach to the languid
swell that in that robust and natural mannered epoch we had encountered."[15] Naturally, then, when Kingsley was restored to the
familiar English atmosphere at Langa-willi, he would have re-
sponded eagerly to it. Also, like Kingsley himself, the principal
characters of the novel are temporary residents in Australia, who
will themselves make their fortunes and return to England. As Sam
Buckley chauvinistically exclaimed: " 'Don't let me hear all that
balderdash about the founding of new empires. Empires take too

15. *Old Melbourne Memories*, p. 172.

long in growing for me. What honours, what society has this little colony to give, compared to those open to a fourth-rate gentleman in England? I want to be a real Englishman, not half a one. I want to throw in my lot heart and hand with the greatest nation in the world. I don't want to be young Sam Buckley of Baroona. I want to be the Buckley of Clere' " (Vol. III, ch. 11). It is only later, in *The Hillyars and the Burtons*, that Kingsley will depict the permanent immigrants and their place in the developing nation. But even in that novel, the gentry, although influenced more by new customs and manners than the Buckleys are, remain English to their very marrow.

Geoffry Hamlyn reveals, however, that Kingsley was not totally unaware of the shifting societal pattern in England—the declining aristocracy and the rising middle class. Major Buckley, of necessity, sells Clere to a prosperous brewer who can afford to maintain the estate and the position of title-holder. And it is the new land of Australia that enables Buckley to recoup his position. Kingsley's succeeding novels, as the discussion of *Ravenshoe* will note, clearly show that he becomes more conscious of and concerned with the decline of the old order that he loved so well. But in writing *Geoffry Hamlyn*, Kingsley is not concerned with detailing the difficulties either English or Colonial, either of adaptation to an established society or of the creation of a new one; he depicts, instead, his ideal Englishman molding, at will, a good life in a new land.

Happily, though, as Scott had realized the fictional possibilities of Scotland, as later Rider Haggard and Olive Schreiner would utilize Africa and Hudson South America for the same end, Kingsley set out intentionally to charm the British readers with the strangeness of Australia. Although his bush-rangers and transported convicts are only Rob Roy, Bill Sykes, and the later Abel Magwitch spiced with a foreign flavor, Kingsley's firsthand account gives them a reality that transforms them from familiar characters in ordinary actions into fresh characterizations. In essence, George Hawker's escape ride at the end of the novel is just another chase scene of the kind used, for example, in Scott's novels and later in Blackmore's, but the frozen uplands by Lake Omeo metamorphosize the scene, and Kingsley's writing gives the reader a fine piece of suspenseful narrative. In fact, as Ernest Baker states, "Few episodes in English fiction surpass the paralysing tension of fear and suspense in the chapters telling how these desperadoes are foiled in their attack on the stations, hunted down by settlers and mounted police, and shot or captured in a beautiful defile of the Snowy Mountains."[16]

Even though Kingsley refines the life observed in Australia, this refinement is not especially distracting, for his low-life characters, such as hut-keepers and convicts, are handled credibly. Unlike the Buckleys, the Brentwoods, and the various other colonists who never act or speak naturally, these ordinary people embody the rough, crude aspects of their world. Such is the case of the excellently drawn "currency-lad," who, delivering a note to Jim Brentwood about a new foal, becomes fascinated by a paperweight at Baroona:

> The lad,—I always call that sort of individual a lad; there is no other word for them, though they are of all ages, from sixteen to twenty,—the lad, I say, was so taken up with the contemplation of a blown-glass pressepapier on the table, that Jim had to say, "Hello there, John!"
>
> The lad turned round, and asked in a perfectly easy manner, "What the deuce is this thing for, now?"
>
> "That," said Jim, "is the button of a Chinese mandarin's hat, who was killed at the battle of Waterloo in the United States, by Major Buckley."
>
> "Is it now?" said the lad, quite contented. "It's very pretty; may I take it up?"
>
> "Of course you may," said Jim. "Now, what's the foal like?"
>
> "Rather leggy, *I* should say," he returned. "Is there any answer?"
>
> Jim wrote a few lines with a pencil on half his sister's note, and gave it him. He put it in the lining of his hat, and had got as far as the door, when he turned again. He looked wistfully towards the table where the pressepapier was lying. It was too much for him. He came back and took it up again. What he wanted with it, or what he would have done with it if he had got it, I cannot conceive, but it had taken his simple fancy more, probably, than an emerald of the same size would have done. At last he put it to his eye.
>
> "Why, darn my cabbage-tree," he said, "if you can't see through it! He wouldn't sell it, I suppose, now?" (Vol. II, ch. 16).

The scene not only reveals Kingsley's ear for the developing Aus-

16. *The History of the English Novel* (New York, 1937), VIII, 187.

tralianisms but it emphasizes the great contrast between the two social classes as well as between Kingsley's two types of characters. Jim is the superior Englishman and he acts accordingly.

That Kingsley enjoyed recording this life his leisurely storytelling manner verifies. Although careful to connect the swift succession of incidents, he delights in stopping merely to entertain. Not only does he halt all action to discuss informally "relevant" material such as the enjoyment of smoking pipes or the secrets of housework, but he indulges in copious Thackeray-like asides explaining his purpose and directing the reader. And like Thackeray's, Henry Kingsley's commentary in *Geoffry Hamlyn*, at least, does not arise, one feels, from a distrust of the readers' intelligence, as did Charles Kingsley's.[17] Henry Kingsley's personal enjoyment of life permeates the work, and he seems to want to share it with his readers. His humorous asides, his qualifying footnotes, the overall discursiveness are all part of that pleasure.

Probably the best example of the zest of the novel occurs near the end. After the pairing off of the appropriate lovers, only one character remains unhappy: Sam Buckley wants to leave Australia and to repossess the family's old English estate. With his magical pen, Kingsley obliges Sam with an aside and footnote:

> They are going home to England. Sam . . . is one of the richest of her Majesty's subjects in the Southern hemisphere. . . . "And so," I suppose you say, "he is going home to buy Clere." Not at all, my dear sir. Clere is bought, and Sam is going home to take possession. "Marry, how?" Thus,—
>
> Does any one of my readers remember that our dear old friend Agnes Buckley's maiden name was Talbot, and that her father owned the property adjoining Clere? "We do not remember," you say; "or at least, if we do, we are not bound to; you have not mentioned the circumstances since the very beginning of this excessively wearisome book, forty years ago." Allow me to say, that I have purposely avoided mentioning them all along, in order that, at this very point, I might come down on you like a thunderbolt with this piece of information.

17. Charles Kingsley wrote about the use of asides: "People are too stupid and in too great a hurry, to interpret the most puzzling facts for themselves, and the author must now and then act as showman and do it for them. . . . Women like them better than any part of a book. They like to be taught a little now and then" (*Charles Kingsley: His Leters and Memories of His Life,* **II,** 40).

Kingsley explains the complex family arrangement that led to Sam's inheritance and purchase of Clere. Then tongue-in-cheek, he footnotes: "If you will examine the most successful of our modern novels, you will find that the great object of the author is to keep the reader in a continual state of astonishment. Following this rule, I give myself great credit for this *coup de théatre*. I am certain that the most experienced novel reader could not have foreseen it. I may safely say that none of my readers will be half as much astonished as I was myself" (Vol. III, ch. 15).

The ending of the novel realizes well the philosophy that informs it: Man is good; there can be charity among all mankind. In fact, one can almost hear Laura Bell telling Arthur Pendennis that *Geoffry Hamlyn* is one of those "good books, kind books, with gentle kind thoughts." Kingsley tells us later, during a more distressing time, that "It is disagreeable to me to write about disagreeable things. I would be myself in favour of all sunshine" (*Stretton*, Vol. II, ch. 36). As his life progressed, he found more "disagreeable things," but during the writing of *Geoffry Hamlyn* the sunshine prevailed. So at the novel's end all important characters have been blessed with happiness. The Australian Arcadia has been transported once again to its proper setting—Clere, where the majority of the characters settle themselves around the restored family estate. Characteristically, Kingsley even deals sympathetically with George Hawker. Maintaining a semblance of poetic justice, he allows Hawker to be hanged, but the reader believes that Kingsley is not punishing Hawker for his nefarious crimes so much as he is saving Hawker from a life of madness, for George becomes demented when he learns that he has unknowingly killed his own son, Charles. Kingsley, also whitening Hawker's blackguardism, blames his actions chiefly on the man's perverted childhood, which did nothing to discipline his violent nature. Stressing his conception of man's goodness, Kingsley has Major Buckley make a final pronouncement about George to Hamlyn: "You have taught me that there are bright points in the worst man's character, a train of good feeling which no tack can bring out, but yet which some human spark of feeling may light. . . . There is a spark of the Divine in the worst of men, if you can only find it" (Vol. III, ch. 11).

And as if to emphasize his point that man can change, Kingsley does not allow Hawker's baseborn son (by Ellen Lee) to be hanged.

Separated now from his father and his "workhouse to prison, from prison to hulk" background, this "Arab of society" later proves his bravery in a heroic death in the Australian interior. Likewise, Kingsley develops Charles Hawker. Moody, envious, in many ways like his father—"at seventeen—he got into a most disreputable connexion with a Highland girl"— Charles is not ruined as much by his "small natural capacity" as by having "his selfishness fostered so excessively by his mother's indulgence, and Tom's good-humoured carelessness" (Vol. II, ch. 6). It is mainly Mary's fault that Charles is so inferior to Sam Buckley.

Since Kingsley usually did not bother to investigate the psychological intricacies in his characters, most of them are flat figures, vivid in their external behavior but psychologically uninteresting. It is unfortunate that more of his art did not lie in the direction of character development, for in *Geoffry Hamlyn* he sketches some individuals who have great possibilities. The undeveloped Vicar Thornton, for example, the good but weak man, offers much potentially. Trollope took such a man and turned him into the wonderful creation of Mr. Harding. It is Mary Hawker, however, with whom the reader is most dissatisfied. Although Kingsley spends much time discussing her, she never evolves clearly.

Mary's disobedience sets up the initial disorder that is not settled until Captain Touan is finally hanged. In the interim, Vicar Thornton suffers a stroke and dies; James Stockbridge, after being refused Mary's love, goes to Australia, where he is killed; and her son, Charles, is slain by his own father. Mary displays various outbursts of remorse over her actions, but the reader wonders whether she ever really suffers repentance, for her later life has traces of the stubbornness and flirtations that caused the original trouble. In one scene Miss Thornton, Mary's aunt, is shocked with "Mary's levity of behaviour with men": "Many a time, when the old lady was sitting darning . . . would her tears fall upon her work, as she saw Mary sitting with her child in her lap, smiling, while the audacious Tom twisted a flower in her hair, in the way that pleased him best. To see anything wrong, and to say nothing, was a thing impossible. She knew that speaking to Mary would only raise a storm, and so, knowing the man she had to deal with, she determined to speak to Tom" (Vol. II, ch. 6).

Something faintly perverse emanates from Tom's and Mary's long, long partnership. Kingsley, being Kingsley, would never have in-

cluded an illicit affair between two characters whom he plans to
reward later, and, in fact, Mary is not bad enough to make the
reader actually suspect such a relationship, but then neither is she
good enough to make such an affair unbelievable. Realizing that
he had developed complexities in her character, Kingsley follows
through for a while, but always at a safe distance. He has Frank
Maberly question Mary's sincerity when Frank finds her in the
throes of "misery, wrath, madness, despair" and thinks, " 'What a
magnificent actress this woman would make.' It merely past through
his brain and was gone, and then he felt ashamed of himself for
entertaining it a moment; and yet it was not altogether an unnatural one for him who knew her character so well. She was lying
on the ground in an attitude which would have driven Siddons to
despair; one white arm, down which her sleeve had fallen, pressed
against her forehead, while the other clutched the ground; and
her splendid black hair fallen down across her shoulders. Yet how
could he say how much of all this wild despair was real, and how
much hysterical?" (Vol. III, ch. 11). And the amiable Hamlyn
makes the formal pronouncement on her: "I think, that she, never
a very strong-minded person . . . actually contemplated her husband's death with complacency, nay, hoped, in her secret heart,
that one mad struggle between him and Tom might end the matter
for ever, and leave her a free woman. I may do her injustice, but
I think I do not. One never knows what a woman of this kind, with
strong passions and a not over-strong intellect, may be driven to. . . .
I knew in spite of all her selfishness and violence that there were
many good, nay, noble points in her character; but I cannot disguise
from myself that that night's conversation with Tom showed me a
darker point in her character than I knew of before" (Vol. III,
ch. 5). But Kingsley quits before he gets to the finish line. After
raising doubts about her actions and showing mainly her selfish
and violent side, he, nevertheless, draws her up in his fairy-tale
ending: Mary finally marries her cousin-partner, Tom Troubridge,
and with their two children they are in the process of joining the
other characters at Clere at the end of the novel.

Though finally deficient in the portrayal of characters, *Geoffry
Hamlyn* has a quality of frolicsomeness and sparkle that flows from
Kingsley's schoolboyish, idealistic view of the world. Life abounds
with youthful love and ideal friendships, both feminine and masculine. His insistence upon the latter has given rise to the suggestion

that Kingsley was latently homosexual, even that a sexual abnormality partially accounts for his artistic decline.[18] Such a conjecture is difficult to substantiate. Kingsley, himself, thought of the boy-love that he portrayed as a Jonathan and David relationship: "A love between men, a pure and beautiful love surpassing the love of man for woman."[19] Although his full insistence on the friendship manifests itself more strongly in later works, especially *Stretton*, Jim Stockbridge and Geoffry Hamlyn and the trio Sam Buckley, Cecil Mayford, and Jim Brentwood demonstrate such ties of loyalty and devotion.

Perhaps "Jackson of Paul's," a short story (1871), most clearly depicts Kingsley's interpretation of this love between young men, in this case Charles Jackson and Lord Edward Deverest: "The two boys had that boy-love for one another which I hope none of our readers have forgotten in the turmoils of life: there is no love except the love of a good woman which surpasses it in purity and in the incitement to noble deed" (*Hornby Mills and Other Stories*, Vol. II, p. 42). Through his love for Deverest, Jackson falls in love with Deverest's sister, Edith, only to be refused her hand. Eventually a series of college mishaps cause Jackson to be rusticated, while war tragedies kill Deverest and Edith's fiancé. Later when Jackson is reunited with Edith, her father asks Jackson:

"Did you love him as you said?"
"I only loved her through him" said Charles, very quietly. "I loved him before I ever loved her. My darling lies out on the Crimean hillside, but his sister lives, and loves me as I loved him."
"He was your Xenos," said Lord Eyre, bending his head down.
"He was more than any Xenos to me, my lord: and if you will let me go to her I will be more than a husband to her" (Vol. II, pp. 79-80).

Kingsley adds one final comment: "He had loved the boy so dearly that he had a double love for his sister. . . . And there, if you please, is the whole of my little romance. He loved the brother

18. See Ellis, p. 37; Martin, p. 107; Clive Hamer, "Henry Kingsley's Australian Novels," *Southerly*, XXVI (1966), 40, 43. For the opposite view see Wolff, p. 214; Thirkell, pp. 186–87.
19. *Old Margaret*, Vol. I, ch. 7; see also Vol. I, ch. 15.

with the love of a boy, and now he loves the sister with the love of a man" (Vol. II, p. 86).

Perceptively, Robert Lee Wolff has noted the similarity between "Jackson of Paul's" and Evelyn Waugh's *Brideshead Revisited* (1945), with its comparable boy-love between two college friends (Charles Ryder and Sebastian Flyte), and its theme of loving a sister (Julia Flyte) through a brother.[20] Beside these fictitious male relationships, one may place the real one between Tennyson and Arthur Henry Hallam and Emily Tennyson that expresses itself so vividly, for example, in *In Memoriam, A.H.H.* (1850). The coincidence lies, it would seem, in Kingsley's, Waugh's, and Tennyson's common source: the affection that has its origin in the cloistered life of Oxford and Cambridge, where female students or, for that matter, any females besides waitresses or shopgirls were rare phenomena. One remembers only too well Zuleika Dobson's devastating impact on Oxford in 1906 or Agnes Pembroke's intrusion into Cambridge in *The Longest Journey* (1907)! Thus, when one of Kingsley's boys exclaims, "My darling, where have you been" to another, or confesses, "I only love his sister through him" one has to see these words—intensely emotional and suggestive as they are in our Post-Freudian age—as a David's concern for his Jonathan. It is this love that Geoffry Hamlyn expresses when he cradles the head of the dead Jim Stockbridge in his lap and cries, "Oh! good old friend! Oh! dear old friend, could you not wait for me? Shall I never see you again?" (Vol. II, ch. 7). Additionally, the masculine horseplay that Kingsley (like Waugh) revels in displaying in his novels only serves to highlight the college origin. Hamlyn's teasing of Jim Stockbridge, when he hesitantly confesses that he has "outlived any little attachment" that he had for Mary Hawker, or Jim Brentwood and Sam Buckley's rough-housing in the stockyards is mere schoolboyish pranks and antics.

A related source of this theme, however, may be a fraternal projection. Ellis asserts, credibly enough, that Kingsley's oldest brother, Gerald, was the model of Henry's boyhood "and the original model doubtless for all the 'grand' and 'noble' youths who were to throng the pages of his books in the future—those gallant and strong and strenuous boys who so often come to an untimely end in the pursuit of adventure."[21] Since so many of Kingsley's heroes contain autobiographic strains, the explanation may well be a dream projection instead of an unconscious homosexual drive. Possibly, he has built his ideal boys around an immature reminiscence of Gerald, but if so, in his imaginings, a substitution has occurred, with Henry acquiring some of his brother's heroism. In *Geoffry Hamlyn*, the rather riotous, boisterous, naïve, and noble as well as high-spirited and brave Sam Buckley, undefeated by the hard realities which defeated Kingsley, accomplished everything in Australia that his creator dreamed of doing. In later novels, the heroes nobly cut their swaths in the Crimean War, the Indian Mutiny, and the Battle of the Sedan, feats that the adventurous Henry would have cherished. Interestingly, as Kingsley suffers more defeats, his boys become nobler and more heroic.

Even Kingsley's near heroes and semi-villains are of the same school. Although they swing very close to the cult of exaggerated physical strength and reckless courage promoted in the nineteenth century by George Alfred Lawrence, the "Guy Livingstons" are always tempered by the antithetical "Tom Browns," as patently seen in the representative Captain Tom Silcote, in *Silcote of Silcotes*. A reckless profligate who has deserted his wife and alienated his father, this "magnificent torso[ed]" man can still inspire the innocent boy-hero to exclaim "I like the look of that man. I would go to the devil after that man." Instead of picturing Henry Kingsley as sexually abnormal, I believe that it would be more valid to see him as a perpetual boyish Walter Mitty, who, unfortunately, as this study reveals, turns into more of a Miniver Cheevy.

Artistically, *Geoffry Hamlyn* has many defects. Besides including Kingsley's usual faults such as slipshod grammar, improbable dialogue, careless construction, it is disjointed, at time melodramatic, and populated with some incredible characters. Nevertheless, as a romance the novel amuses; its idealistic philosophy, its vigorous action, and its boyish joviality reflect Kingsley's sheer delight in storytelling. If Kingsley's notion of the novelist's duty differs from that held by George Eliot his was at least one that was still being stressed by important novelists during the literary upheaval of the 1850s and 60s. Kingsley would have agreed with Trollope that "a novel if it fatigues is unpardonable."[22] Although such a concept does not automatically produce greatness, it does insure entertainment.

22. *Thackeray* (New York, n.d.), p. 187.

III

1859-1864

AFTER THE publication of *Geoffry Hamlyn*, Kingsley lived at Eversley until July, 1864, and for a brief period he was a country squire, enjoying a life more idyllic than usually possible because he had no obligations to a tenantry. Not only was he a successful author, who, according to Charles, had written a better book than his own *Westward Ho!*, but he had the comforts of his parents' cottage, which was, in truth, a large but cozy ten-room house with stables and barns and thirty acres of meadowland. Pleasures were all around him. In the garden located behind and to one side of the cottage he whiled away many afternoons cultivating his favorite roses, especially La France, Souvenir de Malmaison, Jaune d'Espray and others newly imported from France. And he rented a few miles of fishing rights on the River Blackwater to practice fly fishing. To his delight and to the disgust of his brothers, both expert fishermen themselves, and his usual fishing companion and neighbor, Captain West, he caught trout when none of the others got a nibble. When the other three finally gave up in despair, he taunted them by dropping his line into gnarled willow roots and other seemingly unlikely places and catching more trout. We have only to read his novels to see that he vividly remembered these fishing experiences.

Relishing this country life to the fullest, Kingsley also leased for shooting a part of the fir-tree wood and heath adjoining the grassland, mainly, it seems, to pamper his teen-aged nephew Maurice, Charles' son, an enthusiastic shot. Kingsley himself cared little for the sport and jested about his poor marksmanship. On one occasion when George wanted to photograph his reluctant brother, Henry

finally appeared with a gun under his arm and humorously said to
his jeering but enchanted nephew and nieces and brother, "My
dear, I likes to be took as a country squire in me preserves, and
divvle a soul but yerselves knows I can't hit a barn, and me preserves is in the back kitchen closet."[1]

For the children assembled at Eversley, Henry's stay there was a
special event, for he showered great affection on them and amused
them with original stories flavored with his wide knowledge of
slang—"Bürschen, Bargee, Parisian, Irish, cockney and English pro-
vincialism." Years later Maurice fondly recalled his uncle's playfulness and how dearly they loved him "in spite of his tormenting
us by making up supposed conversations between us after the style
of the Herries children in 'Ravenshoe,' and solemnly telling our
father and mother of imaginary misdeeds of his nephew and nieces":
"Nothing was better fun than to get our uncle on his 'genteel'
behavior, which, of course, means exactly the opposite, and brought
forth inimitable stories, scraps of old songs and impromptu conversations, the choicest of which were between children, Irish-
women or cockneys. He was the only man, I believe, who ever
knew by heart the famous 'Irish Court Scenes'—naughtiest and
most humorous of tales—unpublished of course, but handed down
from generation to generation of the faithful. Most delightful was
an interview between his late Majesty George the Fourth and an
itinerant showman, which ended up with, 'No, George the Fourth,
you shall not have my Rumptifoozle [sic]!' What said animal was,
or the authenticity of the story, he never would divulge."[2]

During this time, however, Kingsley also nursed his seriously ill
father, slowly dying from complete collapse. When he finally died
on February 29, 1860, Henry was, in effect, his mother's sole companion, and he left his small house attached to his parents' and

1. Maurice Kingsley, "Personal Traits of Henry Kingsley," *The Book Buyer*,
XI (January, 1895), 728–29. Published also in Introduction to *Leighton Court*
(New York, 1895).

2. *Ibid*., pp. 730–31. The Rumtifoozle also makes its appearance in Kingsley's
allegory, *The Boy in Grey* (1871), where it is among "the rarer and more
recently discovered" animals in Prince Philarete's toy Noah's Ark (ch. 1). As for
the mystery of the Rumtifoozle, Wolff has located a possible source for Kingsley's
tale, a satirical sketch called "The Bottle of Hay," by George Augustus Sala,
printed in *Household Words*, IX (March 11, 1854), 69–75, and reprinted in
Sala's *Gaslight and Daylight* (London, 1859), pp. 122-35. The end of the
George the Fourth story is that the King cannot have the animal because the
"Rumtifoozle has a foot like a warming-pan, and a body like the keel of a
vessel, and a tail that would astonish a donkey" (Wolff, p. 203n10).

moved in with her. Charles had been appointed chaplain-in-ordinary to Queen Victoria on May 7, 1859, and was away from the rectory more and more as the demand for him as preacher and lecturer increased. And three months after his father's death he became Regius Professor of Modern History at Cambridge, taking up residence there in February, 1861. George, now an M.D. and soon to be married, visited occasionally, but he had already started to gratify a wanderlust that would eventually take him to Egypt, the South Seas, America, and Canada, and several times to the Mediterranean.

Heartened by the success of *Geoffry Hamlyn*, Kingsley started his second novel, *Ravenshoe*. While he was working on it, his old friend Henry Campbell returned from his unsuccessful gold prospecting in Australia to study for two years at St. John's College, Cambridge. Campbell usually spent his holidays with the Kingsleys and at that time observed Henry's intense and seldom varied working schedule. After dinner with his mother and much smoking either by himself or with an occasional friend, such as Campbell or Captain West, he retreated with a jug of rum and water to his study at the back of the house at about 11 P.M. and wrote without outside interruptions until 6 A.M. Sleeping then until luncheon time, he spent the afternoon either working in his rose garden, fishing, or visiting with the children or friends. One of his "dear personal friends," according to his nephew, was Vic, a black-and-tan rat terrier, only one of a long line of "a dog of dogs" that figures in his life and novels. At Eversley, Vic was Kingsley's confidant. Sitting with her right paw up, head to one side, one ear cocked and the other pointed toward Henry's face, Vic sympathized with her master until the talk became too serious or prolonged. Then she jumped into his lap and licked his face affectionately.

Some afternoons he indulged himself in a favorite hobby that was unknown except to his intimate friends. Accompanied only by Vic, Kingsley left the cottage and walked into the meadowland to paint. Although one writer, Benjamin Ellis Martin, claimed that Kingsley's skill in drawing was "amazing" and that his watercolors and oils were "masterpieces,"[3] a more accurate label for his artistic technique is "amateurish." But looking at them, a reader of his novels instantly knows why Kingsley's word pictures are so

3. "Old Chelsea," *Century Magazine*, XXXIII (1886), 234. Some of Kingsley's Australian paintings are in the Mitchell Library.

vivid. He loved nature and observed it well for his watercolors and small oil landscapes: Welsh scenery near Snowdon, "Yes Tor" in Devonshire (the setting for George Hawker's attempt to shoot William Lee in *Geoffry Hamlyn*), sketches of Australian scenery, and one of "The Auberg," which hung on the left side of Charles' mantelpiece in his Eversley study. Possibly, this inn recalled pleasant memories of the brothers' continental trip.

When Kingsley did interrupt his writing schedule, it was usually to visit Alexander Macmillan at his London home—23 Henrietta Street, Covent Gardens. On Thursdays, the publisher held open house for many of his writers and other celebrities, who gathered to drink "tea and stronger fluids," to smoke "occasional tobacco," and to argue over the latest controversies.[4] These Tobacco Parliaments, as the gatherings were soon named, drew together some of the most famous men of the day. Henry was there on the first of January, 1860, with Charles and his two friends, the novelist Tom Hughes and the theologian J. F. D. Maurice, and David Masson, editor of *Macmillan Magazine* and at that time Professor of English Literature in University College, London. The discussion subject that evening was Darwin's *The Origin of Species*, published less than two months earlier.[5] Although the distance between Hampshire and London and his mother's dependency on him prohibited his being a weekly member of this informal society, Henry immensely liked these meetings and his new acquaintanceship with such prominent men as Tennyson and the Pre-Raphaelite painter Holman Hunt. He even rented on a regular basis convenient rooms at 19 Henrietta Street. How different these gatherings must have been for Kingsley from those of his earlier Fez days!

Macmillan appreciated Kingsley's literary work and between 1859 and July, 1864, published in his magazine not only *Ravenshoe*, running serially from January, 1861, to July, 1862, but Kingsley's *Travelling in Victoria* (also January, 1861), a personal essay of his journey by rail and coach through that land, describing his traveling companions and the country; three other essays, one of which, "The Navies of France and England," was co-written by Augustus G. Stapleton, Charles' friend and neighbor; and Kingsley's fourth novel, *The Hillyars and the Burtons*, which started in November, 1863, but ran to April, 1865. Macmillan and Company

4. Charles Morgan, *The House of Macmillan* (New York, 1944), p. 50.
5. *Letters of Macmillan*, pp. 37–38.

also published both novels in the usual three-volume editions, as well as *Austin Elliot* (1863), Kingsley's third novel, in two volumes.

When William Thackeray died on December 24, 1863, Kingsley hurriedly wrote to Macmillan, beseeching his permission to "do Thackeray by his novels. Showing by his characters how the public came to know him through his characters. Of mere personal biographys [*sic*] you will have galore. . . . If you want it done, telegraph, that is all" (E., p. 124).[6] Receiving quick approval, Kingsley worked "night and day" and had "great hopes of it." In fear of any miscarriage, he solicited Henry Campbell, who had ended his stay at St. John's and was serving as Henry's amanuensis until his planned return to Australia, to deliver the manuscript personally.

When the essay, "Thackeray," was published in *Macmillan Magazine* in February, 1864, Kingsley was disappointed and angry. He accused Masson of cutting out the best part: "the comparison between William M. T. and Smollett and Fielding; as it was the only important thing in the whole article, it was to be expected. It merely contained the highest tribute to the exquisite purity of Thackeray as compared with the eighteenth century novelist. Every word was carefully weighted; every idea had been carefully discussed with clever men" (E., p. 126). Masson, it seems, wanting to add his own impression of Thackeray, eliminated some of Kingsley's copy for the appendage.

Even excised, Kingsley's essay is a fine tribute. As he had suggested, Kingsley discusses Thackeray "through his characters," mainly those in *Vanity Fair*, but he highlights the analysis with personal reminiscences, detailing, for example, his boyhood meeting with Thackeray, mentioned above. Simply, he continues: But "we shall never look on that kind good face again. . . . William Thackeray is dead. He was, at it were yesterday, in the prime of life, full of new projects, surrounded by friends, quite unexpectant of any change. But in the dull winter's night, while he was alone in his chamber, the Messenger came for him, and he arose and followed it. He has passed quietly from among us, without a word of fare-

6. Kingsley's letters to Alexander Macmillan and George Lillie Craik and his correspondence describing the Franco-Prussian War are printed in S. M. Ellis, *Henry Kingsley 1830–1876* (London, 1931). In order to reduce the number of footnotes, I have identified quotations from those letters in the text with the abbreviation E. and the page number to Ellis' book within parentheses following the quotation. The sources for Kingsley's other letters are identified in footnotes.

well, and the riddle of this painful earth is redd to him at last."[7]

Kingsley's literary successes prompted other journals to seek his talents. John Cassell, publisher of *The Quiver* and the extremely popular *Cassell's Family Paper*, wanted a tale with "plenty of incident and a good moral," but Kingsley refused that offer—"I neither can nor will write such miserable bread and butter stuff as I suspect they want" (E., p. 120)—as he refused the offer extended in 1862 by the *Daily Telegraph*, the very successful one-penny daily, to be the paper's special correspondent for the American Civil War. This latter request had been proffered to him by his old King's College and Oxford companion Edwin Arnold, who had joined the newspaper staff in 1861.

Although Kingsley gave several excuses for refusing this adventurous assignment, the real reason has to be assumed. His reply to the *Daily Telegraph* was that he was engaged to Macmillan for the next year, and to Macmillan he wrote, "One of the reasons which would prevent my going under any circumstances is that I should be pistolled in the public streets before I had been there a week. I have a most unhappy temper when politics or religion are being spoken of" (E., p. 120). It is true that he had contracted with Macmillan to write *Austin Elliot* and later *The Hillyars and the Burtons*, but if Kingsley had really wanted to go to America, he could have arranged matters with the congenial Macmillan. And his mother's dependency on him must be dismissed as a valid cause, because two years later he was to leave her for marriage. The real reason, probably, was his present success and comfortable circumstances. After years of insignificance and the failure of his Australian adventure, he was, at last, making a name for himself in the literary world and, importantly, being accepted by Macmillan's coterie. Why endanger that position for a venture that might prove to be disastrous to him!

Kingsley's statement about being pistolled in the streets refers, of course, to his views on the American Civil War. Like his brother Charles, Henry was, as he said, a "Dis-Unionist": "I don't care much what happens so long as the American Union goes to smash: and after, that the Negroes are slowly and carefully emancipated. I like the Northerners better than the Southerners on the whole, but I hate both, and the Union most of all three" (E., p. 118).

Strong and harsh as his Dis-Unionist view is, Henry was never

7. IX, p. 362.

as vehement as Charles, who seemingly saw little good in that "insolent and aggressive republic of rogues."[8] Henry's anti-Americanism seems to reflect not so much a hatred for America as it does a love for and devotion to England that *Geoffry Hamlyn* or, for that matter, all of his novels so clearly reveal. In *Ravenshoe,* he asks, "Is there any land, east or west, that can give us what this dear old England does—settled order, in which each man knows his place and his duties? It is so easy to be good in England" (Vol. I, ch. 14). Kingsley and many other Britishers feared the great power in America that threatened to diminish that of their beloved England; for that reason the Union should be dissolved.

And—to paraphrase Swift—if Kingsley hated and detested that animal called, in this case, the American man, he heartily loved "John, Peter, Thomas and so forth." Kingsley hated the coarse, loud, bumptious stereotyped Yankee that Mrs. Trollope and Dickens, for example, satirized in *Domestic Manners of the Americans* (1832) and *Martin Chuzzlewit* (1844), respectively. But when he himself relied upon that stereotype, it became for him an individual. Mr. and Mrs. Nalder from Chicago, in *The Hillyars and the Burtons,* show the distinction. Mr. Nalder is the typical Yankee: "His way of prefacing half his remarks by saying 'Je-hosaphat' . . . his way of thwacking down his right or left bower at Eucre, his calling the trump card the Deckhead, his way of eating with his knife, and his reckless, noisy *bonhommie*" (Vol. I, ch. 24) disgust the genteel Gerty Hillyar. Comic in their vulgarity, the Nalders are, nevertheless, kind, compassionate people who ultimately treat Gerty Hillyar more understandingly than she does them. Their only crime—at least in Kingsley's eyes—is that they have been born in a traditionless country that had capriciously refused to obey English authority.

Though Kingsley was occupied with other activities while he lived at Eversley, his main concentration during his first two years there was on the writing of *Ravenshoe,* his most perfect novel.

8. Martin, p. 258.

IV

Ravenshoe

"THERE IS an immense body of vitality in this book—humour, imagination, observation in the greatest wealth, and that delightful kind of satire which springs from a warm heart well reined in by a keen intellect": thus began *The Spectator's* contemporaneous review of *Ravenshoe*, an immediate success when it was published in 1862.[1]

Describing the novel for Macmillan, Kingsley admitted that the plot was "very intricate and so overborne by incident that it would be difficult to give a précis of it" (E., p. 117). Not only is the plot complex, but it is melodramatic and a little silly, turning around a duality of Kingsley's favorite devices—infants switched at birth, and children falsely declared to be illegitimate until a secret marriage certificate establishes their legitimacy. The switched babies in this specific case are Charles Ravenshoe and William Horton. Charles, reared as the second son of Densil Ravenshoe and possible heir to the family estate, is discovered to be the son of the gamekeeper, James Horton; whereas Horton's supposed son, William, is, in turn, Densil's actual son. Later, this confusion is

---

1. XXXV (June 7, 1862), 637. In the United States, Ticknor and Fields published seven editions of *Ravenshoe* in 1862, a total of 4,533 copies. Nine years after its publication, *Ravenshoe* was still popular enough for a writer in *Punch* to include its title as a name for an imaginary horse in a humorous essay on the Derby ("Punch's Derby Prophecy," LX [May 27, 1871], 217). According to Richard Walden Hale, Joseph Pulitzer, who was fifteen when *Ravenshoe* was published, shortly before his death awarded Henry Kingsley a then nonexistent Pulitzer Prize for writing "the best novel in the English language" (*Kingsleys* [Boston, 1934], pp. 8–9).

further entangled but finally rectified when an old marriage certificate confirms that the now deceased James was, in reality, Densil's elder half-brother and their father's legitimate heir. Disappearances and minor but related mysteries compound the complications, and overhanging and influencing all is a religious turbulence that initiates much subterfuge.

The charm of the book does not arise from its plot. In Kingsley's own words: "If I thought I was writing for a reader who was going to criticise closely my way of telling my story, I tell you the honest truth, I should tell my story very poorly indeed" (Vol. II, ch. 22). In *Geoffry Hamlyn*, Kingsley introduces a delightful character named Little Burnside, whose "greatest pleasure, the one to which he would sacrifice everything, was retailing a piece of news." Little Burnside's approach, Kingsley reminds us, resembled that of a three-volume novel, introducing the parties involved, slowly building up the suspense, and finally "crash[ing] down on you with the news itself and leav[ing] you gasping." The charm of *Ravenshoe* comes from Kingsley's faithful following of Burnside's manner of conveying his news: "He gloried in dwelling on it, and making the most of it" (Vol. II, ch. 15).

The novel opens with one of Kingsley's intricate genealogies that the reader should simply enjoy, not analyze. Beginning with the Ravenshoe who was "the only Baron who did not sign Magna Charta," it lightheartedly traces the line of the fanatically Roman Catholic house of Ravenshoe down to Densil Ravenshoe, the heir of the estate in 1820, when the main action commences. Over the centuries these Popish squires have staunchly and quixotically defended their faith and maintained resident priests, who have always managed to control the family. But with Densil's advent, it appears that the history of the Ravenshoes may take a new turn. Densil's second wife, a Protestant, has gained from her husband the promise that her second son, Charles, is to be reared in her faith. Thus, the stage is set for the conflict between Charles and Father Mackworth, the family priest.

Essentially, however, the novel is the story of Charles Ravenshoe, Kingsley's most striking characterization, rather than of the clash between two faiths. He is one of the main reasons why *Ravenshoe* becharms some readers while Charles Kingsley's *Westward Ho!* bristles them.[2] Amyas Leigh, Charles Kingsley's hero, emerges too

2. Arthur Quiller-Couch, pp. 67–68; Richard Walden Hale, pp. 7–12; Walter

gigantically, symbolically as well as physically. Besides being a boy "just doing the right thing without thinking about it . . . because the Spirit of God is with him," Amyas Leigh "is a symbol . . . of brave young England longing to wing its way out of its island prison, to discover and to traffic, to colonise and to civilise, until no wind can sweep the earth which does not bear the echoes of an English voice" (chs. 1, 3). Charles Ravenshoe, on the other hand, embodies Henry Kingsley's favorite hero-type—a gentlemanly boy who must learn to assume manly responsibilities—but unlike Sam Buckley (and, indeed, Amyas Leigh), Charles, although idealistically created, has human proportions and flaws. In the first place, his stout build and hooked nose decidedly diminish his physical glamour (imagine a Heathcliff in this mode), and, more importantly, his weak character precludes his attaining deific status.

While *Ravenshoe* is not a *Bildungsroman* based upon the author's own life like *David Copperfield* or *Pendennis*, Charles Ravenshoe does in fact remind one of the young, irresponsible, unsettled Henry Kingsley. In addition to the scenes of college rioting, paeans on rowing, and the tirades against "firsts," mentioned in Chapter I, that surely echo Henry's undergraduate boisterousness and rebellious and exuberant thoughts, Charles' headstrong conduct suggests Henry's romantically animal eagerness that impelled him from one unfavorable situation into another even more unfavorable one. Charles does not ship out to Australia, but he isolates himself in London and finally flings himself into the Crimean War, a situation as foreign to him as life in Australia was to his creator. Kingsley, interestingly enough, links his leaving for Australia with Charles' departure from Ravenshoe:

> In half an hour [Charles] rose again, and put his portmanteau and carpet-bag outside his room door. Then he took his hat, and rose to go.
> One more look round the old room! The last for ever! The present overmastered the past, and he looked almost without recognition. I doubt whether at great crises men have much time for recollecting old associations. I looked once into a room, which had been my home, ever since I was six years old, for five-and-twenty years,[3] knowing I should never see it

---

Frewen Lord, "The Kingsley Novels," *The Nineteenth Century*, LV (June, 1904), 997–1004.

3. More accurately the time was seventeen years. As previously noted, the

again. But it was to see that I had left nothing behind me. The coach was at the door, and they were calling for me. Now I could draw you a correct map of all the blotches and cracks in the ceiling, as I used to see them when I lay in bed of a morning. But then, I only shut the door and ran down the passage, without even saying "goodbye, old bedroom." Charles Ravenshoe looked round the room thoughtlessly, and then blew out the candle, went out, and shut the door (Vol. II, ch. 2).

When William Marston, the narrator of the novel, apologizes for Charles' "mad, impulsive, way of forming a resolution, and his honourable obstinacy in sticking to that resolution afterwards" (Vol. II, ch. 12), we can readily surmise that Kingsley, in 1862, is rationalizing the impulse behind his Australian adventure.

Charles' boyish charm satisfies our liking for sentiment, and though he may be foolish and obstinate, he is so determined to accomplish the noble and right thing that we find it hard to condemn him utterly. We become impatient with him for what seems to be his insistence on unnecessary suffering and for his persisting so blindly in his course, yet we acclaim him for his courage and independence. As Lord Saltire observed, Charles Ravenshoe is an "idle, foolish, lovable creature, with anger for nothing; only furious, blind indignation for injustice and wrong" (Vol. III, ch. 4). Kingsley, of course, agrees with Saltire's pronouncement, and he tells us again and again through the narrator that he "loves that boy Charles." But Kingsley also realizes that his hero must outgrow his childish outlook on life, that he must earn the right to inherit and govern Ravenshoe. His eagerness must be tempered with patience and discipline, and his exuberance must be applied judiciously to worthy causes. In other words, circumstances must "guide [Charles] on the way to being a man" (Vol. II, ch. 2). Alienation, treachery, death, and poverty serve as his tutors. This transition from boyhood to manhood, although inevitable, is sad. Certainly, Kingsley fails to handle this passage of time as skillfully and brilliantly as Arnold Bennett does later in *The Old Wives' Tale* (1908) and the *Clayhanger* trilogy (1910–15), but Bennett's lament over the maturing Edwin Clayhanger is, essentially, Kingsleyan: "It seemed rather a shame, it seemed even tragic, that this

---

Kingsleys moved to St. Luke's, Chelsea, in 1836, when Henry was six years old, and Henry lived there until 1853, when he left for Australia.

naïve simple creature, with his straightforward and friendly eyes so eager to believe appearances, this creature immaculate of worldly experience, must soon be transformed into a man, wary, incredulous, detracting."

Early in the novel Kingsley informs the reader that Charles has naïvely erected his own standards of justice and worthiness and has foolishly judged everyone else by them. In the case of Adelaide, the girl he loves, "she had told him that she loved him. . . . He believed her. As for vanity, selfishness, fickleness, calculation, coming in and conquering love, he knew it was impossible in his own case, and so he conceived it impossible in hers" (Vol. II, ch. 2). Concomitantly, when he flees from Ravenshoe to London, he carries with him the romantic illusion that he will succeed magnificently, that he will "win money and a name for the sake of one who is worth winning it for." Charles dreams, "Very likely I shall go abroad, to the land where the stuff comes from they make sovereigns of, and try my luck at getting some of the yellow rubbish. And she will wait in the old house at Ranford" (Vol. II, ch. 2). His concept of winning success is just as distorted as is his picture of Adelaide. He has yet to learn that an education is a tedious process. Certainly Kingsley, who toiled unsuccessfully in the Australian gold fields, consciously intended the irony found in Charles' making such a statement.

In order to underline Charles' immaturity and pride, Kingsley relies upon a literary device that permeates much fiction. Many novelists suggest the Manichean doctrine of the two warring forces of good and evil through the form of a good brother–bad brother or half-brothers relationship, such as in Stevenson's *Master of Ballantrae,* Hogg's *The Private Memoirs and Confessions of a Justified Sinner,* Dickens' *Oliver Twist,* or Fielding's *Tom Jones.* Other novelists, toying with the idea, have produced variants, probably the best known occurring in Emily Brontë's *Wuthering Heights,* in the characters Cathy and Heathcliff. Kingsley repeatedly uses this device in many of his novels: George and Erne Hillyar in *The Hillyars and the Burtons,* Robert and Harry Pointz in *Leighton Court,* the half-brothers Allan Gray and Roland Evans in *Stretton,* Arthur and Edward Oakshott (cousins) in *Oakshott Castle,* and Arthur and George Branscombe in *The Grange Garden,* to mention the major ones. In *Ravenshoe,* he creates Charles and William Horton, the half-cousins who form a natural whole. Exceptionally close, the boys not only exchange the heir-groom places, but, as Kingsley emphasizes, William is "a handsome likeness of Charles." In the usual sense they do not represent the good-evil duality, for in their individuality neither is perfect: As Charles is exceedingly proud, William is completely humble, although Kingsley does not make him unpleasant. Heir to Ravenshoe, William wants to relinquish all his rights in order to follow Charles into self-exile and eventually marry the privateer skipper's beautiful daughter. The best example of this self-abnegation occurs at Lady Hainault's dinner party. Although the honored guest, "he soon found that there was another cause for his being interesting to them all, more powerful than his curious position, or his prospective wealth; and that was his connection with Charles Ravenshoe, now Horton. *He* was the hero of the evening. Half William's light was borrowed from him. He quickly became aware of it, and it made him happy" (Vol. II, ch. 14). Before the end of the novel, Charles must gain some of William's humility.

Kingsley's romances, however, emphasize adventurous episodes in the lives of heroic-tinged gentry with noble spirits. They do not attempt to unravel the subtleties and ambiguities that occur in psychological transformations. Although Charles must undergo tests to learn that humility is an integral part of charity and that personal moral standards are not absolutes, Kingsley allows no overt moral, or moralizing, to subordinate his main purpose of entertainment.[4] He simply presents Charles and his need to mature and manipulates him into testing situations, describing the external evidence of his struggle.

Kingsley also does not dwell on the gloom of Charles' isolation in London, at least not until the climax demands it. After Charles' flight, Kingsley changes the tragical tone of the experience to what he calls Charles' "light-hearted desperation," and achieves a profluent description of rebirth by contrasting Charles' new life among the lower classes with the renewal of spring. Starting first

4. Concerning a moral, Kingsley obligingly says at the end of the novel: "From this much of the story we may safely deduce this moral, 'That, if a young gentleman gets into difficulties, it is always as well for him to leave his address with his friends.' But, as young gentlemen in difficulties generally take particularly good care to remind their friends of their whereabouts, it follows that this story has been written to little or no purpose. Unless, indeed, the reader can find for himself another moral or two; and I am fool enough to fancy that he may do that, if he cares to take the trouble" (Vol. III, ch. 13).

with the arrival of spring on the seacoast, then moving inland to the country places, his description settles the reader in a London mews, where Charles sits "pondering on his unhappy lot." Although a rambling scene, it conveys in an excellent manner a mixture of visual and auditory impressions.

Kingsley begins the scene with a humorous account of a noisy melee produced by a jackdaw, an Irish washerwoman, a cockatoo, and a pug-dog and then extends his description to the street:

> The mews itself, as I said, was very quiet, with a smell of stable, subdued by a fresh scent of sprinkled water; but at the upper end it joined a street leading from Belgrave Square towards the Park, which was by no means quiet, and which smelt of geraniums and heliotropes. Carriage after carriage went blazing past the end of the mews, along this street, like figures across the disk of a magic lanthorn. Some had scarlet breeches, and some blue; and there were pink bonnets, and yellow bonnets, and Magenta bonnets; and Charles sat on the wheelbarrow by the dunghill, and looked at it all, perfectly contented.
>
> A stray dog lounged in out of the street. It was a cur dog— that any one might see. It was a dog which had bit its rope and run away, for the rope was round its neck now; and it was a thirsty dog, for it went up to the pump and licked the stones. Charles went and pumped for it, and it drank. Then, evidently considering that Charles, by his act of good nature, had acquired authority over its person, and having tried to do without a master already, and having found it wouldn't do, it sat down beside Charles, and declined to proceed any further.
>
> There was a public-house at the corner of the mews, where it joined the street; and on the other side of the street you could see one house, No. 16. The footman of No. 16 was in the area, looking through the railings. A thirsty man came to the public-house on horseback, and drank a pot of beer at a draught, turning the pot upside down. It was too much for the footman, who disappeared.
>
> Next came a butcher with a tray of meat, who turned into the area of No. 16, and left the gate open. After him came a blind man, led by a dog. The dog, instead of going straight on, turned down the area steps after the butcher. The blind man thought he was going round the corner. Charles saw what would happen; but, before he had time to cry out, the blind man had plunged headlong down the area steps and disap-

peared, while from the bottom, as from the pit, rose the curses of the butcher.

Charles and others assisted the blind man up, gave him some beer, and sent him on his way. Charles watched him. After he had gone a little way, he began striking spitefully at where he thought his dog was, with his stick. The dog was evidently used to this amusement, and dexterously avoided the blows. Finding vertical blows of no avail, the blind man tried horizontal ones, and caught an old gentleman across the shins, making him drop his umbrella and catch up his leg. The blind man promptly asked an alms from him, and not getting one, turned the corner; and Charles saw him no more (Vol. II, ch. 6).

During his self-exile in London, Charles meets Billy Wilkins, a little shoeblack.[5] Dickensian in creation and as sentimentally conceived as Tiny Tim and Oliver Twist, Billy serves as a catharsis for Charles. Their first meeting occurs when Charles' mind is jumbled with "anger, indignation and love" for the treacherous Adelaide and overmastering hatred for her husband, Lord Welter, Charles' boyhood and college friend. Trying to conquer such thoughts, Charles comes before St. Peter's Church, where

at the east end . . . there is a piece of bare white wall in a corner, and in front of the wall was a little shoeblack.

He was not one of the regular brigade, with a red shirt, but an "Arab" of the first water. He might have been seven or eight years old, but was small. His whole dress consisted of two garments; a ragged shirt, with no buttons, and half of one sleeve gone, and a ragged pair of trousers, which, small as he was, were too small for him, and barely reached below his knees. His feet and head were bare; and under a wild, tangled shock of hair looked a pretty dirty, roguish face, with a pair of grey, twinkling eyes, which was amazingly comical. Charles stopped, watching him, and, as he did so, felt what we have most of us felt, I dare say—that, at certain times of vexation and

5. According to Henry Campbell, Billy was modeled after Joe, a newspaper-boy, who visited Kingsley at 19 Henrietta Street, Covent Garden (Ellis, p. 63). He also appears as Meerschaum in the short story of the same name: "A boy, large for his age, say about twelve, with very bold, fearless, courageous, handsome features, and most remarkable eyes; head well shaped, and well set on, a curly crop of fine hair in want of the barber; dress, two garments only, a ragged shirt, with no buttons, and an old pair of footman's breeches with but few buttons" (*London Society*, XXVI [Christmas Number, 1874], 21).

anger, the company and conversation of children is the best thing for us (Vol. II, ch. 12).

Before their friendship can mature, undesired encounters with old friends lead the proud Charles into the Crimean War, specifically the Charge of the Light Brigade. While the battle scenes, as well as the tragedies of war, are well done, it is the small touches that stand out. Particularly fine is Kingsley's recording of how fancy works before a man goes into battle, possibly to die. Impatiently waiting for the bugle call, Charles notes that the soldier in front of him has a "patch of grease on his right shoulder" and imagines that it resembles the map of Sweden:

> A long weary two hours or more was spent like this. Charles, by looking forward and to the right, between the two right-hand men of the troop before him, could see the ridge of the hill, and see the smoke rising from beyond it, and drifting away to the left before the sea-breeze. . . . He was reduced to watching the back of the man before him, and studying the map of Sweden. It was becoming evident that the map of North America, if it existed, must be on his left shoulder, under his hussar jacket, and that the Pacific Islands must be round in front, about his left breast, when the word was given to go forward.
> They advanced to the top of the hill, and wheeled. Charles, for one instant, had a glimpse of the valley below, seething and roaring like a volcano. Everywhere bright flashes of flame, single, or running along in lines, or blazing out in volleys. The smoke, driven to the left by the wind, hung across the valley like a curtain. On the opposite hill a ring of smoke and fire, and in front of it a thin scarlet line disappearing. That was all. The next moment they wheeled to the right, and Charles saw only the back of the man before him, and the patch of grease on his shoulder (Vol. III, ch. 2).

This intense concentration on an irrelevancy as a means of relieving anxiety, though differing in mood and intensity, evokes the same poetry that Defoe caught in *Robinson Crusoe*, when, just after the shipwreck, the meditative Crusoe remarked that the only signs he saw of his former companions were "three of their hats, one cap, and two shoes that were not fellows"; or as noted so acutely in the last lines of Rossetti's little poem "The Woodspurge":

> From perfect grief there need not be
> Wisdom or even memory;
> One thing then learned remains to me—
> The Woodspurge has a cup of three.

Charles leaves the war wounded and practically penniless, yet still "no more dreaming of begging from those who had known him formerly than of leaping off Waterloo Bridge" (Vol. III, ch. 8). When Billy's sister finds him and leads him to Marquis Court, Little Marjoram Street, where Billy lies dying, Charles is physically and mentally deteriorating. At Billy's death the saddened Charles realizes the complete waste and despair of his alienated life and is ready for the Thames.

But for Kingsley, Charles' trial has been tedious enough and, with the contrived entrance of his friend John Marston, Charles is saved. Pointedly at the rescue Kingsley comments again on Charles' pride and allows his hero to acknowledge his own stubbornness and vanity. Confessing to Marston, Charles cries, " 'from a silly pride, I have spent all my cunning on losing myself—hoping that you would believe me dead, thinking that you would love my memory, and dreading lest you should cease to love Me' " (Vol. III, ch. 12). As if to evidence Charles' change, Kingsley has his character say (still somewhat priggishly, one believes) later that " 'I have been the object of all these dear soul's [*sic*] anxiety for a long time. [Adelaide] must take my place now' " (Vol. III, ch. 13).

At the end of the novel, Charles has matured, changing from a fanciful, sentimental youth into a thoughtful, melancholy man. We are touched by his struggle and sympathetic with his cause, but we do not really share in his inner conflict as we do in that, for example, of Adam Bede when he undergoes his period of doubt and anguish before Hetty Sorrel's trial. In the case of Charles we merely witness his worsening physical and mental condition, and then we are told that he is a wiser man. The final description of him removes all doubts that he has suffered and is permanently scarred: "But there is a cloud on Charles Ravenshoe's face, even now. I saw him last summer lying on the sand, and playing with his eldest boy. And the cloud was on him then. There was no moroseness, no hardness in the expression; but the face was not the merry old face I knew so well at Shrewsbury and Oxford. There is a dull, settled, dreaming melancholy there still. The memory of those few terrible months has cast its shadow upon him. And the shadow will lie, I

fancy, upon that forehead, and will dim those eyes, until the forehead is smoothed in the sleep of death, and the eyes have opened
to look upon eternity" (Vol. III, ch. 17).

This streak of sadness underlying the gaiety in all of Kingsley's
major romances except *Geoffry Hamlyn* has prompted Michael Sadleir, the English author and bibliographer, to say of him: "No
writer of the mid-Victorian age had so delicate a sympathy for
splendour in decay, so sensitive an admiration for the forlorn
present of a noble past. He is the prose-laureate of wasted beauty."[6]
Kingsley wrote in those mid-Victorian years when Darwinism and
new political and religious concepts were challenging established
theories, when the relative stability of the Victorian world was in
the process of being upended, and the social-economic microcosm
was being re-examined. Although he was certainly aware of these
developments and seemed to admire and respect the intellectual
vitality of the movers and shakers, Kingsley's novels clearly depict
his worship of the old stable order when houses of Ravenshoe,
Silcote, Stretton, Marksworth, Sheepsden stood proud and secure.
One of his greatest assets as a literary artist is his power to transfer
to prose the beauty of those old, naturally landscaped houses, as he
does, for example, in the description of Ravenshoe. After describing
the surrounding landscape and the seacoast, the village and its inhabitants, Kingsley says:

> But it is not upon horses, men, boats, ship, village, church,
> or stream, that you will find your eye resting, but upon a noble,
> turreted, deep-porched, grey stone mansion, that stands on
> the opposite side of the stream, about a hundred feet above
> the village. . . .
> The house itself is of grey stone, built in the time of Henry
> VIII. The facade is exceedingly noble, though irregular; the
> most striking feature in the north or sea front being a large
> dark porch, open on three sides, forming the basement of
> a high stone tower, which occupies the centre of the building.
> At the northwest corner . . . rises another tower of equal
> height; and behind, above the irregular groups of chimneys,
> the more modern cupola of the stables shows itself as the
> highest point of all, and gives, combined with the other
> towers, a charming air of irregularity to the whole. The win-

6. "Henry Kingsley: A Portrait," *Edinburgh Review*, CCXL (October, 1924),
330.

dows are mostly long, low, and heavily mullioned, and the walls are battlemented.

On approaching the house you find that it is built very much after the fashion of a college, with a quadrangle in the centre. Two sides of this, the north and west, are occupied by the house, the south by the stables, and the east by a long and somewhat handsome chapel, of greater antiquity than the rest of the house. The centre of this quad, in place of the trim grass-plat, is occupied by a tan lunging ring, in the middle of which stands a granite basin filled with crystal water from the hills. In front of the west wing, a terraced flowergarden goes step by step towards the stream, till the smooth-shaven lawns almost mingle with the wild ferny heather turf of the park, where the dappled deer browse, and the rabbit runs to and fro busily. On the north, towards the sea, there are no gardens; but a noble gravel terrace, divided from the park only by a deep rampart, runs along beneath the windows; and to the east the deer-park stretches away till lawn and glade are swallowed up in the encroaching woodland (Vol. I, ch. 3).

For Kingsley, as he later wrote in *Stretton,* this was a "land lapped in order and tradition, good landlords, good tenants, well-used labourers, if ever there were such in late years in England. Surely a land of peace!" (Vol. I, ch. 1).

But even then, as Kingsley's novels reveal, the great houses—Ravenshoe and Stretton and their kind—were slowly vanishing: decay had begun to tarnish their splendor. In *Ravenshoe* the approaching decline is reflected in Charles' lasting melancholy, in the childlessness of Lord Welter, the last of the Ascots, and especially in the death of Lord Saltire, the prime representative of the old order. It is a pernicious decay, eating away not only the basic structure of the country life but traditional concepts of moral principles as well. In *Leighton Court,* Sir Charles Seckerton, the "perfect gentleman and gallant horseman," unable to face the disgrace of financial ruin and the concomitant loss of social respectability, asks his daughter to marry the supposed "disreputable" man who holds his debenture. Yet Kingsley, as if trying to hold on to the past, treats these people sympathetically. His young men still undertake heroic tasks "to govern [their] Empire of nearly 200,-000,000 of souls," and his gentry still pride themselves on their "well-set, well-ordered, well-trained houses [where] you get almost all the things which . . . make life valuable" (*Stretton*, Vol. I, ch. 12). But Kingsley is regretfully aware that the world of his ancestors is crumbling, and he sets himself to capture its fading grandeur.

Evelyn Waugh in *Brideshead Revisited* and E. M. Forster in *Howards End* both attempt something comparable. Discussing the links of similarity between Waugh and Kingsley, Robert Lee Wolff writes that "In twentieth-century idiom, and with all its twentieth-century sophistication, *Brideshead Revisited* is a Henry Kingsley novel." He continues: "The atmosphere that surrounds Waugh's Catholic noble family, the role of the priests in all the intimate concerns of his personages, the sense of being alien to the English nobility because of their membership in something so much older, the very ruin that Catholicism brings them: all this recalls *Ravenshoe*. Waugh's dialogues sometimes strangely echo Henry Kingsley's in pace and manner. With loving attention to detail, both Waugh and Kingsley evoke, in a thoroughly English way, the idyllic beauty of the great houses, Brideshead and Ravenshoe, and the surrounding country with its sights and sounds and smells."[7] In setting and general atmosphere *Brideshead Revisited* is closer to *Ravenshoe* than is *Howards End*, but the tone of Forster's novel recalls more accurately the melancholy suffusing Kingsley's. Waugh seems more fascinated than saddened by the decline of the noble families, whereas Forster and Kingsley both lament the slow erosion of their ancestral homes by the red rust of modern life. For these two writers, Howards End and Ravenshoe, respectively, symbolize the spirit of a vanishing England. Although at the end of each novel the rightful heir has possession of the ancestral home, the picture is not an entirely happy one; the erosion has only been slowed, not stopped.

More personal reasons may also account for this melancholy strain in Kingsley's novels. As previously shown, most outward appearances indicate that Kingsley was happy at Eversley, but signs of anxiety present themselves even during his country-squire days. His constant worry—his financial difficulty—rears its head early. Complaining to Macmillan in 1861, Kingsley asks: "Would it be too much if I were to ask you to send me a cheque for the first number of [*Ravenshoe*], for I am very low at my bankers" (E., p. 117). And in the novel itself, talking about William Horton Ravenshoe, Kings-

7. Wolff, p. 215.

ley muses: "At this time he is master of Ravenshoe, with certainly nine, and probably twelve, thousand a year—a most eminently respectable person. One year's income of his would satisfy a man I know, very well, and yet I am talking of him apologetically. But then we novel writers have an unlimited command of money, if we could only realize it" (Vol. III, ch. 14). There can be no doubt about the personal reference, and within just three years, in fact, Kingsley will be pushed to the verge of bankruptcy, where he hovered for the rest of his life.

Another prevalent fear is Kingsley's great feeling of insecurity, which leads, at times, into a "persecution complex." Although this dread evidences itself more strongly during that period when he was feverishly boiling the literary pot, hints underlying his fear of competition with his brother Charles appear during—and even before—his Eversley days. On February 21, 1859, for instance, while corresponding with Ticknor and Fields about the pending American edition of *Geoffry Hamlyn,* Kingsley compares the length of his novel with Charles' most recent one.[8] By itself, this comparison signifies little, if any, fraternal competition, but viewed as the first in a series of comparisons in which Henry pits himself against his brother, it is of consequence. By 1862, Charles' four major novels and his important religious and academic appointments had made him a great success. Meager by comparison, Henry's achievements were two successful novels. A year after the publication of *Ravenshoe,* he wrote to Macmillan, confidentially informing him that Charles planned to write another "high fellooting historic novel. . . . Scene Babylon, Time Nebuchadnezzar." After taking credit for pointing out to Charles that "a man who has forced his way to the front rank by literature must not throw literature overboard," and "besides, with his literary reputation, it is actually wicked not to make use of that reputation to increase his fortune," Henry ends the letter somewhat apprehensively. His own novel, *The Hillyars and the Burtons,* was soon to begin its serialization in *Macmillan's Magazine:* "I should be glad if he wrote his book from end to end and published it all at once: for these reasons. 1st. It will rather take the wind out of my sails if he starts at once in your Magazine. 2nd. That two brothers writing two novels at one and the same time in one Magazine is a new and astounding spectacle to gods and men. And 3rd. That his book will be far too

8. *Ibid.,* p. 217.

good to be parcelled out into monthly doles. I should almost
wish now that we had kept my book back, sooner than that we
should clash" (E., pp. 121–22).[9]

The evidence of the novels—to whatever extent it is valid testimony—unmistakably hints that his aversion to fraternal competition
arose from a general fear of an inability to match not only Charles'
successes but also his ancestors' heroics. As the discussion of
Geoffry Hamlyn suggested, Kingsley was only able to dream of great
adventures and achievements; he could never realize them. The-
matically, his novels stress the problem that man must prove himself, but Sam Buckley's easy victories are in the past. Charles Ravenshoe and later Austin Elliot, Erne Hillyar, and Mathilde D'Isigny
suffer needless hardships to demonstrate their worthiness; in fact,
at times, their compulsion to suffer and to seek forgiveness for
trivial errors verges on monomania.

The attempt to account for—most of all identify—an author's com-
plexes by the actions of his fictional creations is a pastime that
invites abuse as soon as entered into. Pedantry, according to a well-
known definition, is someone else's scholarship, and by the same
token psychological explanations of authors or of their creatures
persuade nobody except the man who does them. Nonetheless, it
seems to me impossible for anyone to read the whole corpus of
Henry Kingsley's work, as I have done more than once, without
being convinced that this reduplicated pattern of compulsion in his
major characters is not only a main fixation of his own sense of
inferiority and need for heroic fulfillment but also a catharsis.
There can be no doubt that such insecurity existed—the wonder
would be, in fact, if it had not existed—and we know that the
Australian ordeal proved to Kingsley that he was no hero. To
explain the pervasive melancholia in the novels by such psychol-
ogizing is therefore such a small step that only a foolish timidity
could deter one from taking it.

Despite its melancholy undercurrent, *Ravenshoe* is delightful to
read. Kingsley, like Forster (and Beethoven), blows the goblins
away whenever he wants and replaces them with mirth and wonderfully funny imps. Merrily, he follows Lord John Russell and Lord
Palmerston, "walking airily arm-in-arm," through the London
streets; he encourages Squire Humby to remove the "slight cloud"

9. Charles apparently gave up this idea. His next historical novel was *Here-
ward the Wake*, which was not published until 1866.

of seven hundred and eighty-nine years' duration that hangs over his house and Ravenshoe, now that the latter is Protestant; he mixes up the mortal enemies, Lady Ascot, Lady Hainault and her daughter, the "long Burton Girl," at an unplanned dinner; and he treats us to the inimitable behavior of the Herries children, Gus, Flora, and Archy, at the wedding where all the lovers are properly matched. William Marston describes the scene:

> I am sorry to say that these dear children, with whom I had no previous acquaintance, were very naughty. The ceremony began by Archy getting too near the edge of his hassock, falling off, pitching against the pew door, bursting it open, and flying out among the free seats, head foremost. Nurse, a nimble and dexterous woman, dashed out, and caught him up, and actually got him out of the church door before he had time to fetch his breath for a scream. Gus and Flora were left alone with me.
>
> Flora had a great scarlet and gold church service. As soon as she opened it, she disconcerted me by saying aloud, to an imaginary female friend, "My dear, there is going to be a collection; and I have left my purse on the piano."
>
> At this time, also, Gus, seeing that the business was well begun, removed to the further end of the pew, sat down on the hassock and took from his trousers' pocket a large tin trumpet.
>
> I broke out all over in a cold perspiration as I looked at him. He saw my distress, and putting it to his lips, puffed out his cheeks. Flora administered comfort to me. She said, "You are looking at that foolish boy. Perhaps he won't blow it, after all. He mayn't if you don't look at him. At all events, he probably won't blow it till the organ begins; and then it won't matter so much". . . .
>
> When I looked at Gus again, he was still on the hassock, threatening propriety with his trumpet. I hoped for the best. Flora had her prayerbook open, and was playing the piano on each side of it, with her fingers. After a time she looked up at me, and said out loud—
>
> "I suppose you have heard that Archy's cat had kittened?"
>
> I said, "No."
>
> "Oh, yes, it has," she said. "Archy harnessed it to his meal cart, which turns a mill, and plays music when the wheels go round; and it ran downstairs with the cart; and we heard the music playing as it went; and it kittened in the wood-basket immediately afterwards; and Alwright says she don't wonder at

it; and no more do I; and the steward's-room boy is going to
drown some. But you mustn't tell Archy, because, if you do,
he won't say his prayers; and if he don't say his prayers, he
will," &c., &c. Very emphatically and in a loud tone of voice.

This was very charming. If I could only answer for Gus, and
keep Flora busy, it was wildly possible that we might pull
through. If I had not been a madman, I should have noticed
that Gus had disappeared.

He had. And the pew door had never opened, and I was
utterly unconscious. Gus had crawled up, on all fours, under
the seat of the pew, until he was opposite the calves of his
sister's legs, against which calves, horresco referens, he put
his trumpet and blew a long shrill blast. Flora behaved very
well and courageously. She only gave one long, wild shriek, as
from a lunatic in a padded cell at Bedlam, and then, hurling
her prayerbook at him, she turned round and tried to kick
him in the face (Vol. III, ch. 17).

Kingsley also creates for us some memorable minor characters,
especially Lord Saltire, a "great dandy of the Radical Atheist set."
Saltire, a reformed roué, is a traditional figure in English fiction,
probably evolving from the elderly profligate in Restoration comedy
or possibly from Milton's Satan. In varying degrees of respectability, this type populates Victorian pages, either translated, for example, by Disraeli into a Lord Monmouth (*Coningsby*) or by
Meredith into a Lord Mountfalcon (*The Ordeal of Richard Feverel*). Kingsley, however, has vivified the stereotype and has carefully shaped Lord Saltire from the components of his heraldic
name. Noble Saltire is of the old school, a gentleman worthy of his
title and ancestry, but the bend sinister, visible in the St. Andrew
cross that his name denotes, hovers over his reputation, as he
emanates an aura of past wickedness. The young Saltire, we learn
early in the novel, had been regarded by many as Satan incarnate,
whose "tongue no woman could withstand." Now over sixty, Saltire
has lived down his previous indiscretions and is not only reformed
but exceptionally respectable. As a character Saltire's brilliance
lies in his suavity and wit, in his absolute command of situations:
he angers with sarcasm, ridicule, and humor; he conquers with
scorn and understanding; he comforts with compassion and sympathy.

Another stereotype in nineteenth-century fiction that Kingsley
draws upon is the sinister and mysterious Jesuit priest, who has

schemed and glided from Gothic novels to Scott, Le Fanu, and Collins and who had especially raised the ire of such minor Protestant writers as William Sewell and Catherine Sinclair in their vitriolic Anti-Jesuit novels *Hawkstone* (1845) and *Beatrice: of the Unknown Relatives* (1852), respectively. Father Mackworth, Charles' adversary, is as pernicious and furtive as his fictional predecessors: he slips in and out of doors, overhearing secrets and using them at opportune moments. Although Father Mackworth is an undeveloped stereotype, he figures importantly in two excellently written chapters. The first is "The Black Hare" (Vol. I, ch. 13).

Prior to this chapter Charles has jokingly accused Mackworth of being more than religiously concerned with Ellen Horton, the gamekeeper's beautiful daughter and, in reality, Charles' sister, who has been clandestinely meeting a dark figure in the woods. Agitated, Mackworth suspiciously blushes at the accusation. A little later Kingsley skillfully leads his characters into the Horton cottage, where Charles and another family priest, Father Tiernay, overhear an argument between Ellen and William Horton about her nightly rendezvous. At that time Father Tiernay becomes attracted to an unusually large and dark stuffed hare. James Horton explains:

> "That, sir . . . is old Mrs. Jewel, that lived in the last cottage on the right-hand side, under the cliff. I always thought that it had been Mrs. Simpson, but it was not. I shot this hare on the Monday, not three hundred yards from Mrs. Jewel's house; and on the Wednesday the neighbours noticed the shutters hadn't been down for two days, and broke the door open; and there she was, sure enough, dead in her bed. I had shot her as she was coming home from some of her devilries. A quiet old soul she was, though. No, I never thought it had been she". . . .
>
> "Our witches in these parts, Father, take the form of some inferior animal when attending their Sabbath or general meetings. . . . There's another of them out now, sir. . . . Master Charles, dear, if you're going to take the greyhounds out tomorrow, do have a turn at that big black hare under Birch Tor—"
>
> "A black hare!" said Father Tiernay, aghast.
>
> "Nearly coal-black, your reverence," said James. "She's a witch, your reverence, and who she is the blessed saints only know."

Ellen Horton's surreptitious meetings with a suspected lover and

Father Mackworth's flustered denial of any irregularities on his part have been interwoven with black magic.

The next day the greyhounds are taken out, and Father Tiernay, wondering whether James' witch was going to be caught that morning, initiates a conversation which shifts topics from Mrs. Jewel and the black hare to the Witch of Endor and the biblical command that "Thou shalt not suffer a witch to live." The hunt, with James at the head, continues:

> James approached them with the dead hare, and Densil asked where he was going to try. He said, just where they were.
>
> Densil asked, had he seen Father Mackworth? and he was in the act of saying that he was gone over the down, when a shout from Charles, and a still louder one from James, made them all start. A large *black hare* had burst from the thorns at Charles' feet, and was bowling down the glen straight toward them, with the dogs close behind her.
>
> "The witch," shouted James, "the witch! we shall know who she is now."
>
> It seemed very likely indeed. Densil broke away from William, and, spurring his pony down the sheep-path at the risk of his neck, made for the entrance of the wood. The hare, one of such dark colour that she looked almost black, scudded along in a parallel direction, and dashed into the grass ride just in front of Densil; they saw her flying down it, just under the dogs' noses, and then they saw her dash into a cross ride, one of the dogs making a strike at her as she did so; then hare and greyhounds disappeared round the corner.
>
> "She's dead, sir, confound her; we shall have her now, the witch!"
>
> They all came round the corner pell-mell. Here stood the dogs, panting and looking foolishly about them, while in front of them, a few yards distant, stood Father Mackworth, looking disturbed and flushed, as though he had been running.
>
> Old James stared aghast; William gave a long whistle; Mary, for a moment, was actually terrified. Densil looked puzzled, Charles amused; while Father Tiernay made the forest ring with peal after peal of uproarious laughter.

Although Kingsley excessively foreshadows the event, the chapter is amusing and efficient, and, apart from the humor, Ellen's unexplained mysterious meetings and Mackworth's suspected villainy—both, as we ultimately learn, wholly functional—further the action.

The other memorable chapter involving Mackworth sensitively depicts the drowning of Cuthbert, Charles' supposed brother and heir to Ravenshoe (Vol. II, ch. 22). Tyrannical and cruel, Mackworth, nevertheless, has a passionate affection for the ethereal Cuthbert. Despite a few false notes in the description, Kingsley's elegiac mode moves us as he contrasts the serenity of Cuthbert's death with the intensity of Mackworth's feelings:

They saw his head go under water, and, though they started on their feet and waited till seconds grew to minutes and hope was dead, it never rose again. Without one cry, without one struggle, without even one last farewell wave of the hand, as the familiar old landscape faded on his eyes for ever, poor Cuthbert went down; to be seen no more until the sea gave up its dead. The poor wild, passionate heart had fluttered itself to rest for ever.

The surf still gently playing with the sand, the sea changing from purple to grey, and from grey to black, under the fading twilight. The tide sweeping westward towards the tall black headland, towards the slender-curved thread of the new moon, which grew more brilliant as the sun dipped to his rest in the red Atlantic.

Groups of fishermen and sea boys and servants, that followed the ebbing tide as it went westward, peering into the crisping surf to see something they knew was there. One group that paused among the tumbled boulders on the edge of the retreating surges, under the dark promontory, and bent over something which lay at their feet.

The naked corpse of a young man, calm and beautiful in death, lying quiet and still between two rocks, softly pillowed on a bed of green and purple seaweed. And a priest that stood upon the shore, and cried wildly to the four winds of heaven. "Oh, my God, I loved him! My God! My God! I loved him!"

The characterizations of Cuthbert and Father Mackworth also point up not only Kingsley's religious prejudice but his tolerance. Quiet, studious, and very religious, the Roman Catholic Cuthbert is "a reserved methodical lad, with whom no one could find fault, and yet whom few liked" (Vol. I, ch. 5). It is unknown whether Henry was influenced by his brother's attack on Roman Catholicism and the Oxford Movement, but, in any event, Cuthbert

personifies the effeminacy that Charles Kingsley attributed to both.[10]
Cuthbert's spineless character evolves not from a mental or physical weakness but from a religious philosophy which instructed
him that it is holier to prepare oneself to be a saint in heaven
than to be an upright, industrious member of society, or, in other
words, a muscular Christian. In *Geoffry Hamlyn*, Kingsley had
drawn a comparison between those two philosophies. Commenting
on James Stockbridge's voyage past the cliffs of Madeira to Australia, he notes, "Borne upon the full north wind, the manhood and
intelligence of Europe goes past, day by day, in white winged ships.
And about all, unheeding, century after century, the old monks
have vegetated there, saying their masses, and ringing their chapel
bells, high on the windy cliff" (Vol. I, ch. 8). Cuthbert's religious
abasement is best illustrated after Charles nearly drowns in a shipwreck. Overcome with remorse for the way he had sided with
Mackworth in his argument against Charles, Cuthbert, barefoot,
carries his brother pickaback for a quarter of a mile, an act of
penance that humiliates Charles as much as it transfigures Cuthbert, "glorying in his penance."

Henry may have agreed with his brother concerning Roman
Catholic effeminacy, but he declared early his independence from
Charles Kingsley's extreme bigotry. Even Cuthbert's action he
qualified: "Is this ridiculous? I cannot say I can see it in this
light. I may laugh to scorn the religion that teaches men that,
by artificially producing misery and nervous terror, and in that
state flying to religion as a comfort and refuge, we in any way
glorify God, or benefit ourselves. I can laugh, I say, at a form of
religion like this; but I cannot laugh at the men who believe in it,
and act up to it. . . . 'Cuthbert, if you are a fool, you are a con-
sistent and manly one at all events' " (Vol. I, ch. 17). In fact,
in no Henry Kingsley novel does a reader find hostility directed
against any specific Christian sect. In his short novel *Hetty* Kingsley stoutly declares, "For my part, I have known many ministers

10. In 1849 Charles Kingsley wrote to a young clergyman who was contem-
plating becoming a Roman Catholic: "If by holiness you mean 'saintliness,' I
quite agree that Rome is the place to get *that*—& a poor pitiful thing it is when
it is got—not God's ideal of a man, but an effeminate shaveling's ideal. Look
at St. Francis de Sale's [*sic*] or St. Vincent Paul's face—& then say, does not
your English spirit loathe to be such a prayer-mongering eunuch as *that*? God
made man in His image, not in an imaginary Virgin Mary's image" (Martin,
p. 107).

of religion. Roman Catholic verbiage, or Dissenting verbiage, may
be offensive to the ear; but in twenty years I have only known two
bad ministers of religion of any sect, and that is not a large per-
centage, after all: one speaks, of course, merely of a large personal
acquaintance. Being on dangerous ground, I will step off it; only
enrolling my opinion, that the ministers of religion, with all their
eccentricities, are nearly the most valuable class in the community" (ch. 25). Like Allan Gray, the "extreme Protestant" in
Stretton, Kingsley would acknowledge that "every one who works
for Christ does good" (Vol. I, ch. 13).

Although Kingsley may ridicule certain Roman Catholic prac-
tices and beliefs, he never condemns that church per se. In *Ravenshoe*, for example, the villainous Father Mackworth is nicely
balanced with the sympathetic priests Father Clifford and Father
Tiernay, with his wonderful homemade saint-legends, just two in
Kingsley's lengthy list of benevolent Roman Catholic priests. And
in *Mademoiselle Mathilde* not only is the heroic Father Martin
very finely and affectionately drawn, but, a year after the novel's
publication, Kingsley fondly recalls that his Catholic heroine,
Mathilde D'Isigny, still remains his favorite female character.
Dickens told us, in a famous preface, that "like many fond parents"
he had in his "heart of hearts a favourite child. And his name is
David Copperfield." And similarly, Kingsley wrote, later on, in
Stretton: "Of all the ghosts of old friends which I have called up
in this quaint trade, called the writing of fiction, only two remain
with me, and never quit me. The others come and go, and I love
them well enough; but the two who are with me always are the
peaked-faced man Charles Ravenshoe, and the lame French girl
Mathilde" (Vol. III, "Conclusion"). Also, interestingly enough in
Mademoiselle Mathilde, Kingsley even discards the idea of Roman
Catholic effeminacy and presents a Jesuit muscular Christian, a
young priest who "had been selected by the order for missionary
work, in consequence of being singularly athletic and powerful."

Actually, Kingsley treats Father Mackworth rather generously.
Two factors, Kingsley tells us, have malignly influenced the priest's
actions. An illegitimate child, Mackworth was first deposited at a
French school, where "six years of friendless persecution, of life
ungraced and uncheered by domestic love, of such bitter misery
as childhood alone is capable of feeling or enduring, transformed

him from a child into a heartless, vindictive man"; then "Rome
. . . polished and turned [him] out ready for the market" (Vol. I,
ch. 4). Denied a familial identity Father Mackworth seeks his name
in the church, with his full security to be found as master of the
Catholic House of Ravenshoe. Moreover, not satisfied in just
explaining, and even excusing, Mackworth's villainy, Kingsley
allows the finally demented man to repent (rather unconvincingly)
in the end. And in a final apologetic flourish, the sympathetic Father
Tiernay says: " 'There have been many worse men with better
opportunities. He was a good man brought up in a bad school. A
good man spoilt. General Mainwaring, you who are probably more
honoured than any man in England just now, and are worthy
of it . . . you, the very darling of the nation, are going to Oxford to
be made an honorary Doctor of Laws. And when you go into
that theatre, and hear the maddening music of those boys' voices
cheering you: then, general, don't get insane with pride, like
Herod, but think what you might have been with Mackworth's
opportunities' " (Vol. III, ch. 16).

The second villain in *Ravenshoe* is Lord Welter, the Ascot heir,
who shows Charles a world not to be found at Ravenshoe. As
with George Hawker, in *Geoffry Hamlyn*, Kingsley attributes
Welter's blackguardism to his upbringing—in this case, to the
"fast" House of Ranford, the ancestral home of the Ascots, a family
so dedicated to the breeding and racing of horses "that their
marriages with other houses have been to a certain extent influenced by it." Exemplifying this point, Kingsley details Welter's
first visit to Ravenshoe, where seeing a bantam-cock "anxious for
sport," Welter naturally sets it against a great Docking, much to
Cuthbert's consternation.

To the extent that his actions affect Charles' sorrow, Welter
assumes great prominence. Although he loves Charles, his impulsive acts seem to belie the fact: his schoolboy antics cause
Charles to be rusticated; his elopement with Adelaide sends Charles
into a deeper depression after the flight from Ravenshoe; his se-
duction of Ellen Horton mortifies Charles in a sense almost
physical. Thus, our interest in Welter lies in how he reacts to his
betrayal of Charles' trust. Setting up an excellent confrontation
scene, Kingsley takes Charles to Welter's London gambling estab-
lishment, where he sees Welter and his ménage. Locking the door
behind him, Charles boldly walks into the room where Welter

sits alone. The reader expects violence, but, instead, Kingsley opens
the next chapter with seeming indirection:

> There is a particular kind of Ghost, or Devil, which is
> represented by an isosceles triangle (more or less correctly
> drawn) for the body; straight lines turned up at the ends for
> legs; straight lines divided into five at the ends for arms; a
> round O, with arbitrary dots for the features, for a head;
> with a hat, an umbrella, and a pipe. Drawn like this, it is
> a sufficiently terrible object. But, if you take an ace of clubs,
> make the club represent the head, add horns, and fill in the
> body and limbs as above, in deep black, with the feather end
> of the pen, it becomes simply appalling, and will strike terror
> into the stoutest heart.
>
> Is this the place, say you, for talking such nonsense as this;
> If you must give us balderdash of this sort, could not you do
> so in a chapter with a less terrible heading than this one has?
> And I answer, Why not let me tell my story my own way?
> Something depends even on this nonsense of making devils
> out of the ace of clubs.
>
> It was rather a favourite amusement of Charles's and Lord
> Welter's in old times at Ranford. They used, on rainy after-
> noon's [*sic*], to collect all the old aces of clubs (and there were
> always plenty of them to be had in that house, God help it),
> and make devils out of them, each one worse than the first.
> And now, when Charles had locked the door, and advanced
> softly up to Welter, he saw, over his shoulder, that he had got
> an ace of clubs, and the pen and ink, and was making a
> devil (Vol. II, ch.13).

The card-devil symbolism is no doubt too obvious, but it conveys concretely the duality of Welter's character. His friendship
for and love of Charles cling to him even during his most diabolical
periods. The recollection by both of their Ranford days transforms
the conversation into one between two old friends, now estranged,
ironically taking place in the house where both Adelaide and
Ellen are promoting Welter's gambling. Moreover, Welter is little
other than a paper devil, for, like so many of Kingsley's black-
guards, Welter appears more dastardly than he really is. Although it was he who had seduced Ellen and enticed her to become
his mistress, Ellen had been easily tempted. Likewise, his proposal
to the ambitious Adelaide to elope with him without a promise
of marriage cannot be considered villainous because the socially

equal Adelaide eagerly accepted the offer, and, besides, Welter knew that she did not love Charles. Later when he sees the ruined figure of his boy-love, and, realizing the consequences to him if Charles is found alive, Welter still goes to Lord Saltire to report the discovery, knowing well that now Saltire's fortune is lost to him. Kingsley, at that time, pithily sums up Welter's character— "There were some things a fellow couldn't do, you know!" Finally reunited with Charles, reinstated in the good graces of all and eventually becoming aware of his love for Adelaide, Welter, nevertheless, emerges a pitiable man. With his title and incredible fortune, he has been sentenced to childlessness: after her marriage to Welter, Adelaide was permanently crippled, her injury resulting from her greatest vanity, her horsemanship. Kingsley allows some poetic justice to take its course.

Written at the time when his imagination was at its fullest, *Ravenshoe* contains not only some of Kingsley's most attractive characters but his best inventive humor and lovely descriptions. And, above all, it is the work of a disciplined Kingsley, who managed to curb his tendency to fly in all directions. His habit of interpolating random bits of information and of dropping the story thread in order to extend to the reader the right hand of good-fellowship can become ludicrous and tedious if the asides are too irrelevant and the informality excessively whimsical, but in *Ravenshoe*, the author-reader camaraderie is kept at a tolerable level. Kingsley's confidential asides that Charles is a "good, worthy fellow" and that Adelaide is "worthless—Worthless" and his interruptions—such as when he informs us that he will leave the lovers Mary Corby and Charles Ravenshoe alone and follow Lady Hainault upstairs "out of mere politeness" to help her find her blotting-book, for he "decline[s] to go into that drawing-room at present"—will annoy no reader attuned to the eighteenth- and nineteenth-century novel and prepared to accept conventions that no great English novelist from Fielding to Hardy would have dreamed of relinquishing. Assuredly, a few of his footnotes hit a peak of irrelevance, such as when he informs us that he tried to write a single paragraph "without using a single word derived from the Latin," but they are part of the youthful good humor that saturates the work. Their success in this novel lies, I believe, in their naturalness and simplicity. Later on, his asides become either petulant and priggish or just dismally silly, but in *Ravenshoe*, his hand was sure and he seemed able to judge to what limits he could go.

Kingsley was much less successful in *Austin Elliot,* his hastily written third novel, published just a year after *Ravenshoe.*[11] Although composed during the peaceful Eversley days, the novel displays more objectively Kingsley's inherent artistic deficiencies than do his later novels, mass-produced under the stress of financial burdens and emotional tensions. All of the major defects present in the perfunctory *Austin Elliot* also evidence themselves to a certain degree in the more carefully created *Geoffry Hamlyn* and *Ravenshoe,* but because of Kingsley's mastering of his material in those two works, the inadequacies appear less starkly.

The theme of *Austin Elliot* is young love: Austin's romantic love for Eleanor Hilton and his boy-love for Lord Charles Barty. But discordantly, the novel pivots around two very serious incidents: a famine on the island of Ronaldsay, in which hundreds die, and a duel between Charles Barty and the villain, Captain Will Hertford (a non-sexual George Hawker/Lord Welter), in which Charles is killed and Austin, his second, is imprisoned. Comparable tragedies had darkened *Ravenshoe,* but in that novel Kingsley had lightened them with gentle humor, palatable sentiment, and finely tuned pathos. We find no such appropriate lightening in *Austin Elliot;* the gloom is only accentuated by slapstick, forced humor, and ridiculous puns, for example Kingsley's dreadful use of comic names: The Reverend Letmedown Easy,[12] Admiral Sir Foreland North, who was Lord High Inspector of the Shoals and Quicksands, later Lord Sands of Godwin. (In later novels, Kingsley persists in using this unnecessary and distracting device.) Possibly copying Thackeray, Kingsley, however, lacks the former's personal talent that makes his puns more acceptable.

What is most provoking for the readers is Kingsley's ineffectual characterizations. Kingsley, of course, wants us to like his

11. Critically, the novel was praised by the *Saturday Review* (XV [June 6, 1863], 731–32); it appeared in *La Revue des Deux Mondes* (mars, 1864), translated into French by E. D. Forgues. Prompted, no doubt, by the American success of *Ravenshoe,* Ticknor and Fields published four editions—4,512 copies—of *Austin Elliot* in 1863.

12. Kingsley reuses this name in two other works: *The Hillyars and the Burtons* (Vol. I, ch. 3) and "An Episode in the Life of Charles Mordaunt" (*London Society,* XXI [January, 1872], 2).

hero, who, like Charles Ravenshoe, must be tested. At the beginning of the novel, Austin is "full of health, hope, honour, courage, and curiosity," eager to pursue his path "across that world,
which at that time, seemed . . . only a sunny fairy-land lying be-
twixt" him and the grave, "only some enchanted land full of
glorious adventures." But Austin—"a pure, noble, high-minded man,
utterly incapable of anything mean"—is a priggish and moralistic
Charles Ravenshoe. Imprisoned with murderers and experienced
thieves, for example, he decides to elevate their moral tone by
talking to them about Shakespeare and musical glasses until the
convicts "should become penetrated with an abstract love of virtue . . . and should all become reformed" (Vol. II, ch. 13). And
when he wants Austin to be an orphan, Kingsley, prefiguring E. M.
Forster's cold-blooded efficiency in this respect, dispatches Mr. Elliot
conveniently in one sentence.

Also Kingsley doesn't seem to understand his heroine, Eleanor
Hilton. He depicts her as a deeply religious girl, who is keeping
the "disgraceful secret" that her brother is a thief, a swindler,
and a forger from Austin, because he would be incapable of understanding anything so base. Yet it is precisely her self-righteous will-
fulness that brings down the whole catastrophe. If she had told
the secret to Austin, Captain Hertford, who knows her secret and
hates Austin, would have lost his hold over her, Charles Barty
would not have fought the duel to protect Austin and, thus,
would not have been killed, and Austin would not have gone to
prison. Yet Kingsley never attaches any blame to her actions.

And annoyingly Kingsley fails to realize the full potentiality
of scenes that cry for exploitation. Such an example occurs between
the blind Edward Barty, Charles' brother, an ethereal boy who
has dedicated his life to doing good, and Captain Hertford. Discovering Hertford's supposedly secret plot to assassinate Austin,
Barty confronts Hertford with the information. Kingsley prepares
the scene well. Hertford sits, staring at Barty's eyes:

> Those sightless eyes! The darkened windows of a house in
> which sight lies dead, shrouded in grave-clothes of strange
> misconceptions, until the dawn of the Resurrection shall begin
> to gleam in the East, and the dead shall rise upon their feet.
> The eyes of the blind are more awful to look at than the
> eyes of the dead. . . .
>
> "It is uncommon curious to think of," thought the Captain,

"but that fellow has never seen any other fellow in his whole life. There is something very horrid about it."

There was. Lord Edward was feeling his way softly round the table, towards Captain Hertford, in sightless silence, getting nearer and nearer every instant with his long thin fingers; it *was* very horrid. Hertford held his breath, and felt a strange creeping come over him. One of his big hands was on the table, and Lord Edward's long hands were coming slowly towards it, feeling their way through the books, and press-papiers, and paper-knives,—and yet Captain Hertford kept his hand still on the table; there was a kind of fascination about the blind man's eyes (Vol. II, ch. 5).

Barty then divulges the information. Not knowing how Barty came by his knowledge and already superstitiously fascinated and terrified by the blind man's eyes, Hertford ought to have assumed that Barty's prescience had a supernatural origin. But instead of playing upon this element, thus making the scene effectively sinister, Kingsley changes course and merely describes Hertford's anger, disregarding completely the suspense that he had already created.

It would be unfair to condemn the novel completely, for, as every Kingsley novel contains highlights, *Austin Elliot* has its few outstanding features: the fine descriptive handling of Austin's ascent of Mount Snowdon (Vol. I, ch. 4) that must be a deliberate echo of Wordsworth's in Book XIV of *The Prelude*, and of the island of Ronaldsay, caught in a spreading famine (Vol. II, ch. 19); the characterization of Gil MacDonald, a Carlylean figure, who holds the typically Victorian creed "that a man was born to do the work he found to his hand, and that when the work was done it would get paid for in some form"; the humorous glimpses of the Barty children in the nursery (Vol. II, ch. 6), and of Austin's dog, Rover, another "dog of dogs."

One of the saddest notes about *Austin Elliot* for a Kingsley critic is that it is not just a poor third novel. If it had been succeeded by later *Ravenshoes*, we could excuse it as we do other inferior third novels, such as *Sandra Belloni* or *Romola* (by-passing George Eliot's short fable *Silas Marner*). But for Kingsley no *Egoist* or *Middlemarch* ever appeared; in its place hangs *Oakshott Castle*, which Kingsley took two years to write. The defects of *Austin Elliot* become more and more prominent in his later work. His degeneration was steady and inexorable.

V

1864-1869

ON JULY 19, 1864, Henry Kingsley married his second cousin, twenty-two-year-old Sarah Maria Kingsley Haselwood, a governess in the family of the Reverend Gerald Blunt, who succeeded Kingsley's father at St. Luke's, Chelsea. Kingsley makes no mention of Sarah in his known correspondence from Eversley, but it can easily be assumed that during his frequent London trips to Macmillan's Thursday evening gatherings, he also visited his boyhood home in Chelsea and made friends with Mr. and Mrs. Blunt and their young family. Liking children as much as he did, Kingsley, no doubt, often invaded the nursery, where he soon became acquainted with and, consequently, fell in love with their governess. On the basis of the Kingsleys' wedding picture and later secondhand descriptions,[1] few people would call Sarah Haselwood beautiful or even handsome. Taller than Henry, she wore her dark hair parted in the middle and pulled back behind her ears, a coiffure which emphasized her long nose and protruding chin. Not only was she unattractive but her face reflected a determination—a severity—that her later actions will confirm was her character. If Miss Lee, the governess and a central figure in *Silcote of Silcotes*, published serially just two years after their marriage, represented Henry's bride, one can see how completely he was infatuated with and beguiled by her: "Here she was . . . beautiful, attractive, boisterous, noisy; ready at any moment to enter into an animated and friendly discussion with a policeman, or for that matter a chimney-sweep: with a great

1. Mary McLeod, "Henry Kingsley at Cuckfield," *The Sussex County Magazine,* IV (March, 1930), 251–53.

tendency to laugh loudly at the smallest ghost of a joke. . . . There she was . . . a mass of kindliness, vitality, and good humour" (Vol. I, ch. 12).

They were married by the Reverend Blunt and Charles Kingsley from the Chelsea Rectory, which held so many happy memories for Henry, but his marriage was solemnized to a discordant tune. Mrs. Blunt, possibly vexed because she was losing a governess, curtly noted the event in her journal: "Wedding of Mr. Henry Kingsley and Miss Haselwood at St. Mary's Brompton. Wedding Breakfast at the Rectory. Mr. and Mrs. [Charles] Kingsley, Dr. [George] Kingsley, and about thirty friends. Croquet in the afternoon."[2] One imagines that Charles, who seven years later will vehemently say that he had "know[n] all about" Miss Haselwood's and her mother's wastefulness for "some 20–30 years," maintained an explosive silence.[3] Unfortunately for Henry, Charles' prejudice was well founded; that marriage proved to be a financial and literary disaster for him. Financially dependent upon his writings, Henry Kingsley hardly enhanced his fortunes when he married a penniless ex-governess whose sole dowry was her penniless mother.

But if Henry had any premonitions about future difficulties, he pushed them aside: "I am so much happier than I deserve to be, that I am lost in amazement," he wrote to Macmillan soon after the Kingsleys moved to Wargrave, on the banks of the Thames (E., p. 129). There the newlyweds shortly settled into an eight-room cottage appropriately named Hillside House, for it sided a down and backed a chalk cliff. It was, indeed, a honeymooners' delight. From the terraced garden in front of the house, the Kingsleys viewed the winding Thames, "by day a broad river of silver; in some evenings, a chain of crimson pools," behind which ranged wooded hillsides. To the right of the house stretched the chalky Chilterns and across the river and to the left spread the "dim mysterious wolds" of Oxfordshire, "rolling, hedgeless, uncultivated chalk down, capped always by the dark level bars of woodland" (*Silcote of Silcotes*, Vol. I, ch. 10).

Kingsley, who was fond of good company, still journeyed occasionally to London for Macmillan's social evenings, where once, as he relates, "[Thomas] Huxley, and Dean Stanley made me sit between them for a jolly good jaw. And on the other side was my dear

2. Ellis, pp. 66–67.
3. Una Pope-Hennessy, *Canon Charles Kingsley* (London, 1948), p. 266.

Mat Arnold. And we all talked at once. And Tom Taylor got me and talked theatricals, which I hate. And Arthur Helps twiddled his moustach. It was a jolly evening" (E., p. 192).[4] Also in London he frequented the popular Garrick Club (the place where "actors and men of education and refinement might meet on equal terms") and impressed people with his friendliness and modesty. Joseph Hatton, editor of the *Gentleman's Magazine* 1868–74, first met Kingsley in 1868 and remembered that "he was the kind of man I should have liked to be intimate with. . . . He took no pains to let me know that he had had an University education, nor did he talk about his famous brother Charles, nor in any way try to impress me with his importance socially or otherwise."[5]

Mostly the gregarious Kingsley entertained—freely and too extravagantly for his income—his visiting friends from London and Oxford at Wargrave. C. L. Dodgson ("Lewis Carroll") made at least one visit in 1865 and showed his appreciation by sending Kingsley a copy of *Alice's Adventures in Wonderland*, which had just been published. "The fancy of the whole thing," Kingsley wrote to Dodgson, "is delicious, it is like gathering cowslips in springtime."[6]

Also at Wargrave, but two years later, Kingsley became acquainted with Swinburne, then staying at Holmwood, Henley on Thames, and took great interest in the poet who had just shocked the literary world with his *Poems and Ballads* (1866). Swinburne is "a fine healthy lot," Kingsley said, and he tried to persuade Swinburne to transfer the publication of his poems to Kingsley's own publisher, Macmillan. Swinburne returned Kingsley's affection and

4. Arthur Penrhyn Stanley (1815–81), English divine who became Dean of Westminster in 1863; Tom Taylor (1817–80), Scottish dramatist, best known for *The Ticket of Leave Man* (1863); Sir Arthur Helps (1813–75), English essayist and historian, who edited Prince Albert's *Speeches* (1862) and later Queen Victoria's *Journal of our Life in the Highlands* (1868).

5. Letter to C. K. Shorter, "Introduction," p. xix.

6. Unpublished letter, Houghton Library, Harvard University. Upon the publication of Dodgson's *Through the Looking-Glass* (1871), Kingsley wrote to him: "I can say with a clear head and conscience that your new book is the finest thing we have had since 'Martin Chuzzlewit'. . . . I can only say, in comparing the new 'Alice' with the old, 'this is a more excellent song than the other'" (Stuart Dodgson Collingwood, *The Life and Letters of Lewis Carroll* [London, 1898], pp. 142–43). Interestingly, William Tinsley, sometime publisher of Kingsley's novels, erroneously thought that Kingsley and Dodgson "now and then worked together, for Henry Kingsley had a capital sense of fun and true humour" (*Random Recollections of an Old Publisher* [London, 1900], II, 284). Kingsley's letters do not confirm the suggestion.

became a frequent visitor to Hillside House. Their friendship quickened in their common dislike of the "gross insolence and scurrility" of the *Spectator*, which had attacked both Swinburne's poetry and Kingsley's novels *The Hillyars and the Burtons* and *Silcote of Silcotes*, and in their adoration of "our glorious inimitable Blake."[7] On one occasion Kingsley humorously wrote for Swinburne's inspection "A Shameless and ridiculous ballant . . . principally written in Arabic numerals—Par Exemple":

> Lord Ronald courted Lady Clare,
> And he cut the division with Lowe; for repair
> He loved the Lady faithfully,
> And he met her Pa at 8.43.

> Lady Clare she told her Ma
> That Lord Ronald was gone to speak to her Pa,
> That he would settle on her most willing
> £24,000: I:

> The interest on which no doubt
> Is sufficient for carriage, ball and rout.
> I make it this, pray what do you,
> 5462?

> At five per cent., her mother said,
> My dear, you must have lost your head;
> At *three* per cent., with lease fines if any
> I make it 4562 : 2 : 1 (E., p. 192).

Joining Kingsley and Swinburne on other occasions were Anne and Minny Thackeray and Leslie Stephen, Minny's future husband. Anne and Minny were living at Ivy Gate, Henley, and used to row over to Wargrave to visit Sarah and Henry, who greeted them with "flaming gladioli" from his garden and told them about his latest pet dog, a collie, who "used to come in at meal times and lay his long chin upon his master's knee. 'We never send him away when he does this,' Henry Kingsley used to say, caressing the faithful head."

7. *Swinburne Letters*, ed. Cecil Y. Lang (Yale University Press, 1959), I, 195, 199, 231, 268–69, 271; Ellis, pp. 70–71, 76, 86, 155, 168–69, 191. Swinburne published a critical essay on Blake in 1868. In that same year in a letter to Swinburne, Kingsley states that he too had just finished writing one on Blake. If he got it published, I can find no trace of it. He did, however, discuss Blake in *Hetty*, ch. 27.

From those days, Anne Thackeray remembers Kingsley as "a kind, most kind and hospitable host and friend," who "was usually hard at work, but we used to go out in boats together, and meet at odd moments in gardens. He was perhaps more emphatic in conversation than I could comfortably respond to, but my feeling of respect and regard for him was very great, and my affectionate admiration warm and sincere. . . . Leslie Stephen . . . had a very great regard for him."[8]

In the memory of those times, Kingsley's seventh novel, *Mademoiselle Mathilde*, was dedicated to his wife and Anne Thackeray, for "the pleasant summer days during which the better parts of it were written." And in the novel proper, probably referring to one of Swinburne's visits, he recalls another one of those days: "I was with a poet, and a great one, once, and we were in a boat on a cold, steel-grey river, under a cold, motionless, grey sky, with the yellow willow-leaves showering upon us; and he was reading. Suddenly he looked up, and said, 'This weather is enough to kill one!' —I said, 'I love grey weather.'—'Ah!' he replied, 'if it *moves*, I love it too' " (Vol. II, ch. 16).

While Kingsley was living at Wargrave, the intellectual world of Britain was rocked and bitterly divided by the famous Governor Eyre controversy. In October, 1865, at the town of Morant Bay, in St. Thomas, Jamaica, the Negro peasantry rebelled against the white authority, killing about twenty Europeans. Within a month, the Governor of Jamaica, Edward Eyre, ruthlessly suppressed the revolt by having nearly five hundred Negroes killed and many more flogged and tortured, and at least one thousand native homes burned. Among those executed was George William Gordon, a mulatto landowner who was also a magistrate in St. Thomas parish and a member of the Colonial Assembly. In November of that year,

8. Letter to C. K. Shorter, "Introduction," pp. xx-xxi. About Leslie Stephen, Kingsley said, "I am very civil to another man too, a man I once disliked but am now very much attached to—Leslie Stephen. I am keeping his dog for him" (Ellis, p. 178). Another pleasant glimpse of Kingsley was recorded by Lothian Nicholson in the *TLS* soon after Michael Sadleir wrote an article celebrating the centennial of Kingsley's birth (*TLS*, January 2, 1930). Nicholson writes: "Somewhere about 1866–7 my father took a house on the river at Henley, and while with him in our boat at Wargrave I managed somehow to fall in; I recollect (being seven or eight years old) being taken to a cottage and put to dry before the kitchen fire, and that Henry Kingsley came and told me the most delightful fairy stories during the process" ("Letters to Editor," *TLS*, February 6, 1930, 102).

news of the revolt and suppression reached England, and immediately public protest against Eyre's actions led to the formation of an investigating Royal Commission, which first met on the island of Jamaica on January 20, 1866. After months of deliberation and several thousands of pages of testimony, the Commission reported on April 9, 1866. It praised Governor Eyre for "the skill, promptitude and vigour" he exercised in ending the riot, but censured him for the prolonged use of martial law that had deprived the natives of their constitutional privileges and for the excessive punishments inflicted upon the natives.

When the report was published in England, the intellectuals split into two camps: the Jamaica Committee that wanted Eyre prosecuted for murder; and the Eyre Defense Committee that regarded Eyre as a hero. Mill, Huxley, Herbert Spencer, Darwin, Goldwin Smith, and Thomas Hughes spirited the former, while Carlyle, Ruskin, Charles and Henry Kingsley, with Tennyson and Dickens lending their names, marshalled forces for the latter. For six years the case dragged on, as the two committees hurled bitter accusations at each other, and formerly close friendships ruptured, never to be mended. Finally in July, 1872, Governor Eyre was vindicated, with the Government defraying his legal expenses. A year later he was granted a pension as a "retired" colonial governor, which supported him until he died in 1901.[9]

Henry Kingsley's introduction into this controversy was more coincidental than intentional. In 1862, Kingsley had begun to write a series of articles dealing with famous Australian explorers and starting with an account of a year-long exploratory march (1840–41) around the desolate terrain in Southern Australia known as the Australian Bight. The daring explorer of that march had been Edward Eyre. An Australian sheep rancher in the 1830s, Eyre had —ironically enough in light of future events—first made a reputation for himself in Australia as the "Protector of the Aborigines," because of his consideration of their rights when he was Resident Magistrate for the Murray River Territory. Then when he became

9. For a full discussion of the Eyre Controversy, see Bernard Semmel, *Jamaican Blood and Victorian Conscience* (Boston, 1963); George H. Ford, "The Governor Eyre Case in England," *University of Toronto Quarterly*, XVII (April, 1948), 219–33. For a more detailed discussion of Kingsley's position in the controversy, see my article "Henry Kingsley and the Governor Eyre Controversy," *Victorian Newsletter*, no. 37, (Spring, 1970), 24–27.

the only white survivor of that hazardous expedition around the Bight he was—and still is—acclaimed a hero in Australia.

Kingsley did not finish his article on "Eyre's March" until July, 1865, and then, as fate would have it, the first half of it was published in *Macmillan's Magazine* in October, 1865, just a few weeks before the rebellion; the second half appeared the following month. The narrative concentrated on Eyre's expedition, but early in the article Kingsley had briefly referred to Eyre's treatment of the Australian natives: "He knew more about the aboriginal tribes, their habits, language, and so on, than any man before or since. He was appointed Black Protector for the Lower Murray, and did his work well. He seems to have been . . . a man eminently kind, generous, and just. No man concealed less than Eyre the vices of the natives, but no man stood more steadfastly in the breach between them and the squatters (the great pastoral aristocracy) at a time when to do so was social ostracism. The almost unexampled valour which led him safely through the hideous desert . . . served him well in a fight more wearing and more dangerous to his rules of right and wrong. He pleaded for the black, and tried to stop the war of extermination which was, is, and I suppose will be, carried on by the colonists against the natives in the unsettled districts beyond reach of the public eye. His task was hopeless. It was easier for him to find water in the desert than to find mercy for the savages." When Kingsley republished his two-part article seven years later in *Hornby Mills and Other Stories,* he added two footnotes: "These words were published in *Macmillan's Magazine* one month before we heard of the Jamaica rebellion. I have not altered one word of the narrative"; "This narrative was written . . . at a time when the author believed Mr. Eyre to be dead; not in the least degree knowing that Eyre, Governor of Jamaica, was the old hero Eyre of his youthful admiration. Both parties, therefore, in the great Eyre controversy may read it without prejudice" (Vol. II, pp. 88, 91).[10]

In its lead article on November 29, 1865, *The Times*—which became increasingly pro-Eyre—quoted Kingsley's comments and, unintentionally, set up a public correspondence between Kingsley and Mr. W. Bakewell, who took exception to Kingsley's suggestion that Eyre had been socially ostracized in Australia and that, in fact,

10. Swinburne was especially fond of this "noble narrative." See *Letters,* III, 239; VI, 61.

the squatters had waged war against the blacks. The correspondence between the two men went back and forth from November 30 to December 7.[11]

Although a member of the Eyre Defense Committee, Kingsley always seemed to be on the fringe of the controversy. His letters in *The Times* did not defend, or even mention, Eyre's actions in Jamaica. Kingsley, in fact, states in a letter to Alexander Macmillan during the time of his correspondence with Mr. Bakewell that "I shall keep carefully clear of the Jamaica business" (E., p. 141). His letters—both public and private—attack only the injustices dealt the Australian natives by the squatters, especially "those short-sighted idiots," as he confides to Macmillan, "who have made fortunes on soil drenched with the blood of the natives, and have come home here and turned saint" (E., p. 142). Eyre's critics may have considered Kingsley's description of the Australian squatter to be a perfect one for Governor Eyre, but Kingsley never made that comparison. Because of Eyre's past actions in Australia, he was, for Kingsley, a hero.

Therein lies the difference between Kingsley's motivation and those of the other important members on both committees. The others were fighting for a cause, whether humanitarianism and Radicalism (Jamaica Committee) or colonialism and Anti-Radicalism (Eyre Defense Committee); Kingsley was fighting for a man for whom he had a strong personal feeling: "And so my name stands on his Committee. He may or may not have been wrong, but he must have fair play, a thing he would never have got if we had not clubbed together." Kingsley, in fact, was horrified at the rancor that developed between the two committees (Carlyle had called the Jamaica Committee a "knot of nigger philanthropists"), and even defended the Jamaica Committee's right to bring proceedings against Eyre. He was infuriated when the secretary of the Eyre Defense Committee, Alexander Hamilton Hume, termed those proceedings "disgraceful" (E., p. 164).

Kingsley's interest in the Eyre controversy waned, however, as his financial troubles started to overwhelm him. Pleasant as his Wargrave days may have seemed to an occasional visitor, Charles Kingsley's fears about Henry's marriage were soon realized. Just a year after his marriage, Henry lamented to Macmillan: "I was in hopes that you were going to have a new edition of *Austin*

11. For a summary of the letters see Ellis, pp. 194–99.

Elliot by now, for the fearful expense of pulling a sick wife about
the country, literally to save her life, and setting up a new house,
have superinduced an alarming financial crisis, and left me without
any money at all. I suppose that one's first year is always a squeezer,
but to be forced into extravagance by the doctors is too hard.
However, I can see my way quite clear if I can tide over Christmas"
(E., p. 134).

Sarah's recurrent spells of illness, occasioned in part by her
frequent miscarriages, aggravated their difficulties, of course,
but mismanagement and the extravagance in furnishing their house
on the part of Sarah and her equally strong-willed mother, a ha-
bitual visitor of the Kingsleys, must have been main causes of
their impecuniosity. Hints of Henry's domination by these two
women creep not only into the asides in his novels but into his
letters. In *Stretton*, for example, he speaks of two women whom
he knows who have demanded rooms of their own to furnish as
they please (Vol. I, ch. 9), and in his otherwise jovial letter about
Alice's Adventures in Wonderland to Dodgson, after praising
Dodgson's conception of the Queen of Hearts, Kingsley continues
with an obvious reference to Sarah and Mrs. Haselwood: "I know
two women at least who would be quite as dictatorial and as un-
reasonable if they happened to be Queen of Hearts and Spades
instead of being bound by the rules of human society." One wonders not whether but how often those boyish stories told at the
Fez Club about the frivolity of women returned to haunt Kingsley.

Four later representative letters to the patient Macmillan portray
accurately enough Kingsley's steadily worsening plight:

January, 1866
I have invested every available farthing I could get hold of in
this house, with a view to letting it well in the summer months,
and being able to move, and am dependent on *Leighton Court*,
and some money which you said was to come on *Austin Elliot*,
for satisfying my Xmas creditors. I have not invested my money
badly, but still there is nothing at the bank. . . . You see what
a fix I am in. . . . Do you think you could make it safe for
me to present a cheque at Child's by Wednesday? There is
a carpenter wants his money, not to mention others. Poor
Sarah has a sad cough (E., pp. 146–48).

[1867]
Could you let my debt to you stand a little longer? . . . If I

could only get free again I'd give two of my fingers. What did for me was the fearful expense of starting and furnishing my place. I was an awful lot to the good at one time, but it has all melted like snow. . . . I will work like a cart-horse to repay you (E., p. 165).

[1868]

We have had another wretched disappointment, and Doctor A. Massey forbids the wife to move for a time. I believe that these miscarriages are worse than confinements. He thought nothing much of it, but he blames me very much for bringing her up to him. How was I to have him here at a guinea a mile? Do you think you can lend me £35 out of your private pocket? (E., p. 174).

[February, 1869]

I will, if you please, write to Straham and tell him to pay the money he owes me to you instead of to me, if you could possibly pay £22 for me today to Andrew and Atkins, George Yard, Lombard Street. If it was anything but the interest on a mortgage, to prevent them foreclosing, I would not trouble you. . . . I fear you hate the sight of me (E., pp. 183–84).

Kingsley's pleas were not just to Macmillan; he also begged from George Craik, Macmillan's partner. And, pathetically, when he was not actually asking for money, his thoughts were not far from his need. Soon after Craik's marriage to Dinah Mulock, the novelist, in 1865, Kingsley suggested to Macmillan that he make her editor of *Macmillan Magazine* and then Kingsley added, "You owe me £1,000 for the suggestion" (E., p. 146). In his letters he daydreamed, "What beautiful stories one could write if one was rich and had leisure" (E., p. 173). In his novels he gives his characters unlimited wealth. Even his ballad for Swinburne accented money.

Deepening Kingsley's distress was his extreme disappointment at being childless. His playfulness and patience with his nieces and nephews, his numerous and sympathetic descriptions of children in his novels, demonstrate his great affection for children. Time after time his hopes were raised—"My dearest wife is quite recovered. If she goes on like this, I shall actually begin to believe in the possibility of a cherub, though I see nothing of his appearance yet." But they were always shattered: "We rather thought that affairs were going well, for this time at all events, but it has apparently ended in faintness, sickness, and physical misery" (E., pp. 135, 174).

Nothing shows more clearly Kingsley's desperation than his literary slavery between July, 1864, and September, 1869. Besides finishing the serialization of *The Hillyars and the Burtons* and preparing the novel for a three-volume edition, he published four other novels in book form, *Leighton Court, Silcote of Silcotes, Mademoiselle Mathilde,* and *Stretton,* with the last three being also serialized, and a serialized version of a fifth, *Hetty.* He wrote an allegorical fairy tale, *The Boy in Grey,* for *Good Words for the Young,* and a few short stories.[12]

In addition to fiction and to "Eyre's March," Kingsley also produced many nonfictional essays. He wrote "The March of Charles Sturt," about another Australian explorer; reviewed three books for the *Fortnightly Review* and one for the *North British Review*; wrote "About Salmon," a humorous account of the lives of snared and unsnared salmon; edited with a preface ("for which . . . I am to get £50") Defoe's *Robinson Crusoe,* in which he rather ingeniously discussed "this wondrous romance [as] no romance at all, but merely an allegorical account of De Foe's life for twenty-eight years" (xxi). On top of all that, he struggled for five years on a prodigiously researched series of fourteen essays dealing with ancient and modern travelers entitled *Tales of Old Travel Re-Narrated.*[13] What else but sympathy can we feel for him when he cried in 1868, "Lord, if I could only get a fortnight's rest: not much chance of that" (E., p. 179).

And when payments from that work still did not satisfy his creditors, Kingsley proposed to Macmillan a miscellany of Kingsley's previously printed tales, stories, and articles, most of which had been published in *Macmillan's Magazine.* Macmillan refused, and nothing came of the proposal even though Kingsley, in 1869, admonished Macmillan that Bradbury and Evans, publishers of *Mademoiselle Mathilde,* were willing to undertake the project because "they seem to fancy that I have sufficient prestige to float

12. In his letters Kingsley refers to unnamed editors or magazines which have accepted or have requested him to write short stories. For the ones I have tracked down, see Bibliography.

13. While Kingsley was working on this collection, the North German Arctic Expedition claimed that it had reached the highest known north latitude. In a letter to *The Times,* Kingsley refutes this claim and cites information he had gathered for "Spitzbergen," one of the essays in the collection (October 21, 1868, 11c).

[miscellanies].'' Significantly, in the same letter Kingsley senses that his old partnership with Macmillan was nearing an end, as, in fact, it was. After 1867, Macmillan, probably tiring of Kingsley's pleas and recognizing the decline in his writing, published only one more Kingsley novel. Kingsley speaks of the "old times, when you and I worked together" and complains that now Macmillan's editors will not start printing his copy until they get all of it. Then, apologetically, he asks permission to extract his earlier articles from *Macmillan's Magazine* for Bradbury and Evans' use (E., pp. 182–83).

It is almost anticlimactic to record that when Kingsley and his wife did manage a short holiday both were accidentally poisoned and "were dangerously ill; indeed pretty near gone" (E., p. 179). And less than a year later Kingsley broke his leg and suffered from complications for some months. If his jug of rum and water increased during these years to three or four jugs a night, we cannot much blame him.

VI

The Wargrave Novels

NATURALLY, Kingsley's anxiety was reflected in his novels of this period. Not only are they characterized by pervasive melancholy and a deterioration of the sort of controlled humor that highlights *Geoffry Hamlyn* and *Ravenshoe*, but it is all too apparent that Kingsley is writing with his eye on the critics whose approval he needed in order to make money. In view of his circumstances, it is remarkable, not that his novels declined in merit during this period, but that some of them are as good as they are.

The Hillyars and the Burtons, Kingsley's fourth novel which had been partly written before his marriage, is a much tighter, more closely knit work than either of his two earlier major ones and could have been his best novel. Subtitled "A Story of Two Families," the novel traces the misfortunes of the Burtons, the noble blacksmith family, in England and their astonishing rise to wealth and prominence in Australia. Jim Burton, the oldest son, becomes the Honorable James Burton, a commissioner to the International Exhibition of 1862; and his younger brother Joseph, "a hunchback . . . with the face of a Byron," becomes a famous orator, Minister of Education, a member of the Governor's Council, and the husband of a young, pretty, and rich widow, Mrs. North. The novel also deals with the Hillyars of Stanlake, an old aristocratic house plagued by the problems of heirship, which, like those in *Ravenshoe*, focus on the usual confusion of births and the missing document, in this case a will. The half-brothers involved in the fraternal contest are George Hillyar, a less villainous George Hawker (*Geoffry Hamlyn*), and Erne Hillyar, the amiable and gentle boy who must learn responsibility. Plausibly, Kingsley so entangles the fortunes of these families that they never become separated.

When the novel was first published in 1865, some critics ridiculed the Burtons' gushing goodness and nobility. Twenty-two-year-old Henry James, in particular, entitled his review of Kingsley's novel "The Noble School of Fiction" and, in an attack ostensibly directed toward Charles Kingsley, reprimanded writers for attributing heroic proportions to commonplace characters, especially blacksmiths who have "none but the minor virtues—honesty, energy, and a strong family feeling." Snobbishly, James reminded such writers that "there is no such thing as a gentleman in the rough. A gentleman is born of his polish."[1]

The Burtons, it is true, are larger-than-life. James Burton the elder is "the ideal of all the blacksmiths who ever lived" (Vol. I, ch. 2), and his wife, "the most affectionate and big-hearted of women we [have] ever known" (Vol. II, ch. 4), is unhappy only when the family's newly acquired wealth restricts her from doing her own housework. Together, Mr. and Mrs. Burton "would have made it home even on an iceberg. Their inner life was so perfectly, placidly good, the flame of their lives burnt so clearly and so steadily that its soft light was reflected on the faces of all those who came within its influences" (Vol. III, ch. 2). Unreal as they may be, the Burtons, nevertheless, continue the line that Kingsley had set up with the Buckleys, in *Geoffry Hamlyn*. For him, the Buckleys, the Burtons, and all of the other great-hearted, noble gentlemen, be they impoverished aristocrats or blacksmiths, personify the "good life" that Kingsley cherished.

When Kingsley concentrates on narrating his story of the two families, he creates some meritorious scenes. The loving description of Chelsea and the Burtons' home, Church Place (Vol. I, chs.

1. Originally published in *The Nation*, July 6, 1865 and reprinted in *Notes and Reviews* (Cambridge, Mass., 1921), pp. 59–67. For other reviews see *Athenaeum*, XLI (May 27, 1865), 716–17; *Saturday Review*, XIX (May 13, 1865), 576–77; *Spectator*, XXXVIII (May 6, 1865), 501–2. An interesting sidelight on the subject of the Burtons' nobility arose in a favorable American review of the novel, written just two months after General Lee's surrender at Appomattox. Ending his discussion by praising Kingsley's depiction of the Burtons, the reviewer patriotically acclaims that the North likes and fosters such "great-hearted gentlemen," whereas the Southern system encourages "listlessness" and "indolence" (*North American Review*, CI [July, 1865], critical notice 22, 299). Considering Kingsley's view of the Civil War, one wonders about his reaction to the comparison. Ticknor and Fields published three editions of the novel, totaling 4,140 copies.

2, 5); the Omeo gold mining disaster in which Erne almost dies (Vol. III, ch. 23); old Sir George Hillyar's death as recounted by Samuel Burton, Jim's uncle and young George Hillyar's enemy, in his marvelous letter (Vol. II, ch. 20); George Hillyar's premonitions in the Palmerston Post Office that foreshadow his dreaded meeting with Samuel Burton (Vol. I, ch. 15), as well as the scenes of the Australian terrain and of the cyclone which devastates the Burtons' Australian home (Vol. III, ch. 38) are all first-rate Kingsley. And the incident when Sir George drags the lake for the supposedly drowned Erne (Vol. I, ch. 10) is as entertaining a one as can be found in any Kingsley novel.

The novel suffers, however, from a superimposed moral. In his "Preface" (which was not republished in all subsequent editions) Kingsley wrote:

> In this story, an uneducated girl, who might, I fancy, after a year and a half at a boarding-school, have developed into a very noble lady, is arraigned before the reader, and awaits his judgment.
> The charge against her is, that, by an overstrained idea of duty, she devoted herself to her brother, and made her lover but a secondary person. I am instructed to reply on her behalf, that, in the struggle between inclination and what she considered her duty, she, right or wrong, held by duty at the risk of breaking her own heart.

"Probably no living novelist," generalized the *Saturday Review*, "is less fit than Mr. Henry Kingsley to treat a subtle moral question or to describe a conflict of delicate motives."[2] Basically, this criticism is just. *Ravenshoe* demonstrated that Kingsley's art lies in his humor and in his deft depiction of external life, not in psychological studies. In fact, another Kingsley-Waugh comparison can be noted here. Assuredly, the nineteenth-century Kingsley lacks the twentieth-century Waugh's satirical cleverness, as well as his disciplined intellect, but in their individual ways these two writers, at their best, are witty mimics, handling well the frivolous and the farcical situations. Both seem to look at the world with the eyes of perceptive urchins; but whereas Kingsley wistfully dreams heroics, Waugh (or, at least, the early Waugh), with a child's insensitivity, gleefully smears comedy over social criticism and

2. For Kingsley's reaction to the *Saturday Review* article, see Ellis, pp. 144, 149.

brutal physical suffering alike. Lacking delicacy of perception and, possibly one can say, passionate sensitivity to philosophical/ethical problems, both men seem unable to deal well with serious emotional themes, whether the theme be love/duty, as in *The Hillyars and the Burtons*, or religious faith/secular love, as in *Brideshead Revisited*.

Understandably, then, *The Hillyars and the Burtons* inadequately treats the declared moral, and, actually, the love/duty theme fails to dominate the novel. But since Emma Burton, the uneducated girl torn between her love for Erne Hillyar and her duty—the determination to dedicate her life to her deformed brother Joseph—is a major character, the moral must be satisfied at the end of the novel. Although sensible and loving in all other matters, she pursued her idea of duty so zealously that it seems to be an obsession with her, and instead of being the heroic maiden, as Kingsley planned, she becomes a foolish and spiteful girl who victimizes and ruins her lover.

Since Kingsley greatly admired *The Mill on the Floss* (1860), it is possible that in writing his novel he was influenced by George Eliot's presentation of Maggie and Tom Tulliver and Philip Wakem; and in juxtaposing characters and fitting them to his own purposes, Kingsley transformed the hunchback lover of *The Mill on the Floss* into a dependent brother. If so, once again a comparison makes evident Kingsley's inability to analyze such a profound situation, realizing all of its nuances. Whereas George Eliot carefully builds Maggie's love/duty struggle to its ultimate display of sisterly devotion in the sacrificial flood scene, Kingsley depends entirely upon repetitive statements, such as "I have devoted my whole life to one single object, and nothing must ever interfere with it," and a few contrived circumstances to tell the reader that Emma's sacrifice is necessary. Kingsley fails to convince. If Joseph, like Tom/Philip, had stayed in England, where the social structure may have obstructed his professional rise, Emma's devotion might have had a real cause, but since the action of the novel takes place in opportunity-laden Australia her sacrifice seems rather pointless, for without Emma's help Joseph had enough intelligence to achieve all of the honors mentioned.

Mainly, the reader's disgust and anger are directed against Emma's (and Kingsley's) treatment of poor, gentle Erne, who suffers harsh tests—especially the lacerating severity at Omeo—in order to win Emma's withheld love. Like Charles Ravenshoe and Austin Elliot, Erne matures, changing from a "fanciful sentimental child into a thoughtful melancholy man," but in Erne's case the tragic life has not been fully justified for Erne's misfortunes have been forced upon him by unsatisfactory circumstances.

Erne's maturation recalls George Meredith's handling of a comparable problem in *The Ordeal of Richard Feverel*. Erne's childhood parallels many facets of Richard's. Both boys are secluded young heirs, pampered and dominated by a father whose sense of pride has been wounded by an unfaithful wife. Erne's Rayham Abbey is Stanlake, a "brazen tower . . . filled with grey-headed servants." Finally discovering the female sex—Erne at seventeen, Richard at eighteen—they rebel against the stern parental authority and escape or are thrown into an unfamiliar world, where, at length, they are crushed. Richard's ordeal, however, convinces the reader because Meredith has psychologically analyzed the involved ambiguities that motivated the various familial and societal relationships that led to Richard's disillusionment. Also, although Richard's severe trials were initiated by Sir Austin's misdirected and selfish love, they are furthered by Richard's own stubbornness. But when Kingsley tells us at the end of his novel that the innocent Erne finally "saw that life was not as one would have it: that one must submit to the failures of one's boy-dreams, and not whine over them," we feel justifiable indignation and disbelief because Erne's "boy-dreams" have been perversely shattered by Emma's and his half-brother's refusals to return, fully in Emma's case, Erne's passionate and natural love.

In fact, the entire ending of the novel is a disappointment. Like *Geoffry Hamlyn*, this romance is packed with fun and gaiety; we expect and want another glorious grand finale as we had in that earlier novel. We find, instead, only gloom darkening the last part of *The Hillyars and the Burtons*: the old house at Chelsea has been torn down, Emma has died in a shipwreck, Erne has tried to "purge" himself in the "smoke of Sebastopol," the childlike Gerty Hillyar, George's widow, wanders half-demented over the Australian glades, and the once-spirited Lesbia Burke, a symbol of Australian strength, roughness but nobility, stands looking solemnly out over the waters where Emma had drowned. Here, it seems, we have Kingsley's personal realization that "life was not as one would have it"; the boy-dreams of *Geoffry Hamlyn* have become darkly clouded.

Kingsley was stung by the critics' handling of *The Hillyars and the Burtons*, especially that of the *Saturday Review*, which not only dismissed as absurd Kingsley's love/duty moral but attacked his characterizations of both the Burtons and Gerty Hillyar, who, admittedly, talks a language all her own. At times, her words are little more than nonsense: "Are these pink cups ice-cream! I wonder whether I dare eat some. I have never seen iced cream before in my life. Perhaps I had better not; it might make me cry" (Vol. I, ch. 26). At other times, she reverts to her Australian dialect: "Well! if this don't bang wattle gum . . . I wish I may be buried in the Bush in a sheet of bark. Why I feel all over centipedes and copper lizards. For you to go and see the devil with that dear child, and teach him not to let his mother know, and in Whitley Copse, too, of all places. . . . You ought to be——. You ought to get——. Why, you ought to have your grop stopped——" (Vol. III, ch. 3). "Is this wit, or humour or realism or some new-fangled literary Pre-Raffaelitism?" the critic of the *Saturday Review* asked.

Because of this criticism, Kingsley struggled with his next major novel, *Silcote of Silcotes*. "It would," he declared, "be very dry. There will be no fun" (E., p. 144). His letters, however, show a nagging fear of an inability to produce a different type of novel:

Do give me your frank opinions about *Silcotes*. I want to be correct and thoughtful without being dull. I fear dullness above all things (E., pp. 156–57).

I want to tell about good things and good people without being "goody." I want to be tragical without Braddon and Collins [sic][3] bigamy and poisoning. I want to write a story which shall be interesting and exciting, and make everyone the better for having read it. And I shall do it, if God wills (E., p. 159).

Silcotes is all hardbitten, earnest work, but it must be made more lively. There is a dreary purism about the earlier numbers of *Silcotes* which is, even to myself who understand it, very dull. The slanginess and rapidity of *Ravenshoe* were far preferable (E., p. 162).

Silcotes . . . the terrible pull on my resources (E., p. 163).

3. Mary Elizabeth Braddon, author of the melodramatic and sensational *Lady Audley's Secret*; Wilkie Collins.

> You see I have recast *Silcotes*; it must and shall succeed (E., p. 166).

> [*Silcotes*], as I have revised it, can at least give no offense. I have carefully attended to every word of criticism (E., p. 167).

Even the asides in the novel show his worry and struggle:

> It is not necessary to follow Miss Lee and her charge through their long afternoon's walk. It might be funny! but we don't want to be funny (Vol. I, ch. 12).

> So comes one long story to an end. Nothing remains but to give the various characters their departure, and to finish one of the most difficult efforts of story-telling ever attempted (Vol. III, "Conclusion").

Striving to make accurate all details in the novel in order to avoid adverse criticism, Kingsley made a hurried trip to Normandy the month after the serialization of *Silcote of Silcotes* had begun in *Macmillan's Magazine* to witness the Army Maneuvers of 1866. The final action of the novel revolves around the Italian War of Liberation in Lombardy, specifically the battles of Montevella and Solferino in 1859, where the combined forces of France and Sardinia defeated the Austrians, but because expenses prohibited Kingsley from going to northern Italy he thought that the Maneuvers would enable him, as he told Macmillan, to "see large masses of French troops. I cannot *see* Solferino without that. . . . I can do the Austrian business well enough. I am familiar with German troops, but I want to see these curious swarms of scarlet, grey, and white shifting and changing" (E., p. 158).

But with all of Kingsley's great care, the novel was not popular with most of the critics. The influential *Saturday Review*, for example, wrote that "in many respects, *Silcote of Silcotes* is the very worst story that Mr. Kingsley has ever produced—the only point about it upon which we can congratulate him being that in it he has written a novel without a purpose. As long as he steers clear of that fault, there is a vivacity and good nature about him, even in his worst moments, which will always secure for him a certain amount of popularity."[4] The critic, possibly John Morley, criti-

4. XXV (January 4, 1868), 26. Ticknor and Fields published just one edition, 1,000 copies.

cized Kingsley for relying too heavily upon his stock figure, the muscular hero (in this case, Tom Silcote), the complexity of the plot, and the "too refined" language of the characters, especially that of Mrs. Sugden, a farmer's daughter who had been a Duchess' maid for two years and, as we later learn, was secretly married in a Scottish ceremony to Tom Silcote.

Improbable as her dialogue is for her station, there is, as Robert Lee Wolff has recently noted, a "curious power" in some of Mrs. Sugden's conversation, especially in her answer to Squire Silcote's proposition to make her son his groom:

> "No. Let him stick to his sheep. I, you see, know more of domestic service than most, and my answer is, 'No.' Let him freeze and bake on the hillside with his sheep. Let him stay up late with his team, and then get out of his warm bed in the biting winter weather to feed them again at four. Let him do hedge and ditch work on food which a Carolina negro would refuse; let him plough the heaviest clay until the public-house becomes a heaven and a rest to him; let him mow until the other mowers find him so weak that he must mow with them no longer, lest he ruin the contract; let him reap until his loud-tongued wife can beat him at *that*—for he must marry, O Lord, for he must marry, and in his own station too; let him go on at the plough tail; among the frozen turnips, among the plashy hedgesides, until the inevitable rheumatism catches him in the back, and the parish employs him on the roads to save the rates; and then, when his wife dies, let them send him to the house, and let him rot there and be buried in a box; but he shall not be a domestic servant for all that, Silcote. I know too much about that. We have vices enough of our own, without requiring yours" (Vol. I, ch. 11).[5]

It is unfortunate that Kingsley did not align that rhythmically forceful speech with a more appropriate character.

In order to substitute for the eliminated humor and to fill the standard three-volume edition, Kingsley, unwisely, included too many eccentric characters, along with "balderdash," to use his favorite word, and excessive action. In the case of the characters, he has erred most. Although accustomed to Kingsley's presentation of characters through outward behavior rather than by revelation of their mental processes, the reader, nevertheless, demands that

5. Wolff, pp. 205–6.

the characters act consistently if they are to win his full credulity. The unbelievable characters that dotted the pages of the first two novels, with the possible exception of Mary Thornton Hawker, never upset the reader either because the novel did not depend upon their credibility or because Kingsley had so enwrapped them with a special charm that the reader gladly accepted their improbability. Importantly, all of them seemed to act causally, never shifting out of the mold into which Kingsley had placed them. But Eleanor Hilton (*Austin Elliot*) and Emma Burton sharply reveal what can happen to his novels when Kingsley fails to understand complex major figures.

Actually, the central impetus of *Silcote of Silcotes* is built around an improbable characterization. Supposedly, Henry Silcote, the patriarchal Dark Squire of the family, is a man feared by all—as terrifying as the unexpected "lightening which shattered the ash tree . . . and killed two of the sheep." But the Henry Silcote the reader sees is an irascible though kindly grandfather, as easily tamed as the bloodhounds that guard him. Hinging the initial action on a contrived situation, Kingsley asks the reader to believe that jealousy had led Silcote, a brilliant lawyer, to suspect his first wife of murderous intent against him, a suspicion without any evidence, which finally led to her death. We all know *Othello* by heart and thus realize that similar happenings can be fictionalized successfully, but careful characterization, prepared incidents, intensity of language among other things are needed. Kingsley does little. Dating the occurrence twenty years before the novel opens, Kingsley merely tells us that it happened and demands that we believe it so that the parts of his story may fall into place. The impossible becomes even more ludicrous when Kingsley further informs us that the crimes were initiated by Silcote's sister, the foolish and melodramatic Princess of Castelnuovo, and her cohorts, whom Silcote has always believed to be scheming imbeciles.

Kingsley himself, apparently aware that something was wrong in his characterizations, repeatedly tried to rationalize their actions by stating that outside influences or hypersensitive feelings unnaturally swayed their common sense. Through Silcote, for example, he warns that a novelist would have a difficult time making the Princess a good central figure in a novel because "her folly is too incongruous; the ruck of commonplace fools who read novels will not have sufficient brains to appreciate the transcendental genius of her folly" (Vol. III, ch. 8). But this type of circumlocutory explanation will not suffice when her motiveless action effects major crises in the novel, such as Silcote's twenty-year seclusion. Nor does it explain why Silcote ever believed his sister's accusation about his wife in the first place.

The novel proper deals with Silcote's relationship with his three sons: Algernon, the disowned son of Silcote's first wife, a minister who is converted to Puseyism; Tom, the likeable profligate and the heroic soldier; and Arthur, the priggish youngest son, who loves the governess, Miss Lee. Intermingled with these threads are the Princess' intrigues with foreign spies, do-gooders, and assassins, and the story of James Sugden, Tom Silcote's unknown son, through childhood to young manhood.

Besides packing the novel with the excessive action necessary to tie together all of those threads, Kingsley strangely devotes half a chapter to a colloquy among Charles Ravenshoe, Austin Elliot, and Lord Edward Barty. This practice of introducing former characters into later novels is not unusual with Kingsley. Sometimes they maintain their familiar personalities, as with Lord Saltire and Lady Ascot, who appear briefly in three other novels besides *Ravenshoe*, while others merely retain a former character's name, such as the three different Gil Macdonalds, who appear in *Austin Elliot*, *Old Margaret*, and *The Boy in Grey*. Never are their appearances obtrusive, either because they perform minor functions and leave the scenes quietly or else because they are merely mentioned. But in *Silcote of Silcotes* when Austin Elliot asks "What the dickens are we doing in this room?" the reader wants to know the same thing. There is absolutely no reason to include those three boys in the novel, because, chorus-like, they only reiterate the already told Silcote history. What is even odder is the manner in which Kingsley deals with them. They have aged greatly: "The tallest of the three was a rather pale man, with dark hair and very prominent features; the next in height was pale also, but very handsome. Both of these men looked some ten years older than they were, and spoke in a low and deliberate voice, like men who had been in some way tamed." Their conversation contains the balderdash typical of this period of Kingsley's writings:

"Old Silcote now put the Silcote crown on the head of the second son by his second wife, who, as I am informed by Miss

Raylock, refused it with scorn. If that is the case," said
Charles Ravenshoe, "it is the only good I ever heard of him.
He is an utterly narrow-minded prig, of the worst Oxford
model."

"The stamp of man who rusticated you, for instance," said
Austin Elliot.

"Your remark," said Charles Ravenshoe, "is not only coarse
and impertinent, but also falls wide of the mark. I am trying
to enlarge your little mind, narrowed into smaller limits than
even its natural ones, by your worship of this new gospel of
Free Trade and Cobdenism. You interrupt me with personalities. I wish to tell you about these Silcotes."

"You can't deny that you set the College on fire, and aimed
four-penny rockets at the Dean's window. It was entirely owing
to your evil guidance that that quiet creature Ascot got sent
down, you old sinner!" replied Austin Elliot.

"Don't chaff, you two, or at least wait till we get home,"
said Lord Edward. "I am bored here, and I want to hear more
about these Silcotes. That Charles is an old ruffian we all
know; we will get more of his confessions out of him, and
tell Eleanor if he don't go on."

The history continues with occasional references by Lord Edward
and Austin to Charles' rustication. Then, as Charles continues his
tale:

"Arthur of Balliol has rejected the crown, and has system-
atically bullied and insulted him; he has an awful tongue,
this Arthur. The Oxford fellows who were—

"Rusticated for setting the College on fire," suggested Austin
Elliot.

"I shall have to do violence to this man," said Charles
Ravenshoe; "I shall have to fight a duel with this fellow."

There was such a sharp sudden spasm in Austin Elliot's
face as he said this that Charles Ravenshoe hurried on, cursing
inwardly his wandering tongue (Vol. II, ch. 16).

It is difficult to know exactly what Kingsley had intended to
accomplish with all this. Assuredly, the scene does not jell. The
stressing of the boys' permanent scars of melancholy, which are
only emphasized by the references to the college-days antics, probably reflects Kingsley's personal mood at this time, for his youth also
has passed. But the mention of the duel in which Austin's friend

and Lord Edward's brother, Charles Barty, was killed upsets the reader as a macabre joke. And annoyingly, while Kingsley expected his readers to be familiar enough with references to incidents from previous novels, he seemed to have forgotten the proper identification of his characters. Lord Edward says that he will "tell Eleanor" if Charles does not continue with the story. Charles is married to Mary Corby, whereas it is Austin Elliot who is married to Eleanor Hilton.

The disillusionment with life that jarred the ending of *The Hillyars and the Burtons* also affects *Silcote of Silcotes*. At the close of the novel, Dora, the wife of the young hero, James Sugden Silcote, and now the recognized mistress of Silcotes, laments that "the old house will never be what it was before. I know that the new order will be better than the old, but I am wicked and perverse, and I hate it." She then relates her earlier impression of Silcotes: " 'In old times this house was a very charming one. There was a perfectly *delicious* abandon about it. . . . Coming as I did from the squalor of my father's house, this was a fairy palace for me. True, there was an ogre; my grandfather Silcote was the ogre; but then I liked ogres. There was a somewhat cracked princess—a real Italian princess—in velvet and jewels; and I like people of that kind. Then there was a dark story, which we never could understand, which was to us infinitely charming; there was almost barbarous profusion and ostentation, which *everybody* . . . loves in their heart of hearts; there were these bloodhounds which I hated at first . . . but which I have got to love as the last remnants of the *ancien régime*; there were horses, grooms, carriages, ponies, deer, as indeed there are now, with all their charm gone; and lastly, one could do exactly as one liked; one could revel in all this luxury and beauty, set here like a splendid jewel among the surrounding forest, without a soul to control one. And this was very charming' " (Vol. III, ch. 20). Besides recording Kingsley's lamentation for bygone days, Dora's words sum up well the reader's feelings concerning most of Kingsley's works of this period. Although a romantic aura still hangs over the novels, Kingsley's despondent meditation has dispelled most of their charm and liveliness. Whereas *Geoffry Hamlyn* and *Ravenshoe* seemed to have been spontaneous endeavors, these later works strike the reader as tedious struggles.

On January 1, 1867, while *Silcote of Silcotes* was still running serially in *Macmillan's Magazine*, Edward Walford, the editor of *The Gentleman's Magazine and Historical Review*, wrote to Kingsley, "I am authorized by Messrs Bradbury Evans & Co to offer you the sum of £600 (six hundred pounds) for the copyright of a novel which shall run through eight or nine numbers of the Gents Mag. & afterwards be published by themselves on their own account."[6]

This proposal is significant because it shows that even with the adverse criticism received by *The Hillyars and the Burtons*, Kingsley, in January, 1867, had enough of a reputation for Bradbury & Evans & Co. to ask him "to write the first story which has ever appeared in the 'Gentleman's Magazine' in a course of 137 years."[7] Also the finished story, *Mademoiselle Mathilde*, reveals how Kingsley adapted his style of storytelling to editorial restrictions. Walford admonished Kingsley that "Neither Messrs B&E as proprietors, not I as Editor, wish to fetter you as to your subject; but you will doubtless remember that the readers of the GM are a particular and special class, with rather retrospective tastes, & a story which has its scenes laid chiefly in the colonies would scarcely be as likely to interest them as one which deals with Old England, or at all events with Europe."[8]

Needing the money, Kingsley readily accepted the restrictions and assured Walford that the magazine would receive a "sedate gentlemanly thoughtful story," interesting and original, "thrown into the past, and bringing the reader face to face with some one or more of great men of whom he has heard, and whom he will see reappear familiarly with the deepest interest." Probably thinking

6. Printed in William Buckler, "Henry Kingsley and *The Gentleman's Magazine*," *JEGP*, L (1951), 90. Mr. Buckler prints the correspondence leading up to the publication of *Mademoiselle Mathilde* in the magazine and discusses the textual changes between the serialized novel and the later three-volume edition. Additional unpublished letters between Walford and Kingsley concerning *Mademoiselle Mathilde* are in the Houghton Library, Harvard University. *Mademoiselle Mathilde* ran through fourteen numbers instead of "eight or nine," from April, 1867, to May, 1868.

7. "Preface" to first edition. Kingsley's story was intended to boost a sagging circulation. As Buckler notes, "We do have indications . . . that the condition of *The Gentleman's Magazine* was not good at this time: The very fact that it was thought necessary to add the attraction of a serialized novel in the face of opposition from many of the subscribers; the fact that Trollope refused to allow *The Vicar of Bullhampton* to be published in it; the fact that its contents were completely revised—to one of general literature—after May, 1868 [completion of *Mademoiselle Mathilde*] and the price reduced from two shillings and sixpence to one shilling" (p. 97n31).

8. Buckler, p. 90.

again of past critical disapproval of his "new-fangled literary Pre-Raffaelitism," Kingsley added that he was looking "forward with great eagerness to this engagement. I wish very much to see whether or not I can succeed at a more sedate style of story, and I feel sure that I can."[9] Decidedly then, the story could not be Kingsley's usual rambling type dealing exclusively with the history of old declining families nor could it rely upon his Australian experiences, for it had to be directed to "a particular and special class" of readers whose interest was historical. In his "Preface" to the three-volume edition, Kingsley acknowledged his apprehension when he accepted the proposal: "I was extremely diffident, feeling somewhat like a modest young curate, who has to return thanks for the clergy before a large audience principally composed of dissenters; I was not reassured by being told, before I began, that a large number of the subscribers strongly objected to the arrangement."

"The choice of a story," Kingsley also tells us in the "Preface," "was extremely difficult" until someone, possibly Anne Thackeray, to whom, as previously stated, *Mademoiselle Mathilde* was dedicated, suggested that he relate the one that he had heard the previous summer at St. Malo when he had gone to France to get background material for *Silcote of Silcotes* and that he had "so often spoken [of] since." This story focuses on the English-French D'Isigny family, especially the daughter Mathilde, and their involvement in the French Revolution. The climax of the story is Mathilde's sacrificial death on the guillotine for her sister, Adèle.

Taking "liberties" with the original story in order to turn it "from a simple narrative to a dramatically-written fiction" ("Preface"), Kingsley carefully tailored the story to his special audience. In the serialization, footnotes (some so long as three-hundred words); asides which quoted sources for historical information; and direct references to the readers of the magazine, such as "It seems to me that *The Gentleman's Magazine* is the periodical of all others in which the names of heroes, with their performances, should be embalmed," all attest Kingsley's great concern. The direct references and many of the asides and footnotes were dropped in the three-volume edition.[10]

9. *Ibid.*, p. 91. Kingsley's fear of the critics and of waning popularity is also implied in one of the unpublished letters to Walford: "I desired to give you this story for reasons of my own. And it was absolutely necessary that it should be a first rate one, and should not be written in a hurry" (Houghton Library).

10. See Buckler, pp. 93–96.

Aware that his previous novels had been criticized for their loose construction, Kingsley endeavored to tighten this one, and, on the whole, his handling of structural problems is unusually fine. He repeatedly tells Walford that he is taking care to write a novel "which will pay *as a whole.*" He has not, he says, "confined myself to a sensational ending to each No."[11]

Within the first three paragraphs of Chapter 1, "A Chapter Which Will Have To Be Written Several Times Again: Each Time In Darker Ink," Kingsley reveals his heroine's character as she is about to sacrifice her comfort by venturing into a tempest to visit a dying woman:

> It is quite impossible, so Mademoiselle Mathilde D'Isigny concluded, that any reasonable being could dream of going out on such an afternoon. It was not to be thought of. Nevertheless, she began thinking at once about her sabots and her red umbrella.
>
> A wild revolutionary-looking nimbus, urged on by a still wilder wind, which seemed, from its direction, to have started from America, had met the rapidly-heated and rapidly-cooled strata of chalk in the valley of the Stour in Dorsetshire. The nimbus, chased by the furious headlong American wind, met the chalk downs while they were cooled by a long winter's frost, and at once dissolved itself into cataracts of water; into cataracts more steady, more persistent, and, in the end, more dangerous, than any which ever came from the wildest and noisest summer thunderstorm.
>
> It was quite impossible that any reasonable woman could go out on such an afternoon; still the sabots and red umbrella dwelt on her mind, for it might under certain circumstances become necessary, although impossible.

Mathilde, the "sacrificial act," and the "revolutionary" atmosphere, natural and manmade, are interlinked, and, as both the title of the chapter and Kingsley's words at the end of the first chapter predict, this trinity will reappear rhythmically (and in darker ink) during the rest of the novel: "Mademoiselle Mathilde is already developed. The circumstances around her will develop; but she will remain the same."

Relying upon parallelisms and antitheses, Kingsley introduces the setting, characters, and circumstances for Mathilde's future

11. Unpublished letter, Houghton Library.

sacrifices. The novel focuses on the two countries, England (chs. 1–4) and France (chs. 5–8); and then specifically on the D'Isignys' two great houses, Sheepsden and Montauban, the former being struck by an atmospheric tempest, while a war storm rages over the latter; and on Mathilde's antithesis, her weak-willed sister, Adèle. Most of the action during the first half of the novel occurs in peaceful England, but the Revolution for Mathilde enters in the figure of the French soldier, Louis de Valognes, whom she loves. In "The First Sacrifice" (Vol. I, ch. 17) the ink darkens. Mathilde dies "one of her deaths" when she denies herself Louis after seeing him and Adèle embrace.

Near the middle of the novel Kingsley pauses to tell his readers (and probably to point out to his critics that he knows the rules of artistic unity) that he has placed before them all of the causes and motivations and is ready to show the effects.[12] Moving Adèle to France as the Marquise de Valognes, a member of a family especially targeted by the Revolutionists and, thus, into the heart of the Revolution, Kingsley, in an aside about two-thirds through the novel, sets up the final sacrifice: "So the interest of our story concentrates now, I hope naturally, upon the two sisters, and, to some extent, on the two houses in which they lived so entirely separated from one another" (Vol. III, ch. 2). In "The Journey" (Vol. III, ch. 8), a chapter title which recalls Mathilde's first journey out into a storm, Mathilde undertakes her unwilling trip to France, which ends darkly in her sacrificial death for Adèle.

Kingsley also strengthens the novel with minor character antitheses: Mathilde's French lover, André Desilles, is set against her English one, Sir Lionel Somers; the villainous French servant Barbot, who attempts to kill André, against the friendly English groom William the Silent; and the termagant Madame D'Isigny against the noble Lady Somers, Mathilde's English surrogate mother.

Although Kingsley attributed the sole inspiration for *Mademoiselle Mathilde* to the story heard at St. Malo, a reader cannot help but notice the similarities between Kingsley's novel and Dickens' historical romance *A Tale of Two Cities*, published nine years earlier. Kingsley, himself, even calls attention to the connection

12. "It seems to me, in any good story which I have ever read, that there is a kind of pause, or breaking line, about the middle of it. The author, in spite of himself, puts the causes before you in the first half of his story, and gives you the effect of them in the second. I do not know a readable story which does not fulfill this rule. I fancy it is the great rule of story-telling" (Vol. II, ch. 8).

between the two novels. About to describe a mob scene he stops to say, "Who can *describe* a mob? Dickens himself has to be very general when he does so" (Vol. II, ch. 11), and, later, he refers directly to Dickens' novel: "The weather was as white and hot, and fierce, as were the Parisians, and the smell which Mr. Dickens, in his 'Tale of Two Cities,' calls 'the smell of imprisoned sleep,' was hot and heavy" (Vol. III, ch. 18).

It is an exaggeration, however, to assert, as George Saintsbury has, that *Mademoiselle Mathilde* is a direct imitation of *A Tale of Two Cities*.[13] A reading of the two works clearly shows that *Mademoiselle Mathilde* is no more that than *A Tale of Two Cities* is a direct imitation of, let us say, Bulwer-Lytton's *Zanoni* (1842), another tale which utilizes the French Revolution setting and the sacrifice-on-the-guillotine device. Kingsley, like Dickens, was too original a writer to copy wholesale another writer's novel. Not only do Dickens' and Kingsley's story lines have obvious differences but *Mademoiselle Mathilde* is filled with usual Kingsleyan characteristics: a history of a family group; the concentration on a central character who must suffer, must undergo tests before he realizes his goal (or dies obtaining it); an emphasis on the nobility of man; and the loving depiction of ancestral homes. Also, unlike Dickens, Kingsley followed the pattern of English historical fiction set up by Scott of including historical personages as characters in the novel: Marat plays an important part, while Robespierre, Camille Desmoulins, Henri de LaRochejaquelin, among others, are introduced briefly.

Familiar as he was with Dickens' works, Kingsley would have immediately seen the basic similarities between the St. Malo story and *A Tale of Two Cities*. These similarities, plus both Kingsley's desire to write a successful novel and Walford's restriction and admonition, may have led Kingsley to rely even more heavily on Dickens' formula for a historical romance. Some of the "liberties" Kingsley took with the original story tend to substantiate this assertion.

In the "Preface" Kingsley makes no mention that any of the action in the St. Malo story was set in England. Indeed, the implication is that the original story was set entirely in France. But Kingsley followed Dickens' lead and placed part of the French

13. "On Writing Out and Henry Kingsley," *Collected Essays and Papers* (New York, 1923), II, 352.

family in England. To make this living arrangement possible, he gives Mathilde and Adèle—like Lucie Manette—an Anglo-French parentage. Then, when Kingsley needed to move the action to France, he relied upon the same device Dickens had of having a daughter's marriage with French nobility force the French family living in England into the Reign of Terror. Not only did this change from the original story offer Kingsley the contrast between the two countries which had worked so well for Dickens, but it gave him an opportunity to describe his beloved English countryside.

Another alteration of the original story is Kingsley's characterization of Mathilde. In the St. Malo story she was not Adèle's rival in love but her married sister. The love triangle did not exist. In the finished novel, even though Mathilde has other lovers, her sacrifice resembles Carton's. Both characters deny themselves the one they love and finally sacrifice themselves for their love's spouse. Sidney Carton's words to Lucie, "I would embrace any sacrifice for you and those dear to you" (Book II, ch. 13), reflect Mathilde's unspoken words to Louis. Also both Mathilde and Carton are involved in actions that forebode the substitution on the guillotine. Carton had saved Darnay in the English Court scene; Mathilde, as stated above in the discussion of the chapter "The First Sacrifice," had died "one of her deaths" when she gave up Louis to Adèle.

Other less conspicuous resemblances, slightly altered, exist between the two novels. Madame D'Isigny is pictured as a Royalist Madame Defarge, who constantly mends fishnets instead of knitting aristocrats' names in a scarf. Like Madame Defarge's, her fury is monomaniacal, caused by a frenzied desire for personal revenge. Whereas Madame Defarge wanted to avenge herself on those who had destroyed her family, Madame D'Isigny wanted to infuriate and belittle her republican husband, who had never yielded to her. Mathilde's Mrs. Bone, a typically down-to-earth English housekeeper, is a less determined and heroic Mrs. Pross; William the Silent, Kingsley's "solid young Englishman," is a more refined Jerry Cruncher, but like Dickens' character, William adds a light touch to the serious novel; the two sisters imprisoned in the Abbaye with Mathilde suggest Sidney Carton's little seamstress; and a child's death in the street initiates the mob's admiration for D'Isigny's kindness instead of its hatred for the Marquis St. Evrémonde's inhumanity.

But even with Dickens' romance as a model and even with its tight structure, *Mademoiselle Mathilde*, which was Kingsley's favorite novel,[14] is, for the most part, dull reading today. The major reason must lie with its place of publication. In trying to satisfy the readers of *The Gentleman's Magazine* while always keeping his eye on the critics, Kingsley wrote the novel without his usual lightness and humor, and lacking the "slanginess and rapidity of *Ravenshoe*," the novel is too weighted down with historical references and serious political evaluation. When Kingsley attempted to lighten the novel, he unfortunately relied again upon eccentric characters, in this case the exasperating Monsieur and Madame D'Isigny with their impractical and ridiculous attempts to alter the course of the Revolution.

Much can be said in favor of Mathilde herself. Although, like Emma Burton, Mathilde gives up love for duty and always seems to be striving for perfection, she has human faults, and, like Charles Ravenshoe, she is not the epitome of human beauty: "Every one called her plain, and yet Sir Joshua Reynolds . . . painted her. Her figure was almost deformed, and her gait was very clumsy. She was very broad, though not fat; and above her shoulders was that half-Norman, half-Teutonic head, which gave rise to so many theories as to what was inside it. A short clumsy woman, with such a head as I have mentioned" (Vol. 1, ch. 1). What with her near-deformed shoulders and rather masculine look—modeled, possibly, after Marian Holcombe, in Collins' *The Woman in White* (1859–60)—Mathilde is actually a fascinating character. The scenes that could have been mawkishly sentimental, such as Mathilde's view of her fellow prisoners, especially the two sisters, in the Abbaye, and Mathilde's death are treated with remarkable restraint.

In the first of these scenes, Mathilde, recently imprisoned, has just entered the Abbaye and looks around her:

Against the whitewashed wall sat a girl with a square, fine face, of great beauty and power, who was sewing; in her lap lay the head of her sister, a golden heap of splendid beauty. The younger sister lay there utterly wearied, utterly idle, and petulant in her idleness; playing at times with the string of her sister's apron, at times with the hands which sewed so diligently; at times sighing in her *ennui*, at times rolling her restless head into some new position. Mathilde watched this

14. Ellis, pp. 168, 173, 180.

pair with intense eagerness. They suited her. The younger
sister was only another Adèle, and she thought how Adèle
would have been in the same situation but for her; but then
without her. She listened to their conversation.

The younger sister said, "This is so triste and dull, that I
shall die if I stay here: and I have nothing to amuse me,
nothing whatever. I wish that I had brought my squirrel now,
but they said we were to go back again directly."

Mathilde saw the elder sister sew faster, but say nothing whatever. *She* understood her.

"That foolish, giddy Contine will forget to feed him, and he
is petulant if he is not fed. Sister, do you know what I wish?"

"No, dearest."

"I wish I had flowers. My garden will be half-ruined when
we get back, for I took it so entirely in hand myself that none
of our gardeners dare meddle with it. And those balsams
should be in their largest pots now; they will not show beside
Faustine de la Rivère's. Thou are weeping now, sister, for thy
tears fall on my face. Have *I* made thee weep?"

Mathilde sat as rigid as stone listening to this, drinking it
in, every word. The elder sister, with whom she was in deep
friendship that night, told her the bitter truth. Their château
was burnt; their estate was ruined; their father and mother in
the *Conciergerie*; their servants dispersed or faithless; the wolf
in their garden, the hare upon their hearthstone. But she
had kept it all to herself, and had flattered her giddy sister
with the hope of a speedy return to what was gone for ever.

"How could I tell her? She was the little singing-bird in
our house. Would you have me stop her singing forever?"
(Vol. III, ch. 16).

In a few days the two sisters are ordered to the *Conciergerie*
and sentenced to their death. When the order comes for Mathilde,
Kingsley allows the reader to follow her only as far as the main
passage in the Abbaye. "I have seen too many ["harrowing death-
bed scenes"] to describe one," Kingsley wrote in *Silcote of Silcotes*,
and wisely he does not venture to describe Mathilde's death with
the drenching sentimentality Dickens used in Sidney Carton's
final speech. Mathilde's last words are brief. To William, in words
that echo those in "The First Sacrifice," she declares that dying is
not hard because "I have died before now," and to her friend
Journiac de St. Meard she whispers simply, "If you live to see
any one whom I loved tell them I love them still." Then "she

went down the steps carrying her missal, and entering the dark passage was lost to sight." Two later speeches confirm her death. Upon his acquittal, Journiac de St. Meard says, "My friends . . . lead me, for I am going to shut my eyes. One lies here, I doubt [i.e. fear], whom I loved." More directly, William announces Mathilde's death to her parents: "I have escaped by running; but they have murdered Mademoiselle Mathilde" (Vol. III, chs. 19, 20). Kingsley heightens the tragic tone of her death by convening Monsieur and Madame D'Isigny and later Louis de Valognes, each in his own way responsible for Mathilde's death, before their own court of self-accusations, with Mathilde's missal, their only relic of her, lying among them.

One other notable character in *Mademoiselle Mathilde* needs to be mentioned—the fanatic revolutionist Barbot, whose deep hatred for the aristocratic André Desilles, Mathilde's undeclared lover, suggests the inexplicable aversion between characters that Melville achieved so well thirteen years earlier in the Babo–Benito Cereno relationship and perfected later in the Claggart–Billy Budd conflict. Ambivalently, the anguished Barbot cries: "Go thy way, Captain Desilles, I hate thee utterly. I hate thee for thine order's sake, and for thine own. I hate thy delicate white hand and thy delicately dressed hair. You are good, you are brave, and you are beautiful. Curse you! I know you are all three of these things, and I hate you for them" (Vol. I, ch. 6). Kingsley slowly kindles this great antipathy until, in "Barbot's First Revenge" (Vol. II, ch. 8), he skillfully creates a scene in which Barbot's inflamed hatred explodes, foreshadowing Desilles' final doom. After spewing forth his vehemence against all aristocracy and his master, Desilles, in particular and preaching insurrection and wholesale slaughter to the shocked English servant William, the incensed Barbot, infuriated by his inability to slay Desilles legally, accomplished a temporary revenge by cruelly "wounding" him: "He had taken André Desilles down a thick pleached alley in the rectory garden, and had shown him Sir Lionel and Mathilde. Her head was on her lover's bosom, and he was playing with her hair. With one deep sob, and only one, André Desilles turned away; and Barbot saw that his dagger had gone home to the noble heart, hilt deep."

There are many excellent elements in *Mademoiselle Mathilde*, but it is not a first-rate novel, although the potentiality to be one exists in it. Like the reviewer of *Mademoiselle Mathilde* for the

Saturday Review, "one always feels that Mr. Kingsley ought to have written so much better a book than he actually does write."[15]

Kingsley's clumsiest, most confused, and tedious novel during this period is *Stretton*, a novel in which he has evidently lost control over his ability to recognize good taste.[16] So preposterous and exaggerated is the novel in its depiction of four high-spirited, excessively noble and patriotic English boys that it reads like a poor burlesque of the manly adventure stories that flooded the libraries during the 1860s. In presumptuousness these boys outstrip any hero that Kingsley had previously set forth. For Roland and Eddy Evans and John and James Mordaunt, "all possibilities of any disturbing causes seemed absolute nonsense. The chances were so infinitely in their favour. Money was to be had for the picking up; they had talents, prospects, health, high spirits; the world was theirs, in a way, if they cared to go into it and succeed; or if they failed, here were two homes of ancient peace ready for them to come back to. Misfortune, thanks to settled old order, seemed in their cases to have become impossible" (Vol. I, ch. 11).

After carrying his boys through their riotous schooldays, Kingsley gloriously sends three of them into the Indian Mutiny, where, self-righteously, they clamor to save England's "greatest inheritance": "This is the beginning of a great crisis. Now is the time for a lesson to them. The odds against us are not great. We are eighty men to their two thousand. Come, sir, I tell you plainly, it rests in your hands to assist in the saving of India, or to assist in sending back her history for a hundred years" (Vol. III, ch. 16). Although Kingsley had erred before in his characterization of gentlemen, never is his unawareness of good manners, of breeding, of what is a gentleman more flagrant than in the characterization of these boys and their associates. In the scene in which James

---

15. XXV (May 23, 1868), 694.
16. *Stretton* was harshly reviewed; see *Athenaeum*, LXVII (June 5, 1869), 759–60; *Saturday Review*, XXVII (June 19, 1869), 814–16. When *Stretton* was reissued in 1875 by Estes and Lauriat (Boston), the *Atlantic* wrote, "What especial need there was of raking up Mr. Henry Kingsley's *Stretton* from its easily-won obscurity, it would be hard to say. A few years ago this novel appeared, was read, and then disappeared; and now that a new edition is sent into the world, there is but little chance of altering the verdict it received before" (XXXVII [February, 1875], 239). Presumably, neither Macmillan nor Bradbury & Evans would publish the novel, since it first appeared serially in *The Broadway Annual*, from September, 1868, to August, 1869, and then in a three-volume edition by Tinsley Brothers.

Mordaunt has followed Roland Evans to the 140th Dragoons, the Colonel, speaking of Mordaunt, says to Roland:

> "You know him then?"
> "Yes, sir. I know one of the finest fellows who ever walked— in his way—in your way; by Jove, sir, you have strengthened the regiment by ten men."
> "And who is the lady in this case?" said the Colonel.
> "I fear it is my sister," said Roland, quite off his guard. In a moment afterwards, he was praying the Colonel to forget, not to have heard, to ignore, his last speech. And the Colonel said, quietly, "My dear young man, I am the best colonel of cavalry, socially speaking, in the army. Is it likely that I could say one word?" (Vol. II, ch. 9).

One is accustomed to the English in their novels revealing officious conceit, but Kingsley piles Ossa and Pelion on Olympus.

The excessiveness in this novel has prompted Michael Sadleir to suggest that Henry Kingsley was trying to reinstate himself into his family by portraying in his novel qualities which were not inherent in him but which abounded in Charles and his novels.[17] That suggestion may be partly true for Henry's pleas for money had so embarrassed Charles Kingsley and his wife that the two brothers were becoming alienated. And certainly the two Evanses and Jim Mordaunt duplicate if not exceed Amyas Leigh's superhuman qualities. But Sadleir's suggestion cannot explain all of the wild feverishness and carelessness in this novel. For example, at one point Kingsley suspensefully builds up the fact that Roland leaves early one morning on a very dangerous military mission, a distance of one hundred and forty miles. Yet, a few pages later, in the afternoon of the same day, Roland has returned with the mission accomplished. How was the long trip possible in such a short time? What did Roland actually accomplish? Was the trip dangerous? Again, in another scene Roland asks his aunt, Eleanor, who he knows is unmarried:

> "But you did not make such a fool of yourself when you were married, Aunt."
> "My dear, I never was married," said Aunt Eleanor, quietly.
> This so took the wind out of Roland's sails that he had to start on a fresh tack (Vol. I, ch. 20).

17. *Edinburgh Review,* p. 337.

Such absurdities can only be explained by saying that Kingsley was dashing off this novel with his left hand in order to bring in some badly needed money. His reliance upon such stock devices as switched babies, the discussion of family histories, college scenes that echo those in *Ravenshoe,* the usual "sacrificial act" (in this case Allan Gray, the fanatic Christian and legitimate heir to Stretton, who dies to save Jim Mordaunt), as well as the fact that little mention of *Stretton* is made in his published letters, add credence to the assumption. Certainly, the novel shows his concern for money. Besides the great wealth which he gives to his major characters, some of his asides break in discordantly to discuss irrelevant financial information: for example, "One of my neighbours, a commoner, has £20,000 a year; another, just in sight, has £60,000; another, also a commoner, within four miles, has just died worth £5,000,000" (Vol. I, ch. 11). Unpolished and silly, the novel reveals the dismal results of an author so plagued by personal worries that he failed to concentrate upon his work and, instead, strewed on paper his unfulfilled dreams of heroics and wealth.

In the midst of all the eccentricity and absurdities of *Silcote of Silcotes, Mademoiselle Mathilde,* and *Stretton,* however, scenes arise that vividly, yet forlornly by comparison with earlier works, recall Kingsley's old artistic power. Besides the already mentioned scenes in *Mademoiselle Mathilde,* Kingsley carefully describes the great houses of Sheepsden, Silcotes, and Stretton, with their traditional beauty, and, with admirable simplicity, he paints Mrs. Sugden's and her brother's departure from Silcotes: "A very few days afterwards, the steward was standing at his door, in the early dawn, when the Sugdens came towards him, and left the key of their cottage, paying up some trifle of rent. They were expedited for travelling, he noticed, and had large bundles. Their furniture, they told him, had been fetched away by the village broker, and the fixtures would be found all right. In answer to a wondering inquiry as to where they were going, James merely pointed eastward, and very soon after they entered the morning fog, bending under their bundles, and were lost to sight" (Vol. I, ch. 11). Even with the incredible Princess of Castelnuova, Kingsley achieves a very touching scene when she is keening over the dead Tom Silcote, her nephew. Holding Tom's head in her lap, she rocks herself to and fro: "Singing in a very low voice, sometimes in German, sometimes in Italian. Her grief was so deep that Providence in His mercy had dulled it. There was a deep, bitter gnawing at her heart, which underlay everything else; as the horror of his doom must make itself felt in the last quiet sleep of a criminal before his execution, let him sleep never so quietly" (Vol. III, ch. 17). The bodily action wonderfully symbolizes the Babel-like versatility of tongue and both symbolize the Princess' own rootlessness and confusion of values. Finally, Kingsley still retained his talent for rendering in prose the loveliness of the English countryside: "Down below in the valley, among the meadows, the lanes, and the fords, it was nearly as peaceful and quiet as it was aloft on the mountain-tops; and under the darkening shadows of the rapidly leafing elms, you could hear, it was so still, the cows grazing and the trout rising in the river" (*Stretton*, Vol. I, ch. 1).

Overshadowed by the major works of this period is Kingsley's fifth novel, *Leighton Court*, a two-volume romance, which as Kingsley said, "was written so entirely according to [the critics'] orders" (E., p. 144). Undertaking to write a story with "no tragedy and no nonsense—and so AWFULLY genteel" (E., p. 132),[18] Kingsley managed to please the usually hostile *Saturday Review*: "Mr. Kingsley has told his plain story with great skill and taste. He has denied himself almost entirely those senseless oddities and unmeaning freaks which in his last two novels struck everybody as being so wonderfully childish and so offensive. . . . This little comedy . . . though sufficiently slight, is one of the most agreeable things that Mr. Henry Kingsley has written."[19]

The two modern critics who have mentioned the novel either dismiss it as a "rather tame and insipid story of country life," or condemn it as having "a plot which even wet towels round the head will not make any clearer."[20] While the first opinion is superficial, the second is erroneous, for *Leighton Court* is decidedly Kingsley's simplest novel up to 1866. Furthermore, it shows that Kingsley, during this troubled time, could write a better than average work if he kept his subject under control and did not attempt panoramic novels such as *The Hillyars and the Burtons*, *Silcote of Silcotes*, and *Stretton*.[21]

18. See other letters, Ellis, pp. 136, 140, 143.
19. XXI (March 10, 1866), 300. Ticknor and Fields published two editions, 2,750 copies.
20. Wolff, p. 205; Angela Thirkell, "The Works of Henry Kingsley," *Nineteenth-Century Fiction*, V (March, 1951), 279.
21. Even Kingsley's puns are better. A rich suitor is Count Ozoni Galvani,

The novel concentrates on two love triangles. Laura Seckerton falls in love with her father's (Sir Charles) whip, George Hammersley, who, unbeknown to the Seckertons, is really Robert Poyntz, the legitimate brother of Sir Harry, Sir Charles' sole creditor. Rebuked by Laura, George leaves and is presumed to be dead; Laura becomes engaged to a high-minded nobleman, Lord Hatterleigh. Sir Harry, because of a dislike for his younger brother and because of his weakening brain, spreads the rumor that the disguised Robert was really an illegitimate brother. Concomitantly, because of Laura's part in trying to dissuade her friend Maria Huxtable from marrying himself when she really loved the unreceptive Captain George Hilton, Sir Harry plans to disgrace Laura and to ruin her father. He repents, and through a series of incidents the proper parties are united: Lord Hatterleigh frees Laura from the engagement and happily marries someone else; Sir Harry dies, and Maria marries Captain Hilton; Robert returns, assumes his title, marries Laura, and releases Sir Charles from his debt.

There are more things in this novel to praise than to condemn. Opening with one of Kingsley's incomparable descriptions of Devonshire, the novel goes on to demonstrate that Kingsley has not lost his facility for handling descriptive action. In one scene, Tom Squire, the Seckertons' trusted servant, graphically reproduces Robert Poyntz' ride into the ocean: " 'He turned to the left out of the Bell Yard, and broke into a gallop. Then I saw that he was going to try the sands that night, and I cried out, like a man in the falling sickness, "The tide's making! the tide's making!" Perhaps he did not hear, at all events he did not heed. I ran, but what was the good of that? I heard him only a few minutes, but I ran on, guessing which way he had gone; and all I could find of him was the way that the deer still stood gazing as he had startled them' " (Vol. I, ch. 24).

For the first time since *Ravenshoe*, Kingsley has concentrated on his characters. Laura Seckerton is one of Kingsley's best examples of the impudent heroine; she follows faithfully the line of Juliet, Beatrice, Elizabeth Bennet, Diana Vernon, and Lily Dale. Surely England's most wonderful contribution to the art of character

---

brother to the Duke of Pozzo di Argento, later the Duke of Pozzo d'Oro, which are, after all, neither better nor worse that Byron's Strongenoff and Stokonoff, Tschitsshakoff, Roguenoff, Chokenoff, Koklophti (*Don Juan,* Canto 7), or, best of all, Cazzani and Count Corniani (Canto 1).

portrayal, these heroines strike out against the man's world with their tart tongues but never lose their femininity.[22] The valetudinarian Lord Hatterleigh, "a young man of great promise aged twenty-two, who wore galoshes, carr[ied] a bulgy umbrella, and took dinner pills," reveals Kingsley's ability to create a humorous character who does not sink into utter ridiculousness. Kingsley amusingly describes the inept Hatterleigh trying to court Laura at a dinner party:

> He sat next Laura, but his silence continued until he had finished his soup and his fish. He did nothing but smile. He had invented something pretty in the retirement of his chamber which he was to say to Laura, but he had forgotten it, and his soul was consumed in spasmodic efforts to remember it. Laura saw this to her intense amusement. At the end of the fish she thought he had got it, for he brightened up and gave a sigh of relief. She was wrong, he had only abandoned the effort. He slopped out a glass of water, looked sweetly at her, and said—
> "I take it that the great duration of the Liverpool ministry arose mainly from the absence of anything like decision or force of character in the chief. The whole, too, was a mere coalition as profligate as that between Fox and North. The very possibility of a coalition argues an entire absence of principle in the coalescing parties, and of policy in the coalition itself" (Vol. I, ch. 9).

Most outstanding, though, is the Kingsleyan villain, Sir Harry Poyntz, who, Laura believes, "is wicked enough to do anything." Her first meeting with him occurs when she inquisitively visits Berry Morecombe Castle. Sitting in the dark with Sir Harry, Laura is "longing to look on what should be, by all accounts, the wickedest, meanest, most worthless face that ever troubled this unhappy earth." Visualizing the man, "she could see that he was tall, and she pictured him satanic: a dark melancholic man, with sloping eyebrows, wicked little eyes, and an upward curl at the corner of his mouth;

22. George Saintsbury has said in his preface to Jane Austen's *Pride and Prejudice* that "In the novels of the last hundred years there are vast numbers of young ladies with whom it might be a pleasure to fall in love; there are at least five of whom, as it seems to me, no man of taste and spirit can help doing so. Their names are, in chronological order, Elizabeth Bennet, Diana Vernon, Argemone Lavington [C. Kingsley's *Yeast*], Beatrix Esmond and Barbara Grant [R. L. Stevenson's *Catriona* and *David Balfour*]."

the man she knew so well by Cruikshank's art; the swaggering fiendish cavalier who has come home from the Spanish main, and who is no less than the fiend himself; a man with a wicked leer for a woman, and a twopenny-halfpenny, who-are-you, Haymarket scowl for a man." But then: "Huxtable, coming in with a candle, upset all her fine theories. She saw, instead of her corsair, a bland fat, flabby, lymphatic man, with a flat pale blue eye, with less depth in it than a wafer; who was too fat for his apparent age; a man who had apparently, by some mistake in Nature's cookery, been boiled instead of roasted; a man who would not even *grill* well, but would remain mere flabby meat, with a coating of brown. He was so utterly unlike what she had thought, that she forgot Hannah More and all that sort of thing, and burst out laughing. But the nasty, shallow, light-blue, dangerous eye was steadily on hers, with a look of power too; and she stopped laughing" (Vol. I, ch. 14).

It is possible that Kingsley, in depicting Sir Harry, was influenced by the witty and fat Count Fosco, whom Wilkie Collins, in *The Woman in White*, had sprung on his surprised readers, but Sir Harry Poyntz' name plus his corpulence suggests even more that Kingsley was deliberately alluding to *Henry IV, Part I*. The droll Sir Harry is an effective composite of the nobility and authority of Prince Hal, the stealthiness of Poins, and the rascality (and size) of stout Jack Falstaff. Seemingly nefarious in the way in which he plots to ruin Laura, Sir Harry, in reality, deliberately and cunningly contrives to bring Laura and Robert together after the latter's brave conduct in the Indian Mutiny. When finished with his creation, Kingsley takes care to kill him off appropriately: Sir Harry dies laughing at Lord Hatterleigh's sincere but foolish challenge to a duel.

Although no one would call the slight *Leighton Court* a great novel or even a major one, it is, nevertheless, a successful fusion of Kingsley's artistic gifts: the humor is controlled, the description is lyrical, and the characters are not only believable but attractive. In fact, as *Silas Marner* is overshadowed by the great stature of *Adam Bede* and *Middlemarch*, *Leighton Court* suffers primarily from being written by the author of *Geoffry Hamlyn* and *Ravenshoe*.

VII

1869-1873

BURDENED WITH debts and probably wanting a respite from the debilitating pressures of both novel-writing and critical abuse, in 1869 Kingsley forsook Hillside House—the hopes that he had cherished when he had moved there as a young bridegroom and popular novelist crushed—and, as if to start anew, accepted the editorship of the Edinburgh *Daily Review*, an organ of the Free Church Party. He was the last man in the world for such an appointment. Almost immediately he discovered that he was not suited to editorial routine and meeting deadlines. Furthermore, Kingsley lacked the journalistic acumen to be a good editor. An anonymous friend of his remarked that Kingsley's editorial leaders were "dictatorial, self-complacent, egotistical, and ungrammatical."[1] Subjective as that generalization is, Kingsley's novels illustrate his slipshod usage of English grammar; as even his most carefully written novels contain numerous solecisms. Also, within a short time, friction between the proprietors of the newspaper and their new editor grew into open conflict. Provoked, no doubt, by Kingsley's editorial ineptitude, the disagreements between Kingsley, a dedicated Church of England man, and the Free Church Party management, which was not only anti-Anglican but had seceded from the Church of Scotland because of political and civil matters, extended into other areas.

In less than a year, the outbreak of the Franco-Prussian War gave Kingsley an opportunity to separate himself from his editorial desk and the proprietors' nagging supervision. Although years be-

1. Shorter, "Introduction," p. xxii.

fore at the height of his literary successes he had refused an offer to cover the American Civil War, he now welcomed the opportunity to appoint himself the paper's war correspondent.

Without an official pass of any kind, Kingsley sailed from Leith during the first week of August, 1870, journeyed quickly through Rotterdam, Antwerp, and Namur, and arrived in Luxemburg on August 9 to hear that Napoleon III was organizing the Army of the Rhine at Metz. With three officers, Kingsley hurried to the heights overlooking the battlefield of Metz, and, although he was too late to see the actual fighting, he was awed by the incongruity between the "magnificent landscape [that] showed nothing but the most profound peace"—"the rolling woodlands of France, dominated to the south by the splendid cathedral of Metz like a ship in full sail above a sea of forest"—and the fact that three hours before "in the rolling plain . . . the two greatest military powers in the world had been fighting in their fury" (E., p. 202).

Later that night Kingsley crept back to the heights to see or hear whether the fighting had renewed. Refreshed by the atmosphere of virile adventures in which he loved to place his heroes, Kingsley describes the scene with all the conciseness and vivacity that had been so lamentably lacking in his most recent novels. The brutality, the inhumanity of war are colored with his special, strange beauty: "The night was profoundly dark, but there were innumerable stars over head as I sat down to look over the battlefields of that morning towards Metz. I saw nothing but a few fires, which I suppose were watch-fires, dotted about in the broad landscape. There was no movement of any kind; now and then some wandering wind, coming from the battlefield, would whisper in the rye-grass about my head, like the whispers of the dead men who lay heaped below.[2] Knowing what had happened below that morning, the matter became somewhat too solemn, and so I rose and left the night winds to whistle round that desolate down by themselves" (E., p. 202).

2. Kingsley uses variants of this comparison in two of his later novels: "I felt that the gentle wind which was waving the long grass on the down, was also waving the dead men's hair who lay down yonder behind the lights of Thionville" (*Valentin*, Vol. II, ch. 13); "There are few more melancholy places than the glacis of Luxemburg on a dark, rainless, moonless night. It is bad enough on a bright summer's day . . . but it is worse at night, when the wind from the down moves the grass like a dead man's hair, and makes the trees talk secrets to one another about the old wicked slaughters which took place there before they were planted" (*The Harveys*, Vol. II, ch. 10).

After joining other correspondents, such as Sir Henry Havelock (later Allan) and Auberon Herbert, with whom he shared information, Kingsley decided to travel alone through the French countryside, and for about two weeks—in "danger of assassination by an infuriated peasantry every hour" and of imprisonment by either the French or Prussian authorities—he made his way to the frontier, meeting Prussian Hussars "feeling their way from one patch of forest" to another and passing through evacuated French villages. One village was inhabited only by "a Frenchwoman, in deep black, with her baby swathed in such deep black that I thought it was dead, and am not yet sure on the point. She was sitting on a log by herself, but she suddenly arose, clenched her fist, and said several times, 'Dix huit ans! dix huit ans!' What she means, God and herself only know. I only know that it was too sacred and too terrible for my clumsy interference" (E., p. 206).

Then, during the first days of September, Kingsley witnessed the "greatest battle of modern times," the Battle of Sedan, the "butchery" where "80,000 men have capitulated with 600 guns," with at least 40,000 killed. Shocked by the terrible drama of the war, Kingsley, however, seemed unable to shake off his fascination with the death around him. Compassion certainly exists in his accounts, but a boyish innocence that reflects almost pleasure on his part to be in the midst of the bloodshed and slaughter seeps through:

> The *sight* of it is immensely beautiful: the dead men look so pretty from a little distance: they group themselves as they fall, and even when they crawl back to die they look well, for Death is generally beautiful. But I should like the ex-Emperor not only to see his work at a distance, but come near it, to touch it, and after three days to *smell* it, as I have done (E., p. 214).

> One of the dead had his knee up, and they could not get it down. They were trailing him along by his heels with his knapsack still on his back; I looked into his face before he was put into the trench and saw that he had died hard. . . . I found a French sergeant lying apart from the heap of men near him who had died very quietly: he was a splendid young fellow with a slight beard and moustache and lay with his face to the sky perfectly quiet . . . this man had died praying, with his hands over his chest in the Roman manner, and the

ends of his fingers together; as he died . . . his arms stiffened
(E., pp. 224–25).

Yesterday they were dragging a young man to the trench
by his heels, and some inequality in the ground turned his
still open eyes towards me; for an instant, though the man's
face was black with incipient decomposition, I thought that
he wished to speak to me, and I made two steps towards him:
the man had been dead two days (E., p. 226).

Leaving the gore and stench of the battlefield for the town of
Sedan in order to give his readers a firsthand account of its con-
ditions the day after its surrender, Kingsley approached the town
"through a beautiful boulevard of trees" and was struck by the
apparent order that the Prussians had already enforced upon the
inhabitants. "Can we go on into Sedan?" Kingsley asked one of the
Prussian officers. "By all means," was the reply. The gate to the
town still closed, Kingsley and a few other men entered through an
open sewer, "with our bodies bent and our hats off," and immediately encountered a column of 12,000 French prisoners being
marched away: "There were nearly as many disarmed French as
there were armed Prussians." As the French soldiers, many wounded
and almost all of them footsore, tired, and dejected, shambled by,
Kingsley's attention was drawn to the few bemedaled ones who
carried their heads "in the air contemptuously," looking far more
like winners than losers. The German guards, about one to every
hundred French, solemnly accompanied the columns on horse-
back, trying "to look as though there was nothing the matter"
(E., pp. 231–33).

"Half mad with hunger, thirst, and heat," while watching this
procession, Kingsley managed to wind his way through narrow
streets filled with riderless horses and "magnificent confusion" to a
hotel, where he had to settle for some gingerbread he had found in
a little shop and some "intolerably bad claret." All the time the
confusion grew more confounded as wagon loads of captured
rifles and knapsacks and regiment after regiment passed by Kingsley's hotel. Kingsley the artist, always dazzled by the brilliance
of military uniforms,[3] was excited by the Uhlan, "the first I had

3. See, for example, "No one can say that troops in a line, under drill, are
picturesque; but shatter them into heaps and they become picturesque at once.
The mass of scarlet and blue clothes which lies all around you is very beautiful
indeed, and the grouping (to use an artist's term) is always fine" (Ellis, p. 126).

seen," who rode by the hotel window. Prominent in the Prussian Army, especially in the Franco-Prussian War, these lancers in their predominantly blue Oriental dress were picturesque figures. Although some were armed with other weapons, the one Kingsley saw carried only his lance, "with a flag at the end of it" (E., p. 235).

Pro-German as he was, Kingsley, seeing the strength of the Prussians and the utter defeat of their enemy, felt great sympathy for the French: "I wished them to lose, but not like this: they have been ruined by the Charlatan of the Second of December. . . . Let no man say one word against the French Army. The French people chose to be governed by a charlatan and the end has come: but the French army have done what they could: demoralised and abandoned, they fought to the last. When all hope was gone, they fought still. . . . They were beaten, as were the men of Thermopylae. *Vae victis*, glorious old France is not dead yet" (E., p. 237).

The next day Kingsley left Sedan and for the next three weeks traveled mainly with the Red Cross Society, visiting hospitals. But, as he tells his readers, his traveling was severely restricted because of his lack of a pass and, consequently, the "eternal arrestations." Finally, during his eighth week of reporting, Kingsley was weakened by an attack of bronchitis which had begun at Sedan and had been continually aggravated by long periods of his wearing wet clothes, and he left the war zone for Edinburgh.

Kingsley's return to Edinburgh was dismal. After the privations that he had seen and experienced during his eight weeks as a correspondent, he found little comfort in the dark and shabby furnished house that the Kingsleys had rented in Edinburgh. How gloomy it must have been for the wearied Henry, who had loved the sunny loveliness of Eversley and Wargrave, where he could grow roses and relax in well-kept gardens! Anne Thackeray, in Edinburgh for a brief visit during those days, called upon the always hospitable Kingsleys, but she sensed a feeling of despair about her former friends: "The place was full of boxes and packings. Mrs. Kingsley was anxious and troubled, though even then she took me in. I happened to be ill, and she sent for a lady doctor who cured me; she also wrote to Dr. John Brown, my father's old friend, who came to see me. I left them after a couple of days and went south, grateful for their kindness, but feeling as if I ought not to have imposed upon it."[4]

4. Shorter, "Introduction," pp. xxi–xxii.

Kingsley was troubled. The previous disagreements with the owners over the management of the newspaper erupted anew, and, within a few months, Kingsley wrote both to Charles and to Macmillan that the newspaper's owners wanted him to resign, because "the paper is not paying and they want a cheaper editor." Whether Kingsley accepted that probable excuse as a legitimate reason is unimportant; he too wanted to be relieved of the disagreeable experience, but desperate as always for money, he refused to resign until satisfactory financial arrangements were reached. "I was," he told Macmillan, "hired for three years, and I want you and Charles to arbitrate as to what remuneration I must receive for this sudden breach of Contract" (E., p. 185).

Although Charles consented to intercede on Henry's behalf, the strained relations between the two brothers that had, as Sadleir suggested, possibly prompted the extravagances of *Stretton* were now almost at a breaking point. Charles, at first, gladly gave Henry money, but as the requests became more and more frequent, Charles and his wife, Fanny, who was never fond of her husband's younger brother, resented Henry's persistent pleas, especially since they believed that it was Sarah who had caused Henry's poverty. Told that his brother was borrowing money indiscriminately from distant acquaintances, the embarrassed Charles, now the newly appointed Canon of Chester, took it upon himself to warn his friends of Henry's importunity. On March 30, 1871, for example, writing to a friend who had lent him a magazine, Charles added the postscript: "I hear that my poor brother Henry, when you were at Edinburgh, express't his hopes of seeing much of you when he came to Chelsea. I am bound in honour to you, whom I look on also as a brother, to advise you not to ask him to your house. If you can get him any literary work I shall be deeply obligated to you. And your wife must positively see she knows nothing of his wretched wife, who has ruined him. I tell you, of course, in confidence. But I dare not in honour do less. He has gone nigh to break my heart and the hearts of others."[5]

This strong warning suggests that Charles may have feared other actions than merely Henry's proclivity to borrow money. Worry may have increased Henry's drinking. William Tinsley, Kingsley's main publisher during 1869–71, wrote that Henry "stayed often very long in Bohemian haunts, or anywhere where there were

5. Unpublished letter, Houghton Library.

boon companions and the right sort of liquor to keep good wit rolling."[6]

Charles and Macmillan must have reached a satisfactory settlement with the newspaper owners for Kingsley moved to London in 1871. Too exhausted to commit himself to a steady flow of new novels, Henry, to earn money, rushed into print or reprinted previously completed works. In 1871, the allegory *The Boy in Grey*, serialized in 1869–70, was issued as a separate edition as was his one-volume novel *Hetty*, which had not only been serialized in 1869 but had been published in America by Harper and Brothers that same year. In 1872 he also published a collection of nine short narratives, *Hornby Mills and Other Stories*, all of which had been published previously.

Kingsley even persuaded the patient Macmillan to reprint "The Lost Child," a chapter from *Geoffry Hamlyn* (Vol. II, ch. 13), as a Christmas book. This is a sad, tender little tale of a small Australian bush boy who fancies that he sees wonderful fairy children on the other side of the river that he has been forbidden to cross. Disobeying his mother, he crosses it, becomes lost in the bush, and dies. For this edition Kingsley added a very short introduction and conclusion. Though the introduction is unnecessary for the continuity of the story, it reflects Kingsley's depression. Speaking through the character Geoffry Hamlyn, Kingsley writes, "I will go back [to Australia] next year, for I am tired of England, and I will leave my bones there; I am getting old, and I want peace, as I had it in Australia" (p. 12). Interestingly, this same sentiment is expressed in his short story "My Landladies," published a year later, when the narrator describes an Australian scene and sighs, "Oh, the Australian life! how can one exist in Europe after it?" (p. 387). If Hamlyn's and the narrator's thoughts are really Kingsley's own desires, it is not difficult to understand why Kingsley dreams about that earlier time. His Australian years had certainly not been peaceful ones, but in retrospect (his memory of them no doubt revived by his recent limited adventures in the Franco-Prussian War) and in comparison with his present miserable existence, they had been thrilling years, free of literary drudgery, financial crises, and family conflicts.

Kingsley's decision to reprint this tale is ironic, because, symbolically, Kingsley is like the little child who follows the call of

6. Tinsley, II, 118.

his imagination across the river only to discover that hissing snakes and swooping eagles are ready to attack him. All his life, Kingsley strove to be like the noble heroes that populated his novels, but when he allowed the passion of his dreams to lead him into real-life adventures he, also, found the harshness of reality. The frightened little boy dies, "still grasping the flowers he had gathered on his last happy playday"; Kingsley continues to struggle and can only achieve glory by living vicariously through his characters. Both of them sadly find out "what lay beyond the shining river" that tempts them.

The new work Kingsley published during 1871–72 was slight, and most of it had been written before he left for the war. The novel *The Harveys*, he stated in its Preface, was "written seven years earlier," and a second novel, *Old Margaret*, was published just a few months after he had left Edinburgh. The only totally new work was *Valentin: A French Boy's Story of Sedan*, which, as the subtitle implies, was based on Kingsley's war experiences.

Publishing these works quickly in order to pay his creditors but knowing that most of them were inferior, Kingsley understood that he needed to write another major three-volume novel "to gain a fresh lease of popularity." But he still needed money so that he would be free to concentrate on the undertaking, which was to be *Oakshott Castle*. Charles, he knew, would no longer help him, and so, towards the end of 1871, he wrote a pathetic letter to Lord Houghton (Richard Monckton Milnes), almost a complete stranger to him but an important member of the Royal Literary Fund and a champion of Kingsley's friend Swinburne:

In 1865, I had lost everything, since then I have been making a severe and terrible struggle to put matters right. I have nearly succeeded, and should in fact be comfortable with £200. But I have been writing against time in the newspapers for an income and have been republishing things out of my portfolio which in better times would never have seen the light at all. *This will not do.* People naturally suppose that I have written myself out, whereas the simple fact of the matter is that these later things were all written before my hand was as good as it is now. The only new novel in four years is *Oakshott Castle*, which Macmillan and Bentley competed for without looking at it, (Macmillan saw the first chapter) Macmillan has got it, and I am to finish it off by March. Meanwhile I am unable to live. Macmillan's firm will not back me on with any advance on a novel not yet written, and my only hope of making a fine thing of it is to appeal to some member of the literary guild of which I am a humble member for temporary assistance. *My brother* is quite out of the question. Pray never hint to him about this letter. As my wife and I sat with blank faces looking at one another and wondering what would become of us, she said suddenly, "Write secretly to Lord Houghton and ask him whether he will help us over the style [*sic*]. Tell him in a manly way how you are situated and how you refused to relieve yourself of your difficulties by law, but insisted on working them off, then ask him what he can do for you." I have done so.

£40 would be a perfect godsend to us now my Lord: We shall inherit about £12,000 in a few years: *I could not undertake to repay such a loan out of my next novel,* but I could bind myself to do it within a year. If you could help to keep me alive and slightly free from worry until *Oakshott Castle* is done, I honestly venture to think that you would have served literature by £40. Whatever you do let the secret of this application remain in your own bosom. How bitter it has been to make it even to you, you may guess.[7]

This letter to Lord Houghton contains assertions bewildering for a biographer. How had Kingsley "lost everything" in 1865, a year after his marriage? In January, 1866, he had told Macmillan that he had not invested his money badly. If Kingsley is not exaggerating his case for Lord Houghton, this letter seemingly substantiates Charles' accusations and Henry's earlier implications that Sarah and her mother had extravagantly misspent Henry's money when they set up the Wargrave household. Still further, from whom are the Kingsleys to "inherit about £12,000 in a few years"? In that same 1866 letter to Macmillan, Kingsley said, "I have £1,700 to come—£1,200 at my mother's death and £500 at Mrs. Wills's [his aunt]" (E., pp. 146–47). Either the £12,000 is a figment of Henry's imagination or an error in his recording of the amount that he expected to receive at the death of his mother, who was, in 1871, very ill. And it is even possible that the £1,200 was an exaggeration, for when Henry died, one month over three years after his mother's death, his estate was valued at only £450.

7. This letter and the following ones between Charles and Lord Houghton are found in Pope-Hennessy, pp. 265–67.

However exaggerated Kingsley's case may have been, Lord Houghton was sympathetic and sent Kingsley £30. Charles heard of the request but assumed that Sarah Kingsley had written to Lord Houghton, specifically asking his help for a grant from the Royal Literary Fund. Hurriedly, he wrote to Lord Houghton, entreating him in the future not "to entertain any proposal either from her or from her mother Mrs. Haselwood (who is equally likely to trespass on your good nature) without referring to me, who am intimately acquainted with the true state of my most industrious, but most unhappy brother's affairs, and also have known all about these two women for some 20–30 years." On hearing from Lord Houghton that Henry himself had begged for the help and that Lord Houghton had personally lent the money, Charles wrote again, re-emphasizing his reason for Henry's poverty:

> You had a right to express your astonishment that his writings do not provide him with the needful comforts of life. The only persons who can solve the mystery are the two women who have both him and his earnings in their powers.
>
> Let me entreat you to tell me the amount of what you were so kind as to lend him. My honour and conscience will not be satisfied until it is repaid.[8]

Besides giving Henry £30, Lord Houghton presumably assisted him in getting three grants from the Royal Literary Fund, but even they were insufficient to alleviate Kingsley's difficulties. Again he petitions Macmillan in letters that not only display his extreme poverty but his anxiety over his alienation from Charles:

[1872]
Tell me about Charles. They say he is ill, some say very ill, but my mother never mentions it. Do let me know (E., p. 187).

[1872]
I am therefore poor as ever. . . . If you were to advance me £100 on my MS. [*Oakshott Castle*], it seems to me that you

---

8. According to his daughter, Charles was thinking of Sarah Kingsley's pleas for money when he wrote the final lines of his poem "The Delectable Day":

Ah, God! a poor soul can but thank Thee
For such a delectable day:
Though the fury, the fool, and the swindler,
To-morrow again have their way.
(Ellis, p. 100)

are secured in case of my death, and that it is preeminently
my interest to gain a fresh lease of popularity by making it
the best thing I have ever written. It is not altogether easy
to write at one's best with eternal small bothers about one.
I have written nothing new lately, I have not written a new
novel for more than two years, though I have published some
things out of my portfolio.

Think over this and buy me, body and bones (E., pp. 186–
87).

Also in 1872 he writes to Craik: "Strain a point for me and let
me have twenty-five pounds more, and then you shall not hear
one word of me until *Oakshott* is in your hands. We cannot draw
a farthing just now, and the doctors have ordered Mrs. H. [prob-
ably Mrs. Haselwood] to Hastings" (E., p. 188). Small wonder that
Oakshott Castle, his major novel during this period, turned out
to be the fiasco it is.

VIII

The London Novels

KINGSLEY's Australian adventures produced the delightful *Geoffry Hamlyn* and some of the best part of *The Hillyars and the Burtons*, but, unfortunately, his experiences in the Franco-Prussian War produced no comparable novels, only the short stories "Malmaison" and "Miss Milton," and the two-volume *Valentin*, which Kingsley insisted was "merely a slight story for boys."[1] Indeed, *Valentin* is but a slender token of those eight weeks. With his personal knowledge of the war and its locale, Kingsley gives the reader a wonderful sense of place as Valentin wanders through the country where France, Belgium, Luxemburg, and Prussia meet, but the tale, even as a boy's story, is disorganized and confused, besides being filled with irrelevant digressions that a boy would hardly understand in which the hero displays his incredible erudition on subjects ranging from botany and entomology to English education and Eternity. With a wild humor Valentin (i.e., Kingsley) even analyzes Lewis Carroll's recently published "The Walrus and the Carpenter" as a satirical poem on the Franco-Prussian War. And, most awkwardly, Kingsley speaks through the mouth of the young

1. To the *Athenaeum*, which had reviewed the book as "one of the worst novels ever published, utterly devoid of sense, taste, or coherence," Kingsley wrote: "Will you do me the favour to state that 'Valentin: A French Boy's Story of Sedan,' which you reviewed last week, is merely a slight story for boys, written for the *Young Gentleman's Magazine* and reprinted by Mr. Tinsley." The *Athenaeum* curtly replied: "We cannot see that this accounts for the extraordinary blunders that are to be found in 'Valentin.'" Original review, LIV (September 21, 1872), 357; subsequent correspondence, LIV (September 28, 1872), 403.

Frenchman to spout jingoistic accounts of English glory and to affirm his strong belief in liberty.

Valentin himself is the schoolboy's dream of extraordinary nobleness, bravery, daring—a Jacques the Giant Killer. Everyone from William I through Bismarck to Napoleon III either cherishes Valentin's friendship or respects and honors his remarkable merits. To make him even more marvelous (but unusual for a hero of a boy's story), Kingsley awards the seventeen-year-old Valentin the loveliest and bravest of child brides, Marie, who disguises herself as a drummer boy in order to follow Valentin into battle. And furthermore Kingsley continually teases the reader with suggestions that Valentin is really a werewolf!

The carelessness that marred *Stretton* prevails in this novel too. A colonel who is sixty-one years old in 1870 was a drummer boy in the War of 1812. In one chapter Valentin and his mentor, Jacques Cartier, set out on a spying mission supposedly following the "sudden débâcle" of Austria at Sadowa, but, confusingly, after their long trip, they return home so that Valentin's father can leave for his part of the intrigue on the "eve of Sadowa." It seems as if Kingsley either did not concern himself with details or was too worried to comprehend the incongruities.

The last sentence of the novel is "That is all I have to say of Sedan." A reader of the first edition that I examined inked in this comment, "And a very stupid say, too." I have to agree.

Whereas *Valentin* is, at times, unintentionally fantastic, *The Boy in Grey*, Kingsley's other story for children, is a designed fantasy, which was, no doubt, inspired by *Alice in Wonderland*. Kingsley's baffling allegory begins with Prince Philarete's tenth-birthday party and continues with the boy's eleven-year pursuit across Europe, Asia, North America, and Australia and through Fairyland after the enigmatic and elusive Boy in Grey. On his voyage not only does the little prince encounter Wonderland types of animals, but he comes upon a community of literary and historical figures who dwell eternally on the banks and many islands of Minnesswahaha, the River of Happy Recollections. The Pathfinder and Chingachgook stalk out to set their beaver traps, while Cinderella strolls arm-in-arm with Colonel Dobbin and Colonel Crawley; Aunt Clegg, Aunt Pullet, Mr. Pecksniff, and the Queen of Hearts squabble meaninglessly as Alice scampers off with Silas Marner and Tom Pinch to Wonderland to be replaced by the quartet Arthur Pendennis, Don Quixote, Sir Joshua Reynolds, and Dr. Samuel Johnson. And so the list goes on. If nothing else, this work shows Kingsley's wide range of reading.

What this tale exactly means, and, indeed, what the Boy in Grey specifically represents, are difficult to ascertain. Generally speaking, since etymologically "Philarete" means "having a predilection for all of those good qualities that compose the human character" or, in other words, "loving or desiring excellence," the allegory, in essence, suggests a boy's quest for that excellence, which the brave Philarete finally achieves when he kisses the Boy in Grey. Philarete is then twenty-one years old and, thus, a man. Commingled with this allegorical journey is oblique satire directed against, among other things, religious intolerance, the aristocracy, military power, capital and labor, and even the railroad.

In the midst of this jumble, however, stands a simple and enchanting lyric of Mary Magdalen and the blackbird at Glastonbury:

> Magdalen at Michael's gate
>   Tirled at the pin;
> On Joseph's thorn sang the blackbird,
>   "Let her in! Let her in!"
>
> "Hast thou seen the wounds?" said Michael,
>   "Know'st thou thy sin?"
> "It is evening, evening," sang the blackbird,
>   "Let her in! Let her in!"
>
> "Yes, I have seen the wounds,
>   And I know my sin."
> "She knows it well, well, well," sang the blackbird,
>   "Let her in! Let her in!"
>
> "Thou bringest no offerings," said Michael,
>   "Nought save sin."
> And the blackbird sang, "She is sorry, sorry, sorry.
>   Let her in! Let her in!"
>
> When he had sung himself to sleep,
>   And night did begin,
> One came and opened Michael's gate,
>   And Magdalen went in (ch. 4).

Behind the poem, of course, lies the legend of Joseph of Arimathea and the Glastonbury Thorn. According to tradition, it was this devoted disciple who not only offered his tomb for Christ's burial but held the holy Grail to catch His blood at the cross. Then in the course of his missionary travels, he and eleven other disciples founded at Glastonbury the first primitive church. Upon Joseph's death, the other disciples respectfully planted on the grave his staff, which miraculously grew into the bush now known as the Glastonbury Thorn, flowering at Christmas time. Traditionally, this Christmas bush symbolizes Christ's birth and glory and His death and suffering: His sacrificial life and death, which proffers to all mankind hope, love, and forgiveness. This highly symbolic legend Kingsley retells with poetic simplicity and restraint in "Magdalen at Michael's Gate."[2] Frederick York Powell, the English historian and Icelandic scholar, once asked Jack Butler Yeats, the Irish artist and brother of William Butler Yeats, to illustrate this verse, which Powell described as Kingsley's "best thing": "It used to make me cry when I was a boy, and it makes me feel uncommon creepy even now."[3]

Kingsley's other three novels, besides *Oakshott Castle*, can be dismissed without detailed discussion, especially *Old Margaret* (Margaret van Eyck), which shows a new and unsuccessful departure for Kingsley. Set in fifteenth-century Ghent, the novella deals simultaneously with the labor and class struggles near the end of the feudal era and with the van Eycks and their painting of the famous altarpiece "The Adoration of the Lamb." Although Kingsley admits that "we really know very little about this magnificent picture," he definitely assigns the major part of the painting to the historically obscure Hubert van Eyck, whose very existence some art historians contest. Jan van Eyck, Kingsley believes, painted the lamb.

This work may have been Kingsley's attempt to emulate Charles Reade's earlier success *The Cloister and the Hearth* (1861), because Kingsley's letters during this time stress Reade's popularity. But, in this period of his life, Kingsley was no longer a worthy competitor with Reade in ability to create the right combination of theatrical excitement, humor, and sentiment. More a working copy than a finished story, *Old Margaret* is dull, repetitious, and con-

2. For an analysis of this poem see my article "'Magdalen at Michael's Gate': A Neglected Lyric," *Victorian Poetry*, V (Summer, 1967), 144–46.

3. Oliver Elton, *Frederick York Powell: A Life and a Selection from his Letters and Occasional Writings* (Oxford, 1906), I, 379.

fusing, with undeveloped characters milling around and plotting intrigue that just doesn't materialize until very late in the story.

Approximately mid-point in the first volume of *The Harveys*, Kingsley tells his readers that he had written so far "A tale of one of the best and kindest of men, left a widower in the heyday of youth, with his hopes in life blighted, and his faith undermined with squalid poverty for his every-day lot, and a family of helpless, untidy children, whom he had no means of educating decently, and whose future was far more dark, uncertain, and unpromising than that of the young brood of the commonest boiler-hammerer in the land. Next of a high-born woman, sinking without an effort into the habits of those among whom she was thrown, penniless, and hopelessly superstitious, only using her recollections of a higher life to turn the head of a beautiful, passionate, clever, ambitious child. A tale, in short, of decadence and deterioration, settling down darker and darker upon a devoted family." But, as Kingsley continues, he has made the tale as funny as possible because it "would have been too sad to read if I had not" (Vol. I, ch. 10).

One has to disagree with Kingsley's evaluation of his own novel. The "decadence and deterioration" of the "kindest man," Mr. Harvey, and the "high-born woman," Lady Edith, are only background. The novel, instead, concentrates on its narrator, Charles Harvey, and his successful attempt to become a famous painter. Also, the reader does not, as Kingsley later states, "laugh and giggle" through the novel. *The Harveys* is not funny. It consists of little more than a rehash of scenes from previous inferior novels: the duel and prison scene devices from *Austin Elliot*, the classroom balderdash from *Stretton*, and too many similarities from *Silcote of Silcotes* to enumerate. As for characters, the unhandsome, determined, and brave Charles Harvey is a warmed-over Charles Ravenshoe; his "handsome and friendly" brother, Dick, a stupid William Horton; the villain Jack Chetwynd, a undeveloped Lord Welter; and Jack's unnamed brother, an insignificant Cuthbert. And not only are Lady Edith's and Dora Harvey's counterparts found in *Silcote of Silcotes* in Princess Castelnuovo and Dora Silcote, respectively, but Kingsley has reintroduced as a new character the governess Miss Lee, who differs little in actions and appearance from the earlier Miss Lee. This novel must be one of the works, as Kingsley told Lord Houghton, out of his "portfolio, which in better times would never have seen the light at all."

Kingsley, however, tried to enliven the threadbare story line by adding to it a dash of spiritualism, a fad very popular in the mid-fifties and still lingering over England in the early seventies. Its most notorious figure was, of course, Daniel Dunglas Home, the famous exponent of table-turning and levitation, whom Browning immortalized in "Mr. Sludge, 'The Medium.'" There is no indication that Kingsley himself was interested in spiritualism, but we can picture him pitifully grasping for any topical subject that would make *The Harveys* sell.

The sole interesting figure in the novel is the very cruel and heartless Madame D'Estrada, who, like Trollope's Signora Vesey-Neroni in *Barchester Towers*, has had a mysterious marriage and separation and now plays at attracting men. But, unlike the Signora, Madame D'Estrada has little compassion for her victims. After causing numerous duels and the ensuing deaths and utilizing Lady Edith Harvey's musical ability to forward her own singing career, she finally marries an infatuated lover, Von Lieber, whom she proceeds to torment. Kingsley had the material here for a memorable character, but, as too often happened, he merely told the reader about her wickedness, until, unexpectedly, he ends the novel with a short scene that reveals her self-centeredness:

> I saw *her* the other night singing at the Opera. She was rather more handsome than ever, and her success was, as usual, enormous. I stepped round to the stagedoor, and easily, of course, got admission. I met her, and she knew me and smiled.
> "How did I sing?" she said.
> "You know that you always sing well," I replied. "But, do you know that your husband is dying?"
> "Is that so?" she answered. "Give my love to your funny old aunt, Lady Edith."
> And that was the last of Madame Von Lieber, once Madame D'Estrada.

Disappointingly, the rest of the novel failed to concentrate upon character development.

Hetty, one of Kingsley's favorite novels, is the best of these three novels, and as a slight work it almost succeeds.[4] For his setting

4. For Kingsley's opinion of this novel see Ellis, pp. 180, 188–89. *Hetty* received a favorable but odd review in *The Times*. It consisted of two full columns of detailed plot summary and then the final comment: "We think that Hetty Morley is in her way quite as splendid a character as Rebecca Turner, and we

Kingsley returned to the semi-rural Chelsea of his youth, and instead of dealing with a family he concentrated mainly on one character, the impudent heroine Rebecca Turner, her rebellion against her tyrannical father, and her love for a forty-two-year-old muscular missionary, Alfred Morley, the widowed father of Hetty. Essential to the story line is Rebecca's long wait for Morley's return from sea, during which time she must purge herself of her "wild hawklike" nature. In this respect, she is more like Charles Ravenshoe, Austin Elliot, and Erne Hillyar than Kingsley's previous impudent heroine, Laura Seckerton, in *Leighton Court*. Rebecca must suffer, must undergo sacrificial acts before she realizes her goal.

Hetty herself does not enter the novel until five chapters from the end, but she is frequently whispered about earlier. As we later learn, she had, in the eyes of the community, disgraced herself and her minister father by "lowering herself so far as to go to sea as a stewardess." Kingsley favors her decision and makes her an example of courage for Rebecca to follow. As he closes his novel he writes, "I think, if you please, that in honour of the young lady, the reputation of whose deeds kept Rebecca firm, I will call my story after its real heroine, Hetty."

The novel has its defects, a major one being that too many extraneous mysteries complicate the short work. But Rebecca is an appealing character, and Kingsley's description of sweeps, gossips, sailors, and other sea folk has an appealing freshness. For example, the disquisition of Mr. Spicer, a sweep, on dogs springs from the same spirit that enriched Kingsley's earlier works:

> "A warmint dog, Miss, as his name implies, is a dog as is kept for the killing of warmint. Now there's a many kinds of 'em: bull-dog, bull-terrier, fox-terrier, black-and-tan-terrier, toy, Dandy and Skye. Similarly there's varieties in the nature of warmint, as badger, pole-cat, weasel, and rat. Of badgers there is country badgers and old hands. Of pole-cats there is wild and tame. Of rats, why there's as much difference in rats, lor bless you, as what there is in Christians. I've seen big rats as a new-born kitten could kill; and contrariwise, one of my young men went to enter a well-bred year-old toy with an old rat, and I'm blessed if the dog didn't cut and run for his life, howling, round the lanes, and the rat after him."

are quite sure that Mr. Kingsley's *Hetty* is a very amusing and well-written story" (September 16, 1871, 4a).

"I seen it," said Jim Akin.

"But I don't want a dog to kill anything," said Rebecca.

"Miss wants a general dog, I expect, miller," said Jim Akin to the master chimney-sweep. "Tip her some of your advice now."

"General dogs, Miss," said the miller, complacently, "is like warmint dogs, various; and I never seen none that was much 'count, takin' into consideration what dogs was made for. Still Providence made 'em, and the fancy gives prizes for 'em, similarly as they do for fantails and pouters, and other rubbish that were only created for showing and dealing. If I had my will, Miss, there should be no prizes for any pigeons except carriers, and none for any dogs except real warmint" (ch. 9).

Although these five works are inferior, they can be excused because they were hurriedly written and, also, none was a major novel. But the three-volume *Oakshott Castle, Being the Memoirs of an Eccentric Nobleman*, on which Kingsley spent two years, cannot be dismissed that easily.

So confusingly does *Oakshott Castle* relate the multitudinous adventures of its hero, Lord Edward Oakshott,[5] more fantastically eccentric than the subtitle suggests, that when the novel appeared in 1873, the reviewers, justifiably bewildered, were harsh. The *Saturday Review* acrimoniously wrote: "Mr. Henry Kingsley in writing *Oakshott Castle* must, we should think, have engaged in a feat somewhat similar to that of those great chess-players who, without seeing the boards, play half-a-dozen games at the same time. For no other explanation can we give of the utter confusion and absurdity of his latest novel, save the supposition that when he was writing it he had a good many others on hand also, while his memory was not powerful enough to keep the several plots from getting jumbled up together. . . . We will not go so far as to say that *Oakshott Castle* is the worst novel ever written; but, on the other hand, it lacks that one merit which saves many a bad novel, that it puts its readers to sleep. It keeps them awake, not to any enjoyment or good end, but as a gnat or a mosquito keeps one awake."[6]

5. Lord Oakshott was named after Dr. Oakeshott, a friend of Dr. George Kingsley at Highgate (Ellis, p. 102).

6. XXXV (April 26, 1873), 563. In *The "Saturday Review" 1855–1868*, Merle Bevington, on internal evidence, assigns five earlier reviews of Kingsley's novels

A healthier man than Kingsley would have flinched under such an attack by one of the two or three most influential reviews in England. Just imagine, for example, the reaction of the more emotionally stable Charles Reade, who would recoil from even the slightest "disparaging remark from the obscurest critic in the corner of the poorest provincial newspaper."[7] Kingsley's condition was undoubtedly exacerbated. Deeply hurt and evidently suffering a feeling of persecution, he complained to George Craik: "I know perfectly well that if I was to write a book as good as *John Halifax* or *The Mill on the Floss*, I should not have fair play. *Oakshott* was two years in hand, and fast and furious as it looks, was very carefully thought out. It is not more fantastic nor half as improbable as *The Old Curiosity Shop*. Oakshott is exactly what I should be if I had got the money. In my late miserable poverty I amused myself by thinking what I would be if I was rich. The result was Oakshott, a greater fool even than myself. Surely that is legitimate fiction" (E., p. 189).

This extraordinary letter can only be viewed as a further symptom of Kingsley's emotional confusion. The self-pity; the implied comparison between what the *Saturday Review* had almost called the "worst novel ever written" and *The Mill on the Floss*, which Kingsley himself had previously called the "best . . . novel ever written" (E., p. 187); the distasteful, insinuating allusion to *John Halifax, Gentleman*, a third-rate novel published sixteen years earlier that happened to be by Craik's wife, Dinah Mulock; the critical obtuseness and self-delusion evident in the allusion to *The Old Curiosity Shop*, all might seem to verge on paranoia, though Kingsley's reaction is, in any case, a familiar enough phenomenon even in our own day. Everyone remembers a comparable outburst by Ernest Hemingway when *Across the River and Into the Trees* was almost universally damned and mercilessly parodied.

What is so surprising and sad about the book is its complete lack of organization. Although the plot is unnecessarily complex, Kingsley had shown himself capable of handling comparable complexities in his earlier works. It seems impossible that the man who

---

to Thomas Collett Sandars. Since Sandars "remained a regular member of the staff long after 1868," it is probable that he was also the reviewer of *Oakshott Castle*.

7. Justin McCarthy as quoted in *The Library of Literary Criticism*, ed. Charles Wells Moulton (New York, 1910), VII, 527.

had written *Geoffry Hamlyn*, *Ravenshoe*, *The Hillyars and the Burtons*, and *Mademoiselle Mathilde*—even with their improbabilities and meandering digressions—could have been blind to the incoherence verging on lunacy of *Oakshott Castle*. There are no grounds for supposing that the undiagnosed and unsuspected cancer which caused Kingsley's death three years later is responsible for the jumbled condition of the work. His letters of this time make no mention of any physical discomfort, and whether or not the malignancy had affected his mental powers is, of course, purely a matter of conjecture. But insofar as his next novel, *Reginald Hetherege*, shows much less of the recklessness and irrationality that mar *Oakshott Castle*, it seems reasonable to assume a temporary collapse of Kingsley's literary judgment and control, brought on by his extreme poverty and by his fear of permanently lost popularity.

Oakshott Castle starts off well with a storm scene off the Dorset coast: "The weather had been dim and wild all day, and the sea had begun to tumble in heavily from the south-west." From this description, Kingsley shifts the scene to the fishermen gathered round the fire at "Oakshott Arms":

> There was not one single boat out; the catch had been good, the hucksters had been ready, the fish were gone, the money was paid, the women were seeing to the nets, and each man had in his pocket a sum of money allowed him by his wife for liquor. If he chose to spend it that night, he could spend it; if not, he could leave some of it for another night: but so long as he did not come to bed with his boots on, every married man there was as free as if he were a bachelor. . . . The bachelors, it may be remarked, stayed and helped the unmarried girls with the nets, and a kiss or a squeeze of the hand from a handsome young sailor is much the same, whether he be as dry as a dandy or as wet as a shag: and a saunter home to the house with him may be made as pleasant in a furious south-westerly gale on a dark night, as in a bright June day under towering elms, with flowers round your feet at every tread; at least it would seem so, for a great deal of honest love-making went on that night, both on the beach and in front of the cottage-doors, until the bachelors were driven away through the rain and wind by mothers to join their seniors inside the screen at the "Oakshott Arms," down on the beach.

Lord Oakshott enters immediately. He is twenty-two years old, tall and athletic; "his face very brown, with a light yellow beard; his expression dreamy and inscrutable; his dress like that of a sailor." From the convivial remarks, clues emerge as to the tenants' great love for Oakshott and their equally strong hatred for Oakshott's cousin and heir, Sir Arthur, who is thought to be driving his ship through the fierce storm. Then, "one by one the tired fishermen went out into the wild wind to their homes, and at last Lord Oakshott went to bed, with the wind howling at his window as if it would tear his flesh."

The mood of the novel, the influence and amiability of Oakshott, and the suspected villainy of Sir Arthur have been set up concisely and effectively, with traces of Kingsley's old spirit and of his descriptive power. But within a few chapters the novel sinks into a mishmash of morbidity, confusion, and some simply outrageous scenes. Plots and counterplots by Arthur, Oakshott, and others to ruin, kill, and finally help each other motivate some of the action, but the initial loves and hates seem to generate spontaneously. Entangled in the main action are threads of Oakshott's love for Arthur's wife, Marie; his adoption of Arthur's son, Dickie, whom Arthur believes to be Oakshott's, and Dickie's subsequent kidnaping and life among the gypsies; Oakshott's high financial affairs; his oratorical flings in the House of Lords; his mysterious and extraordinary involvements with the Camorrists, the Carbonari, and various Indian tribes in the United States; and his American adventures with his adopted daughter, Dixie, who speaks a British version of Wild West slang:

"Dixie," said Oakshott, "I want you to leave off the old prairie slang."

"All serene," said Dixie.

"But that is not leaving it off," said Oakshott.

"Yes, it is, old hoss," said the outrageous Dixie, "I have done with it, though it comes pleasant to my tongue. You will never hear another word of it from my mouth. You cut upstairs presently, and fig yourself out for Mrs. Rickaby's Pow-wow."

"Dixie!" said Lord Oakshott.

"Well, hoss," said Dixie.

"You said you would not."

"Well, then, I won't; only if you don't go up and rag out, I will kick up the most immortal old tar river Jerusalem

breakdown ever you heard. Molasses to a pineapple! I'll burst
the railings of your lot" (Vol. II, ch. 31).[8]

Eccentric scenes out of control spin throughout the novel—for
example, the one when Oakshott meets for the first time the newly
hired tutor, Mr. Whipple:

> Lord Oakshott went up to him at once, but he had not time
> to speak. Mr. Whipple said—
> "Lord Oakshott, I believe?"
> Oakshott said "Yes."
> "I thought that you or some of your people would have been
> here before. I have been kept waiting for a quarter of an
> hour."
> Lord Oakshott answered, "Let me look at you."
> Whipple set his face. It was a perfectly beardless face, but,
> as Oakshott saw at once, a very good one. He was very ugly,
> whereas Oakshott was very handsome. Oakshott looked at him,
> or rather *down* on him, for a few seconds, and then said—
> "Take off those ridiculous spectacles, and let me look at your
> eyes."
> Whipple did so, and Oakshott saw the grand magnificent
> smile which some of us know so well, come mantling over his
> face. Whipple spoke first.
> "Oakshott," he said, "you will do."
> "And I think that you will do also," said Oakshott. "Come,
> mount your horse and hold your tongue."
> "A thing I never did in my life," said Whipple.
> "Why have you come to *me*?" said Oakshott.
> "In order to be in the same house with Miss Clark," said
> Mr. Whipple, promptly. . . . "I am engaged to be married to
> her. . . ."
> "I see," said Lord Oakshott. "Do you know that I have been
> in love with Miss Clark for twenty-four hours, and that now I
> must get out again the best way I can."
> "Everybody always is in love with Miss Clark," said Mr.
> Whipple, "but she is never in love with any one but myself.
> I want to know—"
> "What?" said Oakshott.
> "I want to know about my cub. Is he good?"
> "How can you tell with a child?" said Oakshott (Vol. I, ch.
> 18).

8. The chapters in the first edition of *Oakshott Castle* are numbered con-
secutively throughout the three volumes.

One more scene of this sort will suffice to show the extent of Kingsley's uncontrolled imagination. This example is the lengthy scene in which Lady Marie Oakshott goes mad, after Lord Oakshott has just saved Sir Arthur from a shipwreck. Granby Dixon is Oakshott's friend. Hearing a shot fired by a coastguard boat in order to warn another ship of dangerous waters, Lady Oakshott

rose, and from that moment her intellect left her for ever. She had refused sin with Lord Oakshott, and she knew well that the rest of her life was doomed to the man who had beaten her and ill-treated her. . . .

Bang went another gun.

"This is from Fort Commorin," said Lady Oakshott. "Save your scalps, ladies—save your scalps and your virtue. These are not Apaches: these are Commanches—they always come from that side. Arthur, the creeping devils are upon us. I tell you that that was a gun from Fort Commorin. . . ."

"Lady Oakshott," said Dixie, holding her among the wondering fishermen, "there is no fort. We are in England. All that hideous time is past—past for ever. Please remember that there are no Commanches here. Why, Big Bear was killed; you must remember that. . . ."

"Commanches! Commanches!" screamed the unhappy lady. "Where is Big Bear? He is here. . . ."

In one instant the whole quiet little village rang with the horrible staccato of the Apache war-cry. . . .

"What noise is that?" said Lord Oakshott. "Tell the boys not to howl like that."

Alas! it was Lady Oakshott giving her wild Indian cry in the street.

She repeated it, more clearly and more terribly than before; it was unmistakable now.

Both men were out of bed in an instant, leaning on their dripping clothes with trembling fingers, and staggering as they did so.

Prostrate as they were before, two mere heaps of humanity, they had a preternatural strength now. It was very odd that both these men had been sane five minutes before. Oakshott knew that he had saved Arthur's life, and Arthur scarcely realized it. Arthur only half knew what had happened to him: that his son was found, and that his wife was in the first stage of hysterics. Though both of them were perfectly sane a minute before, they were both mad now. . . .

"Commanche! Commanche!" cried Sir Arthur. "Oakshott! Oakshott! see to Marie and Dixie. Where the devil are the carbines?"

"In the rack," said Oakshott; "I cleaned them when you were snoring, you fool. Look alive. Marie and Dixie, get your revolvers ready. I'll shoot you, my dears. There is one chance for Big Bear; he is not beyond the creek yet. I'll give it mouth."

He sent the Apache war-cry ringing through the rafters. It was answered feebly from a distance. It was the last ever heard of the unhappy Lady Oakshott.

Thereby proving that Oakshott was not Big Bear, but that some one else was. "What the deuce those four were up to in America," said Granby Dixon often, "I *can't* make out. They discovered the Arizoba Silver Mines, however, and so I have no right to inquire."

As I have not the wildest idea about what those four did in America, I am perfectly unable to assist Granby Dixon in any way whatever (Vol. III, ch. 47-48).

The reader is as confused as every one else.

When Kingsley was writing *Silcote of Silcotes*, he said that he did not want to include Mrs. Braddon's and Wilkie Collins' sensational elements in his work; *Oakshott Castle*, with its numerous tales of ghastly murders and suicides and scenes of madness and death, outsensationalizes both of those writers' novels. But, unlike the sensational writers, Kingsley does not use those elements for melodramatic tears or violence; bizarrely, they serve as a basis for humor, or, at least, what Kingsley intended as humor. At one point, for example, he relates the especially morbid tale of an unmarried woman who decapitated her lover, tied his long black beard around her newly born child's neck, and threw both the head and the baby into a moat. Kingsley as the narrator continues:

For my own part, I do not believe the story at all, because I do not see how you could tie a man's head round a baby's neck; and, moreover, Mrs. Prout's account of the matter is in the last degree vague, though she believes the story; and, indeed, I believe that Lord Oakshott has persuaded himself of it now, in fact ever since he wrote his poem [about it]. . . .

In Lord Oakshott's poem, Lady Florence drowns her baby in the moat by tying its father's head round its neck. How this could be done without putting the father's head in a cabbage-net, Granby cannot see; and Oakshott says not one word of the cabbage-net. Oakshott says—

> "A band round the father's throat,
> A band round the infant's chin;
> Away in the night to the moat,
> And toss them lightly in.

> The lilies will rock and toss
> Under the wind-driven rack,
> Beneath the sedges and moss,
> And I will come lightly back."

When Granby Dixon was getting Lord Oakshott's poems through the press for him, he found that this last line had been originally written—

> "And the ducks will waddle and quack."
>
> (Vol. II, ch. 19)

This story is too gruesome to be the basis for good humor, let alone Kingsley's absurdity.

Not only does this oil and water mixture of morbidity and absurdity permeate the novel, but Kingsley adds a final phantasmagoric scene in which he resuscitates his favorite characters from former novels. Charles Ravenshoe, Austin Elliot, and Lord Edward Barty are again gathered up from their respective novels and their group appearance in *Silcote of Silcotes.* Perversely, though, Kingsley has distorted them. The blind Lord Edward is changed only in appearance—"young, yet grey and partially bald," but Austin Elliot is obnoxiously priggish and Charles Ravenshoe, now Lord Ascot, is imbecilic. For a Kingsleyan, probably the most melancholy part of *Oakshott Castle* is Charles' appearance at the Ladies O'Briens' party:

> "Charles Ravenshoe," said Father Tiernay, "surely you remember Tiernay."
> "Tiernay the groom?" said Charles. . . . "We had Tiernay a groom once, and he went with us to the Crimea. I don't remember anything about Tiernay a priest."
> "Do you remember nothing about a black hare?" said the Father.
> "No, sir. I can remember nothing at all. My wife is not here, and I am all alone. I have come out to these ladies because they bid me. I can give no other answer. I can remember nothing unless I am at Ravenshoe."

"But you can remember the Light Cavalry charge?"

"To tell you the truth about it, My dear sir . . . my memory is utterly going. What did you ask me to remember?"

"The Light Cavalry charge."

"Well, you see, I got heavily hit. I got hit on the head, though I did not know it. You see, sir, that I am not bound to remember. I have left the army. While you stay in the army you are bound to remember, but I have left the army" (Vol. III, ch. 51).

When Lord Oakshott arrives at the party, Kingsley throws off any remaining credibility by having Oakshott say that Charles had not received the cut on the head at Balaclava but had been "hit with a tomahawk by a Blackfoot," after having fallen down "among the rattlesnakes." When a few pages later, Kingsley tells us that "if any one between the four winds of heaven cares about Charles Ravenshoe, they may console themselves by hearing the simple fact that he is quite well again, and that he had a long and affectionate interview with a friend of ours four months ago," the reader no longer knows what to believe; although this scene may reflect Kingsley's own self-doubts and inner turmoils, for the reader the whole situation has become too ridiculous.

Clearly, this incoherent novel projects Kingsley's frantic dreams. The idealistically imagined Sam Buckley, Charles Ravenshoe, and the host of other heroic lads have been replaced by the fantastically rich Lord Oakshott, exactly what Kingsley "should be if [he] had got the money." Besides being wealthy and generous, Oakshott is a talented and famous poet, an honored orator in the House of Lords, and a known and respected financial wizard on the stock market. Importantly, he is unencumbered by marital responsibilities: "You have no responsibilities if you are mad. But you will marry someday, and then you will have responsibilities" (Vol. III, ch. 51). In reality, during this time, Kingsley, the dreamer, was little more than a hack writer, publishing pieced-together sketches from his copybook, burdened with an ailing wife and mother-in-law, and beset on all sides by creditors. Furthermore, his great fear of inferiority, which probably became more acute as Charles won more acclaim, manifests itself in an intense feeling of persecution: he believed that the critics had turned against him. Besides invidiously comparing himself to George Eliot and Charles Dickens in the letter to George Craik, he now condescendingly criticizes the popularity of Charles Reade, whose novels he "can't read" (E., p. 187). For a writer so thin-skinned, so sensitive to harsh criticism, these cries of bravado only make more pathetic the over-bearing feeling of self-distrust that he was suffering. Oakshott's complete indifference to public opinion must have been a glorious fictional release for Kingsley.

As the public-life Oakshott pursues the adventures that the romantic Kingsley wishes, the private Oakshott psychologically reproduces the insecure Kingsley. All of Oakshott's irrational actions are directed toward one object: he is haunted by and lives for the unobtainable Marie Oakshott. She is his reason for his loving Dickie, his helping Arthur, his fantastic sacrifices. In the struggle to gain the object of his obsession, Oakshott exhibits himself ridiculously in the House of Lords, acts fanatically to right Arthur's wrongs, and wildly throws money to anyone who hints that he needs it. This release seems to be yet another form of the self-punishment—or self-justification—that suggested itself previously in Charles Ravenshoe's, Austin Elliot's, Erne Hillyar's and even Mathilde's desires to suffer unnecessarily in order to obtain their respective goals. Certainly, Kingsley's pursuits show him to be a man tormented by the driving thought that he had to prove himself. Early, his overindulgences at college and his quixotic Australian venture bear out his foolhardy attempt to demonstrate manliness. Then when his literary popularity lessened after his first successes, he worked more and more to please his public and critics by rewriting the formerly popular incidents, and, as Wolff asserts, "he strove to conform to his public's desire by giving it high-born heroes behaving perfectly splendidly."[9] Always in the background loom his brother Gerald's heroics, Charles' and George's achievements, and the long line of ancestral greatness, serving to prick Henry with a sense of his own failures. For Henry Kingsley, the goal of respectability and greatness was just as unobtainable as Oakshott's Marie. Undoubtedly while recognizing the futility of accomplishment as he still frantically pursued the goal Kingsley cathartically released his bitter frustrations in Oakshott's extravagances and eccentricities. Thus, instead of being the "legitimate fiction" that he accredited it to be, *Oakshott Castle* is such a farrago of wild dreams and uncontrolled imagination that only by using the most generous of definitions can we even call this work a novel.

9. Wolff, p. 215.

IX

1873-1876

SHORTLY AFTER the Kingsleys moved to No. 29 Fortess Terrace, Kentish Town, the death of Henry's mother in April, 1873, temporarily alleviated their financial difficulties. Also in 1872, before the move, a more distant relative had died, leaving Henry or Sarah a legacy of £50 and appointing him executor of the will. Legal troubles, however, materialized, and Kingsley was unable "to prove the will" immediately (E., p. 186). But, apparently, the case was settled around the time of the elderly Mrs. Kingsley's death. Thus, for a brief while, Kingsley's financial situation was brighter, and he rejoiced in his affluence when he told Craik that "in my altered circumstances I shall of course write more at large" (E., p. 189). Kingsley even had time to supplement the money from his inheritance by taking an occasional pupil.

The countrified Kentish Town offered him more scenic inducements for writing than had the gloomy house in Edinburgh or the city streets of London. Across the road from the line of late Georgian houses on Fortess Terrace was an open green, where Kingsley could walk and describe in his copybook the view of Hampstead Heath and the wooded areas of Kenwood and Highgate. Boys playing cricket on the green and milkmaids and watercress women from nearby farms selling their products were characters he could include in his future novels.

When Henry wanted to escape from the shouts of the vendors or the cricket players—or possibly from Sarah—he found sanctuary at Southwood Lane, Highgate, where his brother George lived from

1863–79. Although George spent most of his time traveling with various members of the peerage to foreign lands, his wife, Mary, always welcomed her brother-in-law and set up for him a study in the attic, where he could write undisturbed. Set back from the road and embowered by trees, the house had a large garden which Henry loved, and on sunny days he basked there, "enveloped in a blue haze of tobacco smoke," and relived his Australian days for his adoring eleven-year-old niece, Mary, and other children, telling them "such tales of corroborees, black snakes, and bushrangers as would have made sleep a curse to you for a week to come."[1] In many ways, Kingsley's short time at Highgate resembled his pleasant bachelor days at Eversley, thirteen or so years earlier, when he had doted on Charles' son Maurice.

George and Charles Kingsley were both in America during 1874, George hunting bears in the Rocky Mountains, and Charles lecturing. Never estranged from Henry, George kept Charles informed of their younger brother's state of affairs, but Charles, although pleased with Henry's contentment, was still apprehensive that it would not last. Writing to his wife on June 18, 1874, Charles expressed anxiety lest Henry or especially Sarah should be worrying her with new financial difficulties.[2]

Henry's contentment was not long lasting, but not for the reason Charles had anticipated. Kingsley was dying from cancer of the trachea and tongue. Whether he knew the exact nature of his illness in 1874 is doubtful, although S. M. Ellis asserts that the doctors broke the news to Kingsley at that time, informing him that "he could only anticipate a few more months of life." According to Ellis, this news prompted Kingsley to leave Kentish Town in order to spend his last days in the country, which he loved. Thus, concludes Ellis, when Henry stood at Charles' grave at Eversley on January 28, 1875, he was well aware of his own killing disease.[3] But contradictorily, Mrs. Sarah Kingsley wrote to George Bentley, publisher of Kingsley's *Reginald Hetherege*, on April 30, 1876, after their move to Cuckfield, that Henry knew "he is in a very dangerous state but the doctors do not wish him to know the nature or hopelessness of his disease. . . . He has been ill for over two months but only three weeks ago the serious nature of his

1. George Kingsley, *Notes*, p. 38.
2. R. B. Martin, *Charles Kingsley's American Notes* (Princeton, 1958), p. 52.
3. Pp. 108–9.

illness was ascertained."[4] In view of Ellis' failure to cite the source
of his information and the unavailability of Mrs. Kingsley's letter
in 1931, when Ellis wrote his book, as well as the tone of Kingsley's
letters postmarked Cuckfield, Mrs. Kingsley's account would seem
to be closer to the truth.

Whatever the case, the Kingsleys left Kentish Town late in 1874
and settled in the little Sussex village, where they rented an old—
possibly fifteenth-century—timbered and gabled cottage, "The At-
trees," named after an old Sussex family. Not a remarkable house
architecturally, it was, nevertheless, picturesque with its oak-beamed
walls and ceilings and its leaded, latticed windows.

The trip to Eversley for Charles' funeral was one of the few occasions Kingsley left Cuckfield during the last years of his life,
and that trip was a sad one for him. Just eight years before,
Kingsley had told Macmillan, "Charles is an *angel* of a man. I know
no one like him at all" (E., p. 165). Then gradually came the
period of heart-breaking estrangement, and, apparently, Charles had
died without a reconciliation between the two brothers. There can
be no doubt that as this gentle, sensitive man stood by his brother's
grave that January morning, he was filled with self-accusations
for the difficulties he had caused first his family and then, specifically, Charles. But as he noticed the presence of so many
celebrities who attested Charles' importance, his sorrow turned
into self-pity and depression when he compared his accomplish-
ments with those of Charles. Overhearing one naval officer present
say, "I have been at many state funerals, but never did I see such
a sight as Charles Kingsley's,"[5] Henry must have asked himself,
"How many such people would come to my funeral?"

When Kingsley returned to Cuckfield, he had sixteen months of
life remaining, and those he spent mostly in semi-seclusion. He was
courteous and pleasant with the Cuckfieldians, who "were very
proud" to have the Kingsleys among them,[6] but they sensed
Kingsley's desire to be left alone. The Reverend Henry Holling-
worth, curate of Cuckfield during those months, remembered seeing
Kingsley at early Communion almost every Sunday, and neighbors
saw him take long walks through the Sussex countryside, always
with his copybook in hand.

4. Wolff, p. 221.
5. *Charles Kingsley: His Letters and Memories of His Life*, II, 463–64.
6. "Letter to the Editor," *Sussex County Magazine*, IV (April, 1930), 340.

Whether it was this countryside that temporarily revived Kingsley's descriptive power, one cannot say, but his rendering of Cuckfield in "Two Old Sussex Worthies" has flashes of his early artistry:

On the rib which divides the infant Adur from the infant Ouse, stands Cuckfield, from the hill above which you can see sixty miles, south, south-west, and south-east; or turning back and looking northwards, you can see St. Leonards, Tilgate, and Ashdown forests, hanging like a purple cloud with gold and green openings. It lies lower than Horsted Keynes, from which place it is distant about five miles, and is supposed to be the healthiest town in England, particularly by the inhabitants. Coming to the summit of the steep little street, on the old London road, the traveller sees the rather steep little street drop suddenly below him, and in the distance over the tops of the houses the pearl grey wall of the downs, between him and the sea, cut almost to the zenith by the tall spire of the church. Reaching the churchyard he finds that he is at the edge of a vast thickly wooded valley, about nine miles broad, bounded on the farther side by the long high mass of the downs, rising to heights of over eight hundred feet; far to the left is the back of Beechy Head, far to the right the hills beyond Chichester. The church is *one* of the most beautiful in England, cared for like a jewel, and the wondrous old houses abutting into it would be highly remarkable elsewhere. In short, there are few places like Cuckfield churchyard; but still more remarkable than church or churchyard is Cuckfield Place, close by, with the finest lime avenue of its length in England, its Tudor house, and its deer park, most artistically broken into glade and lawn: the dearly loved haunt of Shelley, and the original of the "Rookwood" of Harrison Ainsworth (*Fireside Studies*, Vol. I, pp. 158–59).

The Kingsleys must have taken at least one holiday at Brighton—probably in the summer of 1875—where he delighted in meeting Percy Shelley's two elderly sisters, who lived there "with their diamonds, their pictures and there [*sic*] reminiscences of their brother and others." Talking of their friendship and their desire to read the installments of his novel *The Grange Garden*, Kingsley asked the editor of *St. James Magazine*, in which the story was appearing, to send the women issues of the magazine and to "con-

tinue to send it chalking up the expense behind the door to me."[7]
This spurt of sincere generosity on Kingsley's part seems sadly
illogical when one recalls his endless *kyrielle* of financial pleadings.

Most of the time, however, Kingsley spent indoors writing. In
these last years, both at Kentish Town and Cuckfield, he still wrote
prolifically, producing three novels, *Reginald Hetherege, Number
Seventeen,* and *The Grange Garden*; some short stories; a series of
literary essays, *Fireside Studies*; and a children's novella, *The Mystery of the Island,* which was published posthumously.[8]

This last work is an improbable tale dealing with the adventures of a brave sea captain and his equally courageous son in
Australasia and South America. Among the great coincidences and
flat characters in the story, however, are two amusing children,
Ethel, aged twelve, and Mathilde, aged eight, who—influenced by
their reading of Foxe's *Book of Martyrs*—set the house on fire while
playing that they are Mary Tudor and the Pope's legate and burning
their doll, a "wretch," an "enemy to religion and to the peace of
Europe." Delightfully, Ethel explains her reasons to Captain Killick,
a rich and influential sailor:

> "The fact is, that we were burning Tilly's doll for a heretic.
> We have hung her four times and she would not repent, and
> so at last we handed her over to the secular arm. Even then
> she would not burn without setting the house on fire. She
> was a regular beast, and I am glad she is burnt."
> Captain Killick asked, "What were her faults?"
> "Well, she would never go to sleep at nights since we broke
> the thing in her back which made her eyes shut . . . to find out
> how it was done" (ch. 5).

The startling fact about *Fireside Studies* is that this collection
of essays is well written, exceptionally so when one considers the
quality of Kingsley's last novels. Kingsley's hope that this book
"may do my name good"[9] was realized. *The Times* wrote that
"We may say that 'Fireside Studies' show Mr. Kingsley at his very
best," and the *Spectator* ended its favorable review with "The
reader of these brightly-written papers may be inclined to regret

7. Wolff, p. 220.
8. Mary McLeod asserted that Kingsley employed a Cuckfieldian as his secretary, a "big, dark young woman, who was called Barbara Allen," p. 252.
9. Wolff, p. 219.

that Mr. Kingsley did not give more of his time to literary criticism. As a critic, he possessed one virtue which will cover many defects— a sincere and generous appreciation of all noble work."[10]

The literary figures discussed in this collection are Addison and Steele, Andrew Marvell, Ben Jonson, Christopher Marlowe, Fletcher and Beaumont, and Sir Philip Sidney. Kingsley had worked on a few of these essays over the years and had published the Sidney one in the *New Quarterly Magazine* and, as he tells his readers in an introductory note, a couple of the others "anonymously, but the larger portion of the book has never appeared before."[11]

In these essays, Kingsley does not merely breeze over the writers with a secondhand knowledge; he visits with them familiarly and sometimes very perceptively as he contrasts the "Fathers of the *Spectator,*" Fletcher with Beaumont, and Marlowe with Jonson, and both Marlowe and Jonson with Shakespeare. He reveals his admiration for Addison; he proclaims his dislike of Swift and of Pope (but he "was a very great poet"); he qualifies his appreciation of Jonson: "On the whole, the best thing we can liken him to is an English meadow with a flower here and there; when you do get a flower, however, it is a real gem."

As this collection, his novels, and, indeed, *The Boy in Grey* clearly show, Kingsley had read not only the greats and near-greats but the lesser figures of the English literary world from Quarles' *Emblems* to Milton through all of Dickens and Thackeray to Carlyle and Tennyson. Even Mrs. Mary Martha Sherwood's *Infant Pilgrims* and Bulwer Lytton's *Zanoni* impressed him sufficiently that he included references to them in his novels, and, without prejudice, he praised "The Dream of Gerontius," the poem by Cardinal Newman, his brother's main theological adversary. Kingsley's expressions, moreover, are those of a reader who has been captivated by what he has read, and he readily surrendered himself to his favorite author or character.

Of the last three novels, little praise can be given to *Number Seventeen* and *The Grange Garden*; both are dull imbroglios filled with impossible and undeveloped characters. By this time of his life Kingsley's imagination and artistic judgment had been numbed

10. April 24, 1876, 4d; XLIX (June 24, 1876), 803–4.
11. For identification of the essays published anonymously see the entries under *Temple Bar* in Bibliography.

by years of frustration. He was worn out before the fatal cancer killed him.

Although *Number Seventeen* does not focus on any one main character, much of the action revolves around Mary Arnaud, the unrecognized widow of Iltyd Arnaud, the younger son of the very rich Lord Festiniog. To support herself, she sets up a millinery shop at No. 17, Hartley Street, where on the second floor lives George Drummond, the supposed son of the lawyer James Drummond, but, in reality, the legitimate son of Iltyd and Mary. Years earlier James Drummond had told Mary that her child had died when both of them were ill with fever; he had hoped that in her loneliness she would marry him. Twenty odd years later—even after Mary has finally discovered the truth about her son—James is still pressing his proposal. Mixed up with all of that foolishness is Lord Festiniog's concern for a document which he says will ruin him but, in the end, turns out to be worthless. Illogically, however, he has saved the document for over fifty years. Still more improbabilities are scattered throughout the novel.

The Grange Garden, published just four months before Kingsley's death, begins well enough with Lady Madeleine Howard and Lady Alice Browne, two rich old ladies who had retired from the world of society to live in the country.[12] For ten years they have lived undisturbed, but, according to the villagers, the Grange has become haunted: "Farmer Joyce, a most respectable man, with as much imagination as one of his own haystacks, saw the ghost: it was in black, and passed him without any sound. Several other people saw it, but they were contradictory in their accounts of it. Some said that it was dressed in white, some in black. They were both right: the ghost was dressed differently at different times, but farmer Joyce on one occasion utterly horrified the village; *for he saw both the ghosts together*" (Vol. I, ch. 4).

The ghosts are really Lady Madeleine's nephew and niece, Lionel and Clara Branscombe. Believing that his wife, Edith, was unfaithful, Lionel had fought a duel with Edith's cousin, killing him and becoming "a speechless mass of humanity" himself. Clara has rescued her brother and has taken him to the Grange to find "such

12. Kingsley's models for the two old ladies were "Lady Eleanor Butler and Sarah Ponsonby, who withdrew in the 1770's to live together in solitude at Plasnewydd in the vale of Llangollen, where various distinguished visitors sought them out, and they themselves achieved fame as 'the most celebrated virgins in Europe'" (Wolff, p. 220n).

peace as was possible for them." The reader is given all of that information plus further background about Lionel and Clara within the first nine chapters. Then complexities materialize quickly and abundantly as Kingsley introduces Lionel's two cantankerous brothers, Arthur and George, who continually bait each other; the villainous Dr. James Cross, who was the instigator of the false accusations against Edith and is now intent upon poisoning Arthur for money and placing the blame on George; Edith, who has emerged from a convent to live at the Grange; and Robert Struan, the Branscombe's illegitimate half-brother. Although there is a real Struan, the one the reader meets during most of the novel is the miraculously cured Lionel, who is impersonating his half-brother. Even Kingsley gets confused with all of this intrigue. Attempting, for example, to develop the steps in which Lionel impersonated Struan, Kingsley at one time places Lionel (disguised as Struan) in the park where he meets Dr. Cross. After having Lionel offer Cross a cigar, Kingsley asserts, "Struan knew, possibly from his colonial experiences in countries where men smoke but seldom drink, that tobacco was more apt to open a man's mouth than wine" (Vol. II, ch. 15). But Lionel, impersonating Struan and having never been in the colonies, would have known no such thing.

Reginald Hetherege, written during the short time after the death of the elderly Mrs. Kingsley and before the move to Cuckfield, reflects a more peaceful Kingsley. An overabundance of characters along with an excess of superfluous scenes gravely mar the novel, but *Reginald Hetherege* is Kingsley's best book since *Mademoiselle Mathilde*. Gone are the utter recklessness and absurdities of *Stretton* and *Oakshott Castle* and the excessive reduplications found in *The Harveys*. And unlike *Old Margaret* and *Valentin*, *Reginald Hetherege* returns to the depiction of the moneyed class that Kingsley can usually handle, lovingly if not competently. Also, possibly with nostalgia, Kingsley recalls his one great adventure by including a brief Australian episode, in which the kidnapped George Hetherege is lost in the bush. Although Kingsley controls the scene well, the kangaroo hunt that initiates the abduction, as well as the description of the countryside, is just an echo of his early power.

The starting point of the novel is Thomas Digby's eccentric will, which Kingsley based on the famous real-life will of Peter Thellusson (April 2, 1797). After bequeathing his property to "my friend the devil, for his sole use and benefit during his lifetime, hoping that he will repent," Digby provides that if the devil fails to appear to claim the property the money is to be placed in the English funds until Digby's "four principal relations, Hetherege, Talbot, Simpson, or Murdock, *or any of their male descendant living at the time of his death*," are dead. At that appointed time, the money is to be divided among the living male descendants born since Digby's death.

To the disgust of the heirs'-to-be progenitors, Reginald Hetherege, "*the wretched little swindler*," was born two days before Digby's death. Thus, the novel traces Reginald's long life of eighty years: his "most magnificent blunder" in being born when he was; his poverty; his life with his son, Charles, and grandson, George; his reversal of fortune and subsequent life as a country landlord; his loss of fortune; and his final happiness and death. Although referring constantly to the will and the continued lawsuit over it, Kingsley does little with the latter. He is more concerned with Reginald's Job-like struggle through life.

Lacking the heroic dreams of Kingsley's usual boys, the matured Reginald, nevertheless, differs little from those heroes in his nobleness, kindness, and child-like innocence. Moreover, he shares with them that ubiquitous obsession for atonement, but for Reginald the suffering assumes the form of self-abnegation: "Whatever goes wrong it is his fault; he has no powers of self-assertion, no powers of self-defence, when he knows he is in the right" (Vol. III, ch. 3). The humble Reginald seems to represent just another step in Kingsley's shifting dream world. From his romantic lads through to the fabulous Oakshott, Kingsley has arrived during his last years at the "gentle, biddable, unselfish" Reginald, who, like himself, has been troubled during his life by a myriad of misfortunes and plagued by his own "weakness and errors." Fictionally, though, Kingsley still dreams the ideal. Missing from the projection are the humiliating pleas for money and the indignant denunciations against the unfairness of the world that loomed so terribly during Kingsley's last years. Reginald had "lived without blame," honorable and kind during his remarkable successes and patient and noble in his failures. Reginald's last words before his peaceful death could well have been the sentiment that Kingsley hoped would be applied to himself: "And always think of me at my best. Don't think of me as a clever man; I have been that, but then I was at my worst; think of me as I am now—one who never willingly injured anybody, a mere child" (Vol. III, ch. 22). Fittingly, the last glimpse that we have of Kingsley transmits such an impression.

Hearing that Kingsley was very ill, Anne Thackeray and Leslie Stephen went together to Cuckfield to see their friend, and the former wrote: "We walked from the station along a village road with trees on either side to a low sort of farm-house cottage where the Kingsleys were then staying. Mrs. Kingsley was lying down upstairs, he was alone to receive us in the latticed sitting-room. He was himself, and yet different from himself; his eager manner was gone; he was very gentle, but he seemed collected and cheerful only. 'They tell me I am going to die,' he said; 'I can't believe it, I don't *feel* like a dying man.' He said this quite naturally, with a sort of simplicity and courage which were a part of all his life. He went on to talk of books and every-day things; he seemed pleased that we should have come to see him, and made us ashamed by making so much of it. Very soon afterwards we heard that he was gone."[13]

On the morning of May 24, 1876, Henry Kingsley, aged forty-six, died. The next morning a twenty-two line obituary appeared in *The Times* (Charles had rated three full-length columns), and two days later, on Saturday, May 27, an announcement of the funeral: "The Late Mr. Henry Kingsley—We are asked to state that the funeral will be solemnized at noon on Monday next at Cuckfield Churchyard. The train which leaves Victoria Station at 10:05 would reach Hayward's Heath in time. One, too, leaves London-bridge just about the same hour."

How many people rode those trains to Cuckfield for the funeral is unknown, but, although a large number of friends and villagers gathered in the churchyard to pay their respects, Henry Kingsley's funeral did not resemble a state one. Mr. Moberly, the vicar, and his two curates performed the simple service, and Malcolm Lawson, from the Chelsea Apostolic Church, played the organ. Villagers carried the coffin, covered with a purple pall, to the large grave a short distance from the church. Henry's only surviving brother, George, and his wife; his two cousins, Mr. Eversley and his niece, Miss Murray-Allen; George Craik, representing the Macmillans; Edwin Waugh, the "Lancashire poet"; and other mourners fol-

13. Clement Shorter, "Introduction," p. xxii.

lowed, each with a spray of lilies-of-the-valley, which they threw into the grave at the close of the service. Sarah Kingsley placed two wreaths of lilies on the grave. Shortly after Henry's death, there was erected over the grave a low wooden cross on which was inscribed "Entered into rest on the Vigil of the Ascension, May the 24th 1876, Henry Kingsley, aged 46 years. R.I.P. In Thy Presence is the Fullness of Joy."

On May 26, 1876, *The Sussex Daily News* had written a more eloquent memorial for Kingsley. After praising his high culture, general knowledge, and pleasant humor, the tribute ended by describing Kingsley as "a fair, frank, hearty man, pleasant to look upon, always kind, cheery, helpful and hopeful. Though he was a middle-aged man in years, yet he had a boy's pure, fresh, generous heart."

A week later, the *Spectator*, which had severely criticized so many of his novels, wrote that although "Mr. Henry Kingsley was only one of the 'might have beens' . . . the 'might have been' in him was so very good, that we are unwilling to let him pass away as one of the mere crowd, unnoticed and unregarded." "No one," the obituary ends, "can read his books without feeling that his love for his kind has increased, that his fortitude has been strengthened, and that he has been encouraged by no mean help to prefer before all things in life to do the work God has given him to perform. He never wrote a book with a moral, and never drew a character far above the average, but a brisk and clear north wind of sentiment— sentiment that braces instead of enervating—blows through all his works, and makes all their readers at once healthier and more glad."[14]

Kingsley's sad story, however, does not end with his death. As poverty had haunted and humiliated him through life, it followed his name beyond the grave. The £450 Kingsley had left maintained Sarah for just a short time. On July 4, writing to the publisher George Bentley, Sarah ended her note with, "I feel the emptiness of the house more & more and have in addition to my sorrow much pecuniary trouble—But I would not have Hal back to the suffering & trials of this world."[15] Four months later Sarah's plight must have become more desperate, for, on November 7, the following advertisement appeared in *The Times*: "Henry Kingsley—This well-

14. XLIX (June 3, 1876), 706–7.
15. Wolff, pp. 221–22.

known author, having been quite unable to make any provisions for his widow, a fund is being raised on her behalf." Places for subscriptions were then listed. Pained by the fact "that a name so pleasantly familiar should figure in such an appeal," a Mr. Edward Jenkins, of South Kensington, inserted his advertisement in *The Times* on November 9, requesting all of Kingsley's fellow writers and "the multitude who owe him for so many hours of instruction and amusement" to donate to a "Guinea Subscription Fund" which Jenkins had set up and to which some of personal friends had already subscribed. Kingsley would have been gratified by the response of his admirers and friends, but how stricken he would have been by the public disclosure of his failure.

The pathos of the story continued for the next forty-six years as Sarah Kingsley lived without a definite income. In 1879 she wrote a two-volume novel, *Dead Lilies*, which she alleged was written by Cecil Haselwood (her maiden surname) and edited by Mrs. H. Kingsley, and in 1884 she published an eight-page pamphlet entitled *Missions and Missionaries*. Intermittently she made both private and public pleas for assistance. In 1907, for example, she appealed to the Royal Literary Fund, through a Mrs. Sigand, for a pension. To Mrs. Sigand, George Meredith, then President of the Society of Authors, replied on June 11 of that year: "The presentation of the sad case of the widow, coming from you, as a member of the Society, direct to the Secretary, may have a better effect. Write it fully, but plainly. Henry Kingsley has a claim on our literature. A pension, I fear, is precluded by the rules. A donation there may be well. Write immediately. You can, if you please, say what I think of H. Kingsley."[16] It is possible that George Kingsley, who lived to 1892, may have helped to support Sarah in the years immediately following his brother's death, but there are no records of any assistance to her from the Kingsley family.

Moving frequently and seemingly without purpose, Mrs. Kingsley finally settled at Folkeston, where she was active in temperance and other social causes, preserving, we are told, "her forceful and assertive character to the end." According to her neighbors, "her behaviour was eccentric and often antagonistic to the townspeople."[17] She died on August 12, 1922, at the age of eighty, and because of

16. Ellis, p. 110*n.* For J. M. Barrie's interest in Mrs. Kingsley, see Janet Dunbar, *J. M. Barrie, The Man Behind the Image* (Boston, 1970), p. 173.
17. *Ibid.*

her husband's fame, she was given a nineteen-line obituary in *The
Times* (only three less lines than her husband's). Probably because
of her poverty, her body was not moved to Cuckfield to be buried
beside that of her husband's. Nor did she make any provisions to
have Henry's grave maintained.

In 1926, Canon Wilson, vicar of Cuckfield at that time, received
a letter from a Mr. Arthur French, of Victoria, Australia, stating
that the Melbourne *Argus* had described the "crazy, broken-down
condition" of Henry Kingsley's grave, and offering some money to
erect a more fitting memorial because he had "admiring memories
of [Kingsley's] books, 'Geoffry Hamlyn,' 'Ravenshoe,' and others."[18]
Four years later, the Henry Kingsley Fund was organized by Arthur
Quiller-Couch, Michael Sadleir, and others to erect such a memorial
to Kingsley at Cuckfield. Finally, in 1931, fifty-five years after
Kingsley's death, the wooden cross, the only monument that had
designated Henry Kingsley's untended grave, was replaced by a
tall, rather simple memorial stone, designed by Arnold Whittick.
On one side of the monument was chiseled biographical information and on the other side "To The Memory Of Henry Kingsley
(1830–1876) This Monument Was Erected In 1931 By Some Of
His Admirers." Around the flat base were listed titles of eleven of
Kingsley's novels. But like the weather-beaten wooden cross it
replaced, this stone stands today, symbolically like the man's reputation itself, neglected and coated with fungus; many of the letters
are almost illegible.

18. Mary McLeod, p. 253.

Conclusion

THE STORY of Henry Kingsley's artistic decline does not support George Saintsbury's explanation that Kingsley merely depleted "his 'pocket' of invention, rich while it lasted, but definitely exhaustible."[1] That explanation is too pat. Nor is S. M. Ellis' assertion that Kingsley's financial difficulty alone caused the decline totally satisfactory.[2] Ellis, for the most part, ignored the psychological tensions that contributed greatly to the swift deterioration of Kingsley's literary powers. Michael Sadleir's theory that only a progressively worsening mental abnormality explains Kingsley's ruin cannot, however, be dismissed as readily as the other two explanations because three supporting points that Sadleir made need to be discussed. For proof that a severe mental disorder quickened Kingsley's decline, Sadleir offers the "queer oblivion to which the family chroniclers deliberately condemned" Kingsley; Leslie Stephen's curt memorial notice in the *Dictionary of National Biography;* and the illogicality of *Stretton, Valentin,* and *Oakshott Castle.*[3]

The main chronicle in question that allegedly condemned Henry Kingsley to oblivion is Mrs. Charles Kingsley's biography of her husband, which ignores Henry entirely. A critic, however, must be circumspect when he deals with this highly biased work. First, it must be seen in the light in which it was written: a wife's loving account of her husband's public life, especially his Christian in-

1. *Collected Essays and Papers,* II, 357.
2. P. 114.
3. *Edinburgh Review,* pp. 347–48.

169

fluence on the times. Charles' parents and his other brothers are barely mentioned in the biography, since they played little part in that public life. Mrs. Kingsley's book was, as R. B. Martin states in his fine study of Charles Kingsley, "the Victorian conception of biography, or rather the conception held by Victorian widows."[4]

Second, Fanny Kingsley's personal prejudice toward Henry must be considered. Both Charles and his wife abhorred Sarah Kingsley, and both disliked and resented Henry's persistent requests for money. Both probably believed that Henry drank too heavily. Fanny's dislike for her brother-in-law, moreover, had begun earlier than with his marriage. Una Pope-Hennessy, in her life of Charles Kingsley, asserts that Fanny Kingsley had been extremely displeased in 1858 when Henry, penniless and with a common Australian accent, had arrived home in England just when her carefully planned campaign to build up Charles "as a person to be reckoned with as an author unique in his own line" seemed to be achieving success. And, even worse, Henry had written a novel which Charles had proclaimed to be better than her beloved *Westward Ho!*[5] Her dislike for Henry grew during his years of begging and deepened when the two brothers became estranged. Since she published her book only twenty-three months after Charles' death and seven months after Henry's, whose funeral she did not attend, it seems more reasonable to say that she achieved a belated revenge for what she considered past humiliating experiences than that she purposely built a stone wall around a family skeleton.

As for the other members of the family maintaining a guarded silence, Sadleir himself contradicts his assertion when he admits that Mary Kingsley and Maurice Kingsley published recollections of their uncle; Sadleir, in fact, quotes from Maurice's reminiscences in his own essay. In her memoir of her father, Mary referred often and lovingly to Henry, acclaiming his literary gift. Maurice not only published his personal account of his beloved uncle in Charles Scribner's magazine *The Book Buyer* but reprinted it as an introduction for Scribner's new edition of Henry Kingsley's novels in 1895. Also, Dr. George Kingsley, who outlived both his famous brothers, has been reported by G. C. Moore Smith as replying to his question, "You are, I think, a brother of Charles Kingsley?" "I am a brother of Henry Kingsley! Henry was the great man, not

4. *Dust of Combat*, p. 219.
5. Pp. 173–74.

Charles."[6] Whether Dr. Kingsley's known lack of sympathy for Charles' religious principles prompted his strong and partial answer is unimportant; he, at least, displayed no hesitancy in speaking of his younger brother.

The question, however, of Leslie Stephen's perfunctory entry in the *Dictionary of National Biography* is more difficult to answer. With no proof to the contrary, it must be assumed that Stephen himself and not a subordinate wrote the biography. Containing only the most meager facts about the novelist's life, the account is void of recollections and criticism which Henry's personal friend should not only have had in mind but been eager to convey. Stephen's sister-in-law, Anne Thackeray (then Lady Ritchie), gladly wrote her recollections of Kingsley to Clement Shorter for publication shortly after the *Dictionary of National Biography* was published. Since Stephen never publicly explained his brevity, this question must remain an unsolvable literary puzzle. But other solutions, such as editorial deadlines, Stephen's personal problems, instead of Kingsley's mental condition, may be offered for Stephen's brevity.

Stretton, Valentin, and *Oakshott Castle* are indeed incoherent and illogical, and, one may add, so are other novels as well. But a mental abnormality—one so severe that Kingsley's family and friends allegedly sought to hide the fact of it from history—is, as I have shown in my study, not the reason for their jumbled condition. On the whole, Kingsley's novels were good or, at least, sensible when he was happy. After his early literary successes, Kingsley became too preoccupied with personal problems and too concerned with critical disapproval to develop his own special gifts. Instead of firmly entrenching himself as a writer, he did the opposite. By trying to write different types of novels, he turned out many mediocre ones, filled with glaring illogicalities. The poor reception of most of these novels, in turn, intensified his financial problems and personal distress. In addition to his other problems, Kingsley had to combat a feeling of inferiority. Looming before him were thoughts of his own insignificance compared to the importance of his brothers and the prestige of his ancestors. And because of the harsh critical attacks on his novels, he was not even sure of his own talent. This treadmill led to *Stretton, Valentin,* and, finally, *Oakshott Castle.*

6. "Letter to the Editor," *Times Literary Supplement,* January 9, 1930, p. 28.

Kingsley, of course, was emotionally affected by his frustrations. Few men as sensitive as he would not be. But in 1873, when he received an inheritance and, thus, some financial security, he was able to write the more restrained *Reginald Hetherege* and the perceptive *Fireside Studies*. Those works would not have been possible if a disorder had gripped his mental capacities in 1873. His last two novels, it is true, are inferior, but they are not the works of a mentally abnormal man; they are the products of a physically tired and ill man.

Sentimental though it may be, the most appropriate epitaph that can be applied to Henry Kingsley is one which he himself wrote about Daniel Defoe in his preface to *Robinson Crusoe*: "The only rest which his fevered spirit ever had, was in writing his romances and in his grave."

Bibliography

I. Primary Sources

A. First Editions and Serializations

The Recollections of Geoffry Hamlyn. 3 vols. Macmillan and Co., 1859.
Dedication: "To My Father and Mother this book The Fruit of so many weary years of separation is dedicated with the deepest love and reverence."

Ravenshoe. 3 vols. Macmillan and Co., 1862.
Dedication: "To my brother Charles Kingsley I dedicate this tale In token of a love which only grows stronger as we both get older."
Serialization: *Macmillan's Magazine*, January, 1861, to July, 1862.

Austin Elliot. 2 vols. Macmillan and Co., 1863.
Dedication: "To the Reverend John Mill Chanter and Charlotte Chanter, this book is affectionately dedicated by their brother, the Author."
Serialization: *La Revue des Deux Mondes*, mars, 1864 (translated by E. D. Forgues).

The Hillyars and the Burtons. 3 vols. Macmillan and Co., 1865.
Dedication: "This Tale is Dedicated to My Wife."
Serialization: *Macmillan's Magazine*, November, 1863, to April, 1865.

Leighton Court. 2 vols. Macmillan and Co., 1866.
Dedication: "To my brother George this country tale is most affectionately dedicated."

Silcote of Silcotes. 3 vols. Macmillan and Co., 1867.
Serialization: *Macmillan's Magazine*, July, 1866, to September, 1867.

Mademoiselle Mathilde. 3 vols. Bradbury, Evans and Co., 1868.
Dedication: "To my wife and Miss Thackeray, in memory of the pleasant summer days during which the better parts of it were written."
Serialization: *The Gentleman's Magazine*, April, 1867, to May, 1868.

Robinson Crusoe, edited with a biographical introduction. Macmillan and Co., 1868.

Tales of Old Travel Re-Narrated. Macmillan and Co., 1869.

Stretton. 3 vols. Tinsley Brothers, 1869.
Serialization: *The Broadway Annual*, September, 1868, to August, 1869.

The Boy in Grey. Strahan and Co., 1871.
Serialization: *Good Words for the Young*, March–September, 1869; June–July, 1870.

The Lost Child. Macmillan and Co., 1871.

Hetty. Bradbury, Evans and Co., 1871.
Serialization: *Once a Week*, February–May, 1869.

Hetty and Other Stories. Bradbury, Evans and Co., 1871.
The other stories are "The Two Cadets," "Our Brown Passenger," and "Seeking your Fortune."
Serialization: For previous publication of "The Two Cadets" see *Magazines*.

Old Margaret. 2 vols. Tinsley Brothers, 1871.

Hornby Mills and Other Stories. 2 vols. Tinsley Brothers, 1872.
Dedication: "Dedicated by Henry to Barbara [Barbara Murray-Allen Mackay, his cousin]."
Serialization: For previous publication of the nine stories see *Magazines*.

Valentin: A French Boy's Story of Sedan. 2 vols. Tinsley Brothers, 1872.
Serialization: *Every Boy's Annual*, 1873.

The Harveys. 2 vols. Tinsley Brothers, 1872.

Oakshott Castle: Being the Memoirs of an Eccentric Nobleman. 3 vols. Macmillan and Co., 1873.

Reginald Hetherege. 3 vols. Richard Bentley and Son, 1874.

Number Seventeen. 2 vols. Chatto and Windus, 1875.

The Grange Garden. 3 vols. Chatto and Windus, 1876.
Serialization: *St. James Magazine*, April, 1875, to August, 1876.

Fireside Studies. 2 vols. Chatto and Windus, 1876.
Dedication: "To the Earl of Pembroke and Montgomery. My Lord,—To use the words of another, 'I bring you here a nosegay of a few culled flowers, with nothing of my own but the string which binds them.' Henry Kingsley."
Serialization: For previous publication of four of the seven studies see *Magazines*.

The Mystery of the Island. William Mullan and Son, 1877.

B. Short Stories and Essays Published in Magazines

The Argosy
"New Year's Day at Windsor, 1327: Sir Henry Mullory's Story," i (January, 1866), 173–85. [*Hornby Mills and Other Stories*]
"Hornby Mills Garden," i (April, 1866), 394–407. [*Hornby Mills and Other Stories*]
"Why Lady Hornbury's Ball was Postponed," xii (September, 1871), 200–219. [*Hornby Mills and Other Stories*]
"Miss Milton," xviii (November, 1874), 352–60.
"Our Widow," xx (August, 1875), 111–25.

Belgravia
"The Mystery of St. Remi," xxxiii (Holiday Number, 1877), 1-21.

The Dark Blue
"Jackson of Paul's," I (May, 1871), 302–13; (June, 1871), 456–65. [*Hornby Mills and Other Stories*]

The Fortnightly Review
"The Discovery of the Albert N'Yanza; a review of *The Albert N'Yanza, Great Basin of the Nile*, by Samuel White Baker," v (August, 1866), 654–69.
"The Last Two Abyssinian Books: a review of *The Nile Tributaries of Abyssinia*, by Sir Samuel White Baker, and *Narrative of a Journey through Abyssinia in 1862–3*, by Henry Dufton," VIII (November, 1867), 547–58.

Good Words
"The New Church at the Mistibithiwong," IX (May, 1868), 322–28.

London Society
"An Episode in the Life of Charles Mordaunt," XXI (January, 1872), 1–18. [*Hornby Mills and Other Stories*]
"The Wooden Soldier," XXIV (Christmas Number, 1873), 27–38.
"Meerschaum," XXVI (Christmas Number, 1874), 21–34.

Macmillan's Magazine
"The Navies of France and England," II (August, 1860), 249-58. [With Augustus G. Stapleton]
"New Books of Sport and Natural History: A Gossip for September," II (September, 1860), 385–93.
"Travelling in Victoria," III (January, 1861), 140–50.
"Some Account of the Village of Inverquoich," VII (April, 1863), 447-59. [*Hornby Mills and Other Stories*]
"Thackeray," IX (February, 1864), 356–68.
"The March of Charles Sturt," XI (January, 1865), 204–17. [*Hornby Mills and Other Stories*]
"About Salmon," XII (June, 1865), 127–36.
"Eyre, the South Australian Explorer," XII (October, 1865), 501–10; XII (November, 1865), 55–63. [*Hornby Mills and Other Stories*]

New Quarterly Magazine
"Sir Philip Sidney," III (January, 1875), 416–42. ["Sir Philip Sidney," *Fireside Studies*, II, 171–242]

North British Review
"Baker's Explorations in Central Africa," XLIV (June, 1866), 363–88.

Once a Week
"The Two Cadets," XVI (February 23, 1867), 214–20; (March 2, 1867), 246–53.

The Reader
Review of *A Successful Exploration through the Interior of Australia. From the Journals of W. J. Wills. Edited by his Father.* I (February 21, 1863), 183–84.
Review of *Reminiscences of a Thirty Years' Residence in New South Wales and Victoria. By R. Therry.* I (March 14, 1863), 256–57.
Review of *The Varieties of Dogs, as they are found in Old Sculptures, Pictures, Engravings, and Books: with the Names of the Artists by whom they are represented; showing how long many of the numerous breeds now existing have been known. By Ph. Charles Berjeau.* I (June 6, 1863), 547–48.
Review of *Tracks of McKinlay and Party Across Australia, by John Davis, one of the Expedition. Edited from Mr. Davis's Manuscript Journal by William Westgarth.* I (June 27, 1863), 618–19.

Temple Bar
"My Landladies," xxxvi (October, 1872), 371–90.
"Richard Steele," xl (March, 1874), 103–21. ["Fathers of 'The Spectator,'"
Fireside Studies, i, 7–63]
"Addison," xli (June, 1874), 319–37. ["Fathers of 'The Spectator,'" *Fireside
Studies*, i, 70–128]
"Ben Jonson," xlii (August, 1874), 35-50. ["The Master of the 'Mermaid,'"
Fireside Studies, i, 264–310]
"Fletcher and Beaumont," xlii (November, 1874), 460–71. ["Fletcher and Beau-
mont," *Fireside Studies*, ii, 93–112; 120–29; 167–70]

Tinsley's Magazine
"Malmaison," ix (December, 1871), 560–76; (January, 1872), 672–91. [*Hornby Mills
and Other Stories*]

II. Secondary Sources

A. Periodicals 1859–1876

Athenaeum
"The Recollections of Geoffry Hamlyn," xxxii (May 7, 1859), 610–11.
"The Hillyars and the Burtons," xli (May 27, 1865), 716–17.
"Leighton Court," xliii (February 24, 1866), 266.
"Silcote of Silcotes," xliv (November 16, 1867), 643–44.
"Tales of Old Travel Re-Narrated," xlviii (October 16, 1869), 497.
"Stretton," lxvii (June 5, 1869), 759–60.
"Boy in Grey," li (April 8, 1871), 431.
"Old Margaret," lii (July 22, 1871), 109.
"Hetty," lii (August 19, 1871), 232–33.
"The Harveys," lii (December 16, 1871), 790.
"Hornby Mills and Other Stories," liii (June 1, 1872), 686–87.
"Valentin," liv (September 21, 1872), 357.
"_____," liv (September 28, 1872), 403.
"Oakshott Castle," lv (March 22, 1873), 375.
"Reginald Hetherege," lvii (June 20, 1874), 825.
"Number Seventeen," lix (June 12, 1875), 779.
"Fireside Studies," lxi (March 25, 1876), 424.
"Obituary," lxi (May 27, 1876), 731.

Atlantic Monthly
"The Hillyars and the Burtons," xvi (July, 1865), 121.
"Stretton," xxxvii (February, 1876), 239–40.

North American Review
"The Recollections of Geoffry Hamlyn," lxxxviii (October, 1859), 547.
"The Hillyars and the Burtons," ci (July, 1865), 293–99.

North British Review
"The Recollections of Geoffry Hamlyn," xxxi (1859), 384–400.

Punch
"Punch Derby's Prophecy," lx (May 27, 1871), 217–18.

Saturday Review
"Austin Elliot," xv (June 6, 1863), 731–32.
"The Hillyars and the Burtons," xix (May 13, 1865), 576–77.
"Leighton Court," xxi (March 10, 1866), 299–300.
"Silcote of Silcotes," xxv (January 4, 1868), 25–26.
"Mademoiselle Mathilde," xxv (May 23, 1868), 693–94.
"Stretton," xxvii (June 19, 1869), 814–16.
"Old Margaret," xxxii (July 8, 1871), 56–57.
"Hetty," xxxii (December 2, 1871), 728–29.
"Valentin," xxxiv (September 28, 1872), 412–13.
"Oakshott Castle," xxxv (April 26, 1873), 563–64.
"Reginald Hetherege," xxxviii (July 18, 1874), 92–93.
"Number Seventeen," xl (July 3, 1875), 29–30.

Spectator
"Ravenshoe," xxxv (June 7, 1862), 637–38.
"The Hillyars and the Burtons," xxxviii (May 6, 1865), 501–2.
"Old Margaret," xliv (August 19, 1871), 1014–15.
"Hornby Mills and Other Stories," xlv (May 18, 1872), 632–33.
"Valentin," xlv (November 2, 1872), 1401–2.
"Henry Kingsley the Novelist," xlix (June 3, 1876), 706–7.
"Fireside Studies," xlix (June 24, 1876), 803–4.

The Times
"Hetty," September 16, 1871, 4a.
"The Lost Child," December 25, 1871, 5b.
"Oakshott Castle," April 18, 1873, 4e.
"Fireside Studies," April 24, 1876, 4d.
"Obituary," May 25, 1876, 5f.
"Funeral Notice," May 27, 1876, 12e.
"Advertisement for Funds," November 7, 1876, 6d.
"Funds for Henry Kingsley," November 9, 1876, 8b.

B. Books and Articles since 1876

Baker, Ernest. *The History of the English Novel.* 10 vols. New York, 1924–39.
Baker, Joseph Ellis. *The Novel and the Oxford Movement.* New York, 1965.
Bevington, Merle Mowbray. *The "Saturday Review" 1855 1868.* New York, 1941.
Boldrewood, Rolf [Thomas Alexander Browne]. *Old Melbourne Memories.* London, 1896.
Buckler, William E. "Henry Kingsley and *The Gentleman's Magazine*," *Journal of English and Germanic Philology*, l (1951), 90–100.
Byrne, Desmond. *Australian Writers.* London, 1896.
Collingwood, Stuart Dodgson. *The Life and Letters of Lewis Carroll.* London, 1898.
Cruse, Amy. *The Victorians and Their Reading.* Boston, 1935.
Davies, Bryn. "English Novelists in Australia," *Literary Criterion*, vi (1964), 113–25.
Dunbar, Janet. *J. M. Barrie, The Man Behind the Image.* Boston, 1970.
Ellis, S. M. *Henry Kingsley 1830-1876.* London, 1931.
Elton, Oliver. *Frederick York Powell: A Life and A Selection from His Letters and Occasional Writings.* 2 vols. Oxford, 1909.
Ford, George H. "The Governor Eyre Case in England," *University of Toronto Quarterly*, xvii (April, 1948), 219–33.

Graves, Charles. *Life and Letters of Alexander Macmillan.* London, 1910.
Green, H. M. *A History of Australian Literature.* 2 vols. Sydney, 1961.
Hale, Richard Walden. *Kingsleys.* Boston, 1934.
Hamer, Clive. "Henry Kingsley's Australian Novels," *Southerly,* xxvi (1966), 40–57.
————. "The Surrender to Truth in the Early Australian Novel," *Australian Literary Studies,* ii (1965), 103–16.
Hergenhan, L. T. "*Geoffry Hamlyn* Through Contemporary Eyes," *Australian Literary Studies,* ii (1966), 289–95.
Horner, J. C. "*Geoffry Hamlyn* and its Australian Setting," *Australian Literary Studies,* i (1963), 3–15.
Howe, Susanne. *Novels of Empire.* New York, 1949.
Hutton, Laurence. "Henry Kingsley," *The Book Buyer,* xi (January, 1895), 723–35.
James, Henry. "The Noble School of Fiction," *Notes and Reviews.* Preface by Pierre de Chaignon la Rose. Cambridge, Mass., 1921.
[Kingsley, Frances E., ed.]. *Charles Kingsley: His letters and Memories of His Life.* Edited by His Wife. 2 vols. London, 1877.
Kingsley, George Henry. *Notes on Sport and Travel,* with a Memoir by His Daughter Mary H. Kingsley. London, 1900.
Kingsley, Maurice. "Personal Traits of Henry Kingsley," *The Book Buyer,* xi (January, 1895), 727–31.
Lang, Cecil Y., ed. *Swinburne Letters.* 6 vols. Yale University Press, 1959–62.
Lord, Walter Frewen. "The Kingsley Novels," *The Nineteenth Century,* lx (June, 1904), 996–1004.
McLeod, Mary. "Henry Kingsley at Cuckfield," *The Sussex County Magazine,* iv (March, 1930), 251–53. Letters and replies (April, 1930), 340; (May, 1930), 428–29.
Macmillan, George A. *Letters of Alexander Macmillan.* Printed for Private Circulation [Glasgow], 1908.
Maison, Margaret M. *The Victorian Vision.* New York, 1961.
Martin, Benjamin Ellis. "Old Chelsea," *Century Magazine,* xxxiii (1886), 225–36.
Martin, R. B. *Charles Kingsley's American Notes.* Princeton, 1958.
————. *The Dust of Combat, A Life of Charles Kingsley.* London, 1959.
Melville, Lewis. *Victorian Novelists.* London, 1906.
Morgan, Charles. *The House of Macmillan.* New York, 1944.
Moulton, Charles Wells, ed. *The Library of Literary Criticism.* 8 vols. New York, 1901–4.
Norton, Charles Eliot, ed. *Letters of Thomas Carlyle.* 2 vols. London, 1889.
Pope-Hennessy, Una. *Canon Charles Kingsley.* London, 1948.
Quiller-Couch, Sir Arthur. *Adventures in Criticism.* New York, 1925.
Ritchie, Anne Thackeray. *Chapters from Some Unwritten Memoirs.* New York, 1895.
Russell, G. W. E. *Selected Essays on Literary Subjects.* London, 1914.
Sadleir, Michael. "Henry Kingsley: A Portrait," *Edinburgh Review,* ccxl (October, 1924), 330–48; revised and shortened "Henry Kingsley," *Times Literary Supplement,* January 2, 1930, 1–2.
Saintsbury, George. *Collected Essays and Papers.* 4 vols. London, 1923.
Scheuerle, William H. "Henry Kingsley and the Governor Eyre Controversy," *Victorian Newsletter,* no. 37 (Spring, 1970), 24–27.
————. "'Magdalen at Michael's Gate': A Neglected Lyric," *Victorian Poetry,* v (Summer, 1967), 144–46.
————. ed. *Ravenshoe.* University of Nebraska, 1967.

————. "Romantic Attitudes in *Geoffry Hamlyn,*" *Australian Literary Studies,* II (1965), 79–91.

Semmel, Bernard. *Jamaican Blood and Victorian Conscience.* New York, 1963.

Serle, Geoffrey. *The Golden Age.* University of Melbourne, 1963.

Shorter, Clement. "Introduction," *The Recollections of Geoffry Hamlyn.* London, 1894.

Sutherland, Bruce. "Henry Kingsley and Australia," *The Australian Quarterly* (June, 1945), 98–104.

Thirkell, Angela. "Henry Kingsley," *Nineteenth-Century Fiction,* v (December, 1950), 175–87; (March, 1951), 273–93.

Thorp, Margaret Farrand. *Charles Kingsley: 1819-1875.* Princeton, 1937.

Ticknor and Fields Cost Books. Houghton Library, Harvard Library.

The Times Literary Supplement
    Gordon, George, et al. "Letter to the Editor" (April 10, 1930), 318.
    Moore Smith, G. C. "Letter to the Editor" (January 9, 1930), 28.
    Nicholson, Lothian. "Letter to the Editor" (February 6, 1930), 102.
    Simpson, Charles. "Letter to the Editor" (April 10, 1930), 318.
    Toynbee, Paget. "Letter to the Editor" (January 9, 1930), 28.
    Trevelyan, Sir George Otto. "Letter to the Editor" (June 21, 1923), 422.

Tinsley, William. *Random Recollections of an Old Publisher.* 2 vols. London, 1900.

Trollope, Anthony. *Thackeray.* New York, n.d.

Wolff, Robert Lee. "Henry Kingsley," *Harvard Library Bulletin,* XIII (Spring, 1959), 195–226.

Index

Abbot, George, 5
Abbot, Robert, 5
"About Salmon" (Henry Kingsley), 98
Addison, Joseph, 161
American Civil War, 58–59, 101*n*, 129
Arnold, Sir Edwin, 14, 58
Arnold, Matthew, 2, 90
Athenaeum, 2, 27, 139*n*
Atlantic, 121*n*
Austen, Jane, 42, 126*n*
Austin Elliot (Henry Kingsley), 1, 57, 58, 85–87, 95–96, 108, 109, 143

Baker, Ernest, 44–45
Bakewell, W., 94–95
Banks, Sir Joseph, 5
Barnark Rectory, 6–7
Barrie, J. M., 167*n*
Beaumont, Francis, 161
Bennett, Arnold, *The Old Wives' Tale* and *Clayhanger*, 63–64
Bentley, George, 157, 166
Bentley, Richard, 135
Bevington, Merle, 146*n*
Blackmore, Richard, 44
Blake, William, 91
Blunt, Reverend Gerald, 88–89
Book Buyer, The, 170
Boy in Grey, The (Henry Kingsley), 54*n*, 98, 109, 134, 140–42, 161
Brackenbury, Mrs., 21
Bradbury & Evans, 99, 112, 121*n*
Braddon, Mary Elizabeth, 105, 152
Bronte, Emily, *Wuthering Heights*, 64
Browne, Rose, 24

Browne, Thomas Alexander ("Rolf Boldrewood"), 24, 43; *Old Melbourne Memories*, 24
Browning, Robert, "Mr. Sludge, 'The Medium,'" 144
Buckler, William, 112*n*
Bulwer, Edward (Lord Lytton), *Zanoni*, 116, 161
Burney, Fanny, 12
Butler, Lady Eleanor, 162*n*
"Button Cap," 6–7, 11
Byrne, Desmond, 28
Byron, Lord, 5, 124*n*

Cadogan, Lord, 9
Campbell, Henry J., 21–22, 55, 57, 67*n*
Carlyle, Thomas, 9, 93, 95, 161
Carroll, Lewis, 2, 139; *Alice's Adventures in Wonderland*, 90, 96, 140; *Through The Looking-Glass*, 90*n*
Cassell, John, *Cassell's Family Paper* and *The Quiver*, 58
Cavalier, Jean, 10
Chanter, Mrs. J. M., 6, 7
Chelsea, 9–12, 24, 88–89
Clarke, Marcus, 28
Clovelly, 8–9
Coleridge, Derwent, 8
Collins, Wilkie, 77, 105, 152; *The Woman in White*, 118, 127
Craik, George, 57*n*, 97, 138, 147, 154, 156, 165
Cromwell, Oliver, 4

Daily Telegraph, 58

181

Date Due